# TRAVEL PHOTOGRAPHY

For Shimoda-san

# Travel Photography

## How to research, produce and sell great travel pictures

Roger Hicks and Frances Schultz

OXFORD BOSTON JOHANNESBURG MELBOURNE NEW DELHI SINGAPORE

Focal Press
An imprint of Butterworth-Heinemann
Linacre House, Jordan Hill, Oxford OX2 8DP
225 Wildwood Avenue, Woburn, MA 01801-2041
A division of Reed Educational and Professional Publishing Ltd

A member of the Reed Elsevier plc group

First published 1998



**British Library Cataloguing in Publication Data**
A catalogue record for this book is available from the British Library

**Library of Congress Cataloging in Publication Data**
A catalogue record for this book is available from the Library of Congress

ISBN 0 240 51514 5

Printed and bound in Italy by Vincenzo Bona - Torino

# Contents

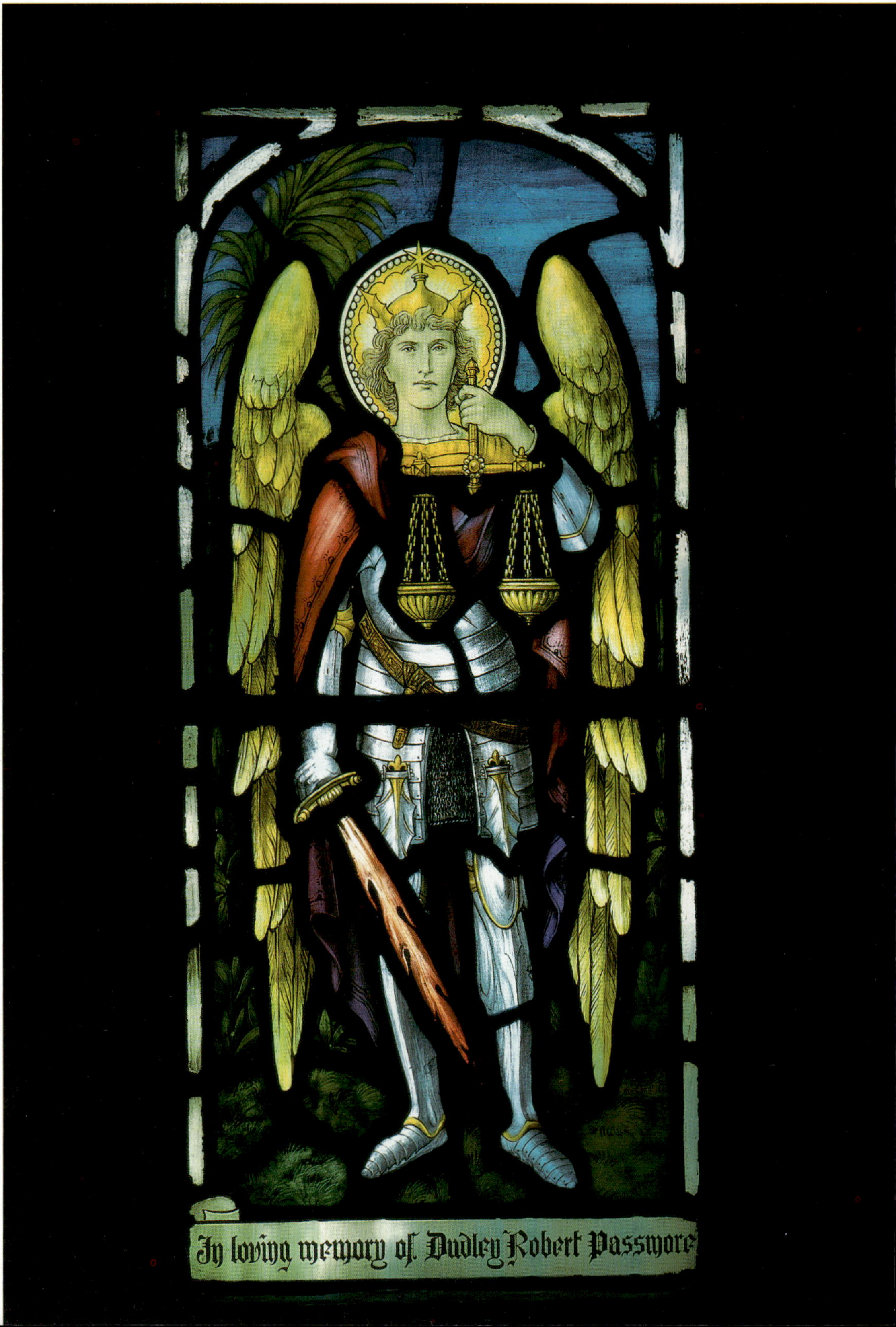
In loving memory of Dudley Robert Passmore

# 1 The dream and the reality

From the outside – and often, from the inside too – travel photography looks very like the perfect way to earn a living. What you are doing as a business is, after all, what most people do for fun.

Of course, the dream doesn't take any account of getting up before dawn, or of collapsing into bed at past midnight; of arguing with surly, armed and intransigent border officials; of six days' rain and one day's decent weather in a week-long shoot; of suddenly realizing, with sinking heart, that the most expensive single lens that you own has been stolen...

But then again, the dream cannot fully encompass the moments of elation. Waking in the morning at a hotel where you arrived at dead of night, throwing back the curtains, and seeing Braganza Castle float above the mist like something from a fairy tale. Watching the sun set over the 'Chinese' fishing nets on the coast at Cochin. A team of unexpectedly beautiful schoolgirls helping to renovate a twelfth-century church in rural France. A few seconds break in the dawn clouds on Tiger Hill, so that Kangchenjunga is framed in rose-tinted clouds. A ruined late-mediaeval chapel, dramatic under a stormy spring sky, at the point where a muddy Portuguese farm track finally became impassable. Spring flowers framing Mdina, the ancient capital of Malta.

## The limits of travel photography

Much of what you experience, you will never be able to photograph at all. You have to reconcile yourself to this, early on. You will never capture on film the smell of a huge pan of paella cooking over a wood fire. You cannot record the damp of pre-dawn, or the frost crunching underfoot as you photograph a river crossing used by Union soldiers during the Civil War, 125 years ago to the day. No picture can communicate the seemingly endless walk from the end of the paved road in Sougia, up the canyon, across the top and down to the next canyon to photograph the ancient Greek theatre at Lissos, a ruin for twenty centuries.

There is much more that you will never be able to photograph adequately. The deep cave in Crete where Zeus was born. The bustle of the Old Bazaar in Istanbul. The timelessness of a Tibetan cham dance, at once rooted in centuries past and in the immediate moment. The traffic of the Etoile at the end of the Champs Elysées. The fishermen on the coast of Coromandel, leaving at dawn and coming back an hour or two later with their pitifully small catches.

All of these things – the good, the bad, the beautiful, the impossible – have been a part of our life in travel photography. Anyone else in the same field could give you a hundred similar examples. So what does it take?

***Figure 1.1*** *Everywhere you go, there are intriguing stories waiting to be documented. Many are aware that Dante Gabriel Rosetti is commemorated by a window in All Saints' Church, Birchington, and this is what we went to photograph; but his is not the only memorial window. This one commemorates a young motorcyclist who was killed in a traffic accident in the 1930s. The window next to it commemorates his fiancée, who was killed at the same time. We arranged with the church to remove the external wire mesh grids which protect the windows from vandalism and accidental damage, and got much better pictures as a result. We shot duplicate sets and gave the church a set: an easy, inexpensive and very welcome 'thank you' for being allowed access. (RWH)*

## No 'royal road'

The very idea of a guide to being a successful travel photographer is something of a joke, because progress is far from automatic. There is no royal road: if there were, everyone would take it. All that anyone can offer you, and all that is on offer in this book, is a guide to getting started in travel photography.

Even this is a complex and multi-faceted subject, though it begins with one simple question. Ask yourself this: 'What would I do to become a travel photographer?' If you are to have any hope of success, the only possible answer is, 'Whatever it takes.' If you answer anything else, you won't be able to do it.

If you want a reliable and predictable income; if you want a comfortable house; if you want a new car – all of these things which many people take for granted as early rewards in starting a career will be beyond your reach for a considerable while (perhaps forever) unless you are very, very lucky, or very, very good, or preferably both.

## Loneliness and worse

The majority of travel photographers are either single, or have very understanding partners who are willing to put up with prolonged and erratic absences. Many relationships fail under the strain, the more so when the

*__Figure 1.2__ There is a steady demand for pictures of ante-bellum houses in the American South; this is the Sturdivant House in Selma, Alabama. As a general rule, it is as well to shoot colour, as it can always be converted to black and white, but a well-made black and white print has a charm of its own and might even sell better than colour, especially if sepia-toned. Shooting on 35mm is normally acceptable; demand is rarely high enough to justify using larger formats. (RWH)*

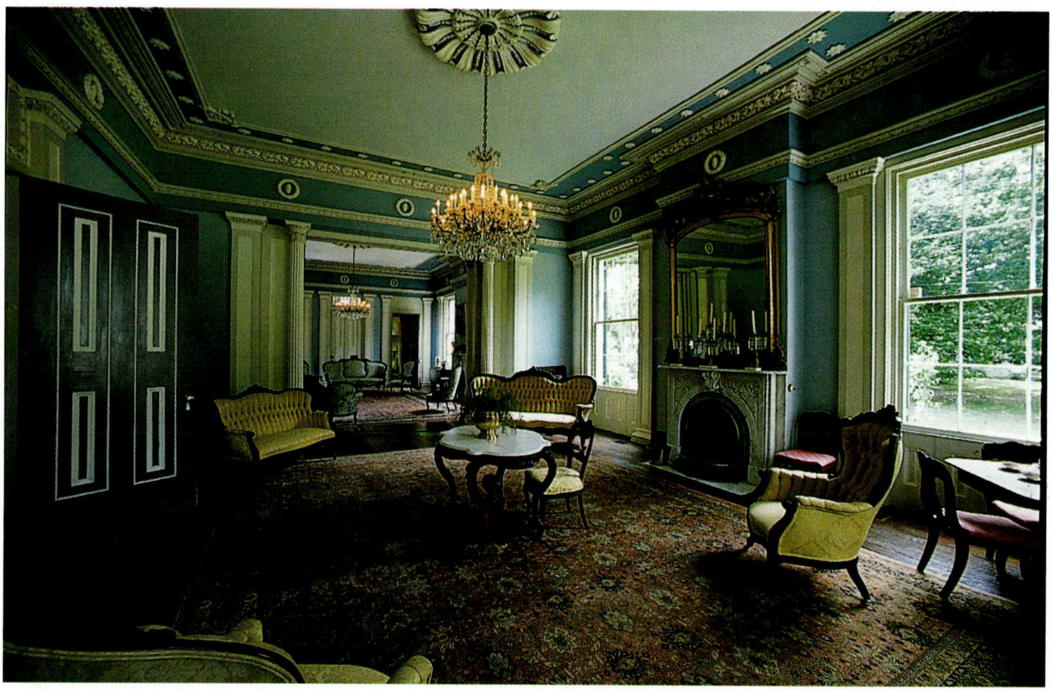

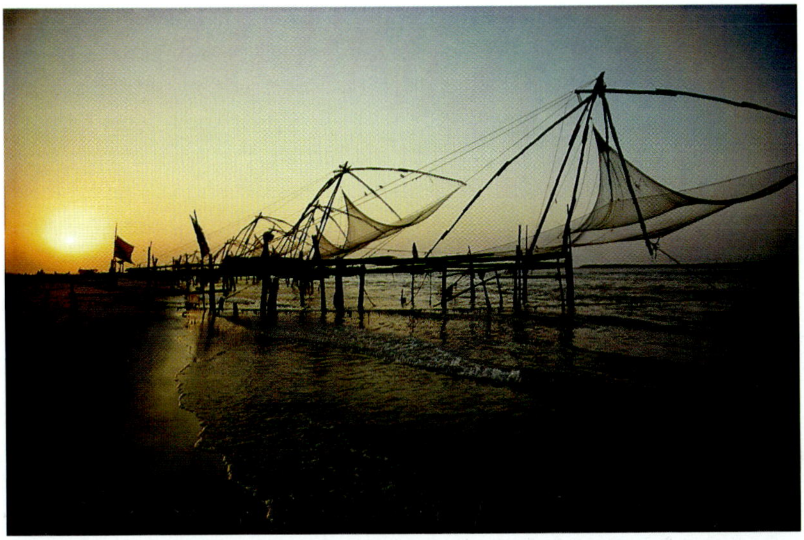

***Figure 1.3*** *These 'Chinese' fishing nets are something that everyone wants to see in Cochin and Ernakulam – and something that everyone remembers. The travel photographer must however bring back more than just a snapshot: people want pictures of what they remember, not of what they saw. Early in the morning and late in the evening are the obvious times to shoot, provided there are enough people around to lend meaning and context to the picture. (FES)*

photographer comes home full of anecdotes and excitement, and the partner has been slaving away at a nine-to-five job.

A few – a very few, but we are among them – travel as couples. The classic combination is a writer plus a photographer, for reasons which will become clearer in Chapter 4, but occasionally you find two photographers together. We are unusual in that we are both photographers and writers, though Frances's strength lies more in photography and Roger's is more inclined towards writing.

Although working with someone else has many advantages, from companionship, to someone to watch your back, to a friend to get you out of trouble, there are also two major disadvantages. The first is that the 'comps' (complimentary tickets, accommodation, and so forth) are hard enough for one person to get; for two, the difficulty is a lot more than twice as great. The other is that because there are lows as well as highs on photographic trips, you have to be pretty well adjusted to one another if you are not to fall out. Constant proximity can be as destructive to a relationship as constant separation. We met in Los Angeles in 1981 and have survived so far.

## Where do you start?

In large measure, the answer to the question, 'Where do you start?' depends on the answer to the question, 'Where do you want to end up?' There is no more a single monolithic entity called 'travel photography' than there is a single monolithic entity called 'photography'. Do you want to take holiday brochure shots? Cutting edge reportage? Adventure travel pictures? Stock pictures for library use? Editorial feature work? Single shots or picture essays? Can you supply packages of words and pictures, which tend to be much more saleable than pictures on their own?

Each route into travel photography, each goal, has its own requirements and its own starting points; but equally, you cannot rule out the possibility that you will change direction. There are all sorts of reasons for doing so, but the most pressing are, first, that some types of travel photography pay better than others, and second, that when opportunities present themselves, the wise travel photographer will normally go for them. Photography does not exactly present a career path. The closest analogy is probably with a rugger player, or an American football player. Having gained possession of the ball, in itself no mean feat, he runs like fury. He jinks to avoid tackles, jumps over recumbent players, swerves and twists in any direction necessary, but always has the touch line in mind. Finally, he slams the ball down to general applause. For that matter, the analogy can be continued: like rugger, travel photography can be pretty wet, cold and muddy at times.

## Technical skill

No matter what your intended goal, skill at photography has to be taken for granted. There is little point in going into this here, except to say that your 'hit rate' needs to be fairly high, merely in order to keep your expenses down. To put it another way, one top-flight, saleable picture in every ten exposures is more than adequate; one top-flight, saleable picture in every 100 exposures is probably going to tip you over the edge financially. When you are better established, you can start shooting like the *Life* photographers of old – one in a thousand was quite acceptable, provided it was great enough – but until then, you have to watch the pennies.

## Equipment and materials

As with skill, a certain level of equipment quality is taken for granted, but the truth is that this level need not necessarily be very high. Most professional cameras made since the 1960s, and many so-called 'amateur' cameras, are more than adequate. There is a 'quality plateau', above which the skill of the photographer is far more important than the equipment used, and it no longer costs a fortune to get above that plateau.

The same is true of materials as for skill. The days are gone when magazines would accept only large-format transparencies, or when, if they accepted 35mm, they insisted on Kodachromes. Both equipment and materials are sufficiently important that they are the subject of Chapter 2, but this chapter is aimed more at the amateur who wishes to turn pro than at the professional photographer or student.

## Originality

Dr Johnson once told an aspiring playwright that his work was both good and original, but that unfortunately the original parts were not good and the good parts were not original. A major problem for students in particular is that colleges often prize originality over quality, so that when the unfortunate graduate tries to show his or her 'book' to prospective clients (Chapter 20), there is too much in it which is unquestionably original but which is also, unfortunately, not good.

There is no doubt that a great deal of what is demanded in travel photography is conventional in the extreme, though this is not necessarily the same as hackneyed. As with technical skill, this is not a subject to be explored at too great a length here, but a thread which runs through the book is the need for originality, which has been defined as the art of remembering something while forgetting precisely where you saw it.

Do not be afraid to try to copy the style of a photographer you admire, whether they are commonly regarded as a 'travel' photographer or not. Likewise, it can be a very useful exercise to try to copy an individual picture or style of picture from a brochure, company report or advertisement. You can learn a great deal by trying to replicate a particular picture or style, and the technical rigours of doing so will almost always force you to pay attention to details which you might previously have failed to consider. Also, you are unlikely ever to replicate another's style entirely, so copying is, paradoxically, one of the best ways of developing your own style.

## Business skills

This is where most books on professional photography start to become seriously forbidding. They talk about business plans and bank managers and accountants and taxes and all the things you would rather not think about. Indeed, like equipment and materials, this is a subject which warrants a chapter to itself, Chapter 5; but like them, it is not something to get too excited about.

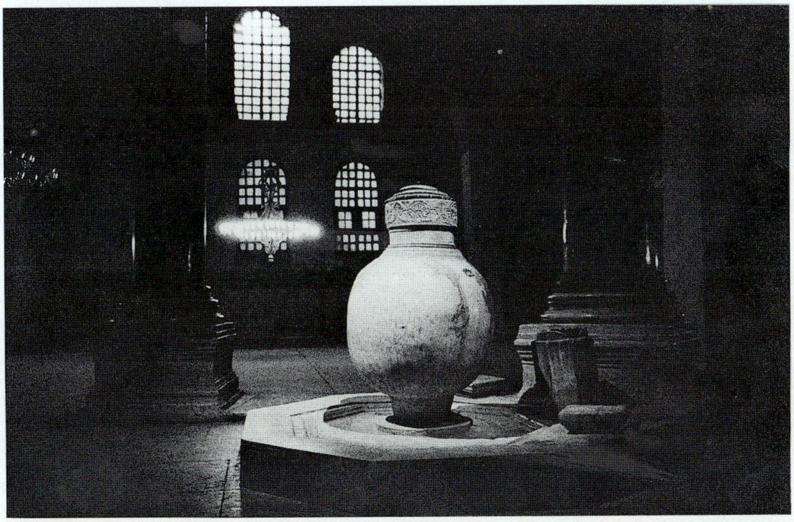

***Figure 1.4*** *The interior of Hagia Sofia in Istanbul is one of the most magical places we have ever been: a huge, substantially empty space. It is all the more impressive when you realize that for a thousand years after it was built, it was the biggest man-made enclosed space on the planet. It is however very dark, and although we shot a few rolls of fast colour film (Fuji RSP, pushed to EI 2500), we were happier with the monochrome shots, mostly on Kodak TMZ rated at EI 12,500. (FES)*

The simple truth is that business plans and financial structures and pension plans and the like are not how most photographers get into the travel business. For that matter, they are not how most photographers get into any kind of photography. No matter what aspect of photography you choose, there's a lot of luck, and being in the right place at the right time, and meeting the right people, and working on a shoestring, and doing things which make no business sense whatsoever, just because they are fun.

Many photographers also end up somewhere quite different from where they started, because of a sequence of happenstances. Roger has a law degree, is a qualified secondary school teacher, and his first professional job as a photographer was as an assistant in an advertising studio. Frances has two degrees in theatre. We both studied accountancy. Now we take pictures; write books and magazine articles; and travel as much as we can.

Most of the photographers we know, whether in the field of travel or elsewhere, could have made more money if they had stuck to something more respectable and dull, but they didn't: they worked on the principle that we are on this earth for a good time, but not necessarily for a long time.

## Roughing it

We have already made one reference to personal or character qualifications, referring to relationships, and we hope we have made it clear that travel

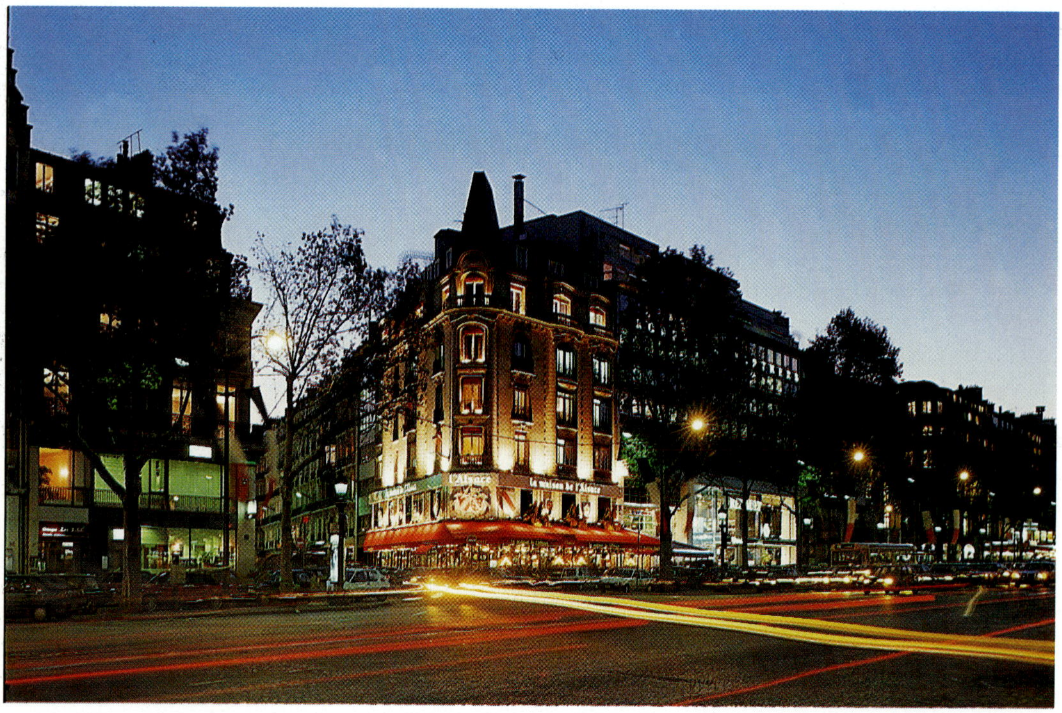

***Figure 1.5*** *Pictures of people sitting outside cafés are one of the staples of Paris brochures, articles and books. Shooting a brasserie from across the Champs Elysées does however manage to convey a totally different mood: part of the energy of Paris and (to be frank) just how tiring it can be. (FES)*

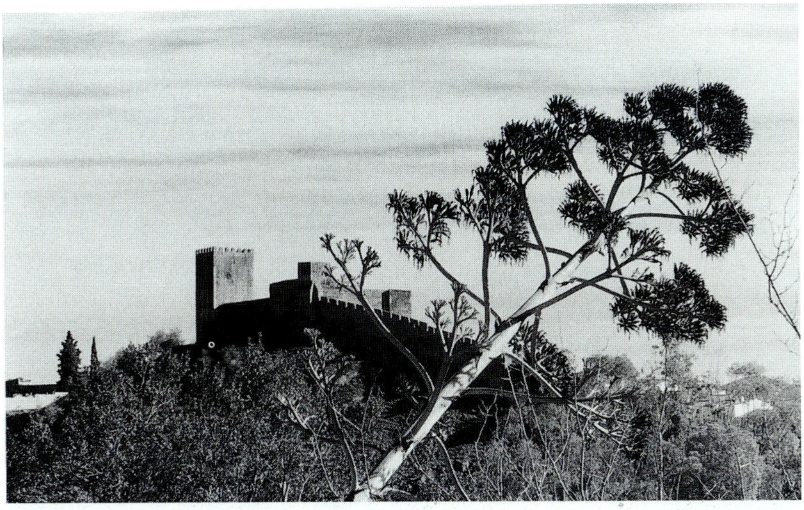

***Figure 1.6** Mertóla – Roman Myrtillis – in south-central Portugal is a perfect mediaeval (and earlier) town crowned with an ancient castle. On our way there, we stopped to shoot a general view of the fortress and were seduced by the parallels between the tree and the castle: nothing lasts forever. This is at once a literal shot, and one with an off-beat slant: remove the tree, and it is rather a dull picture. (FES)*

photography is rarely a road to riches, but these are only some of the potential drawbacks. Can you put up with, and indeed be grateful for, free accommodation on the floor in a temple which is 50 miles from the nearest flush toilet? If there is a flush toilet, how happy are you with the hole-in-the-floor variety? Can you survive for three days on dhal, raw onions and chapatties, and drink neat rum at seven in the morning with a sorcerer? Can you go for a week or ten days without a bath, and not particularly worry about it? Could you handle being ill, with bronchitis say, 5000 miles from home?

Don't look at all this stuff in a romantic glow: think hard about shivering in an unheated room at 2000 metres (6600 feet, for the unmetricated), about how your digestion will cope, about how you'll smell after a few days without a bath, about running to that hole-in-the-floor toilet with Delhi Belly. None of what I have described is an exaggeration: indeed, everything in the paragraph above happened to us on one three-week trip.

## Other personal qualities

You must be able to get on with people. You need to be able to get on with clients, photographic subjects, petty officials, bank managers – just about anyone with whom you come into contact. You survive by your wits, or not at all.

Not surprisingly, most travel photographers are great raconteurs; get them sitting around with a cup of coffee or a drink in their hands, and the stories just keep on coming. Some talk a better picture than they shoot, and others shoot a better picture than they talk, but they almost all talk as well as shoot. In the business schools they call it 'networking', but to most photographers, it's just fun.

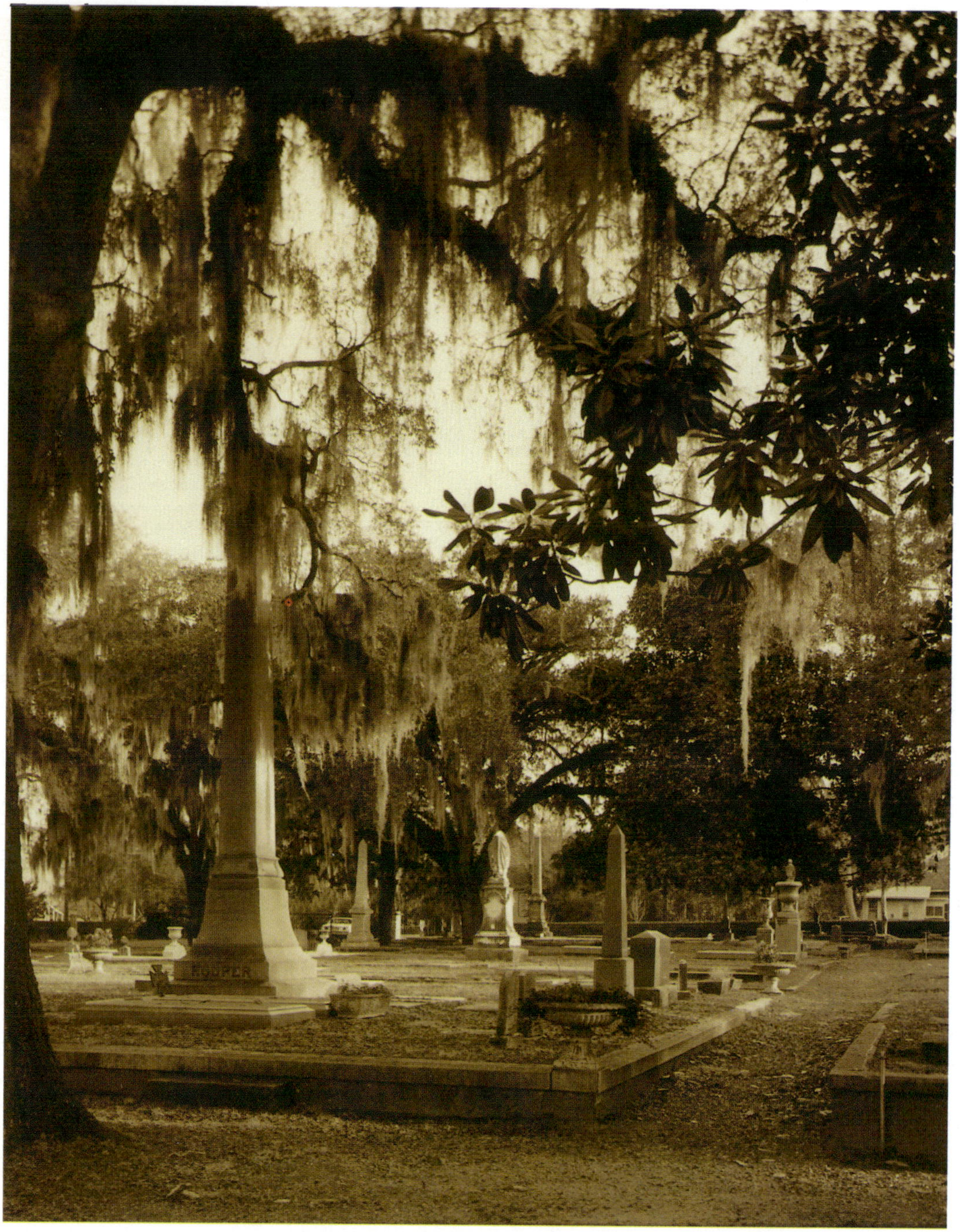

**Figure 1.7** *Part of the travel photographer's job is to capture mood as well as making record shots. This Southern graveyard seemed to cry out for dark, mournful sepia, and Polaroid's excellent 4 × 5 inch material allows you to fine-tune the colour on the spot. For submissions, though, it would probably be best to copy this onto 6 × 7cm colour slide. (RWH)*

You have to be resourceful, and persuasive. You have to know when to push your luck, and when to quit. You have to be able to run with the hare, and hunt with the hounds; you must be flexible.

Above all, though, the travel photographer must have twin burning desires: to travel, and to take pictures. Unless these take precedence over pretty much everything else, there is little chance of success. Does this indicate an unbalanced outlook? Perhaps, but an unbalanced outlook is what you need for success. You can't just take pictures in order to pay for your travel, and you can't just travel in order to find subjects for pictures.

## OTHER NON-PHOTOGRAPHIC SKILLS

You need to be well informed, and you need to be able to find information that you don't have. There is much more about this in the rest of the book in general and in Chapter 7 in particular, but for now, an example will do. Unless you have a very specific project in mind, you don't want to be on the plains in India during the hottest part of the dry season, just before the burst of the monsoon, and you don't want to be there during the monsoon itself. Where would you find out about weather statistics in, say, Bombay? It took us just two minutes to find them (and, admittedly, ten minutes to find the book which we had mislaid).

You also need to be reasonably well organized: not in the sense of having a clear desk with all pencils sharpened and pointing in the same direction, but in the sense of being able to do what you say you will, pretty much when you say you will. The golden rule with delays is always to let the client know as soon as possible that things may not happen quite as fast as they should. Ninety-nine times out of a hundred, things can be rescheduled if there is enough warning; but if you wait until past the agreed delivery date, and then explain that, um, you haven't quite finished yet, then trouble normally ensues rapidly.

## WHEN YOU'RE NOT TRAVELLING

Few photographers make a full-time living from travel, and even if they can, most of the ones we know are happier not to. We probably could, but we've never really tried. First, you have to spend some time at your home base, sorting and captioning and labelling, as described in Chapter 3. Then you have to spend time selling. And you do need some time just to rest and recuperate.

Our all-time record was no more than six months away from home in one year, and we generally find that three to four months a year travelling is about right, but then, we are writers as well as photographers and we need time to write as well as time to caption, file and sell pictures. Even with the few photographers we know who travel constantly, few if any spend more than half the year away from home.

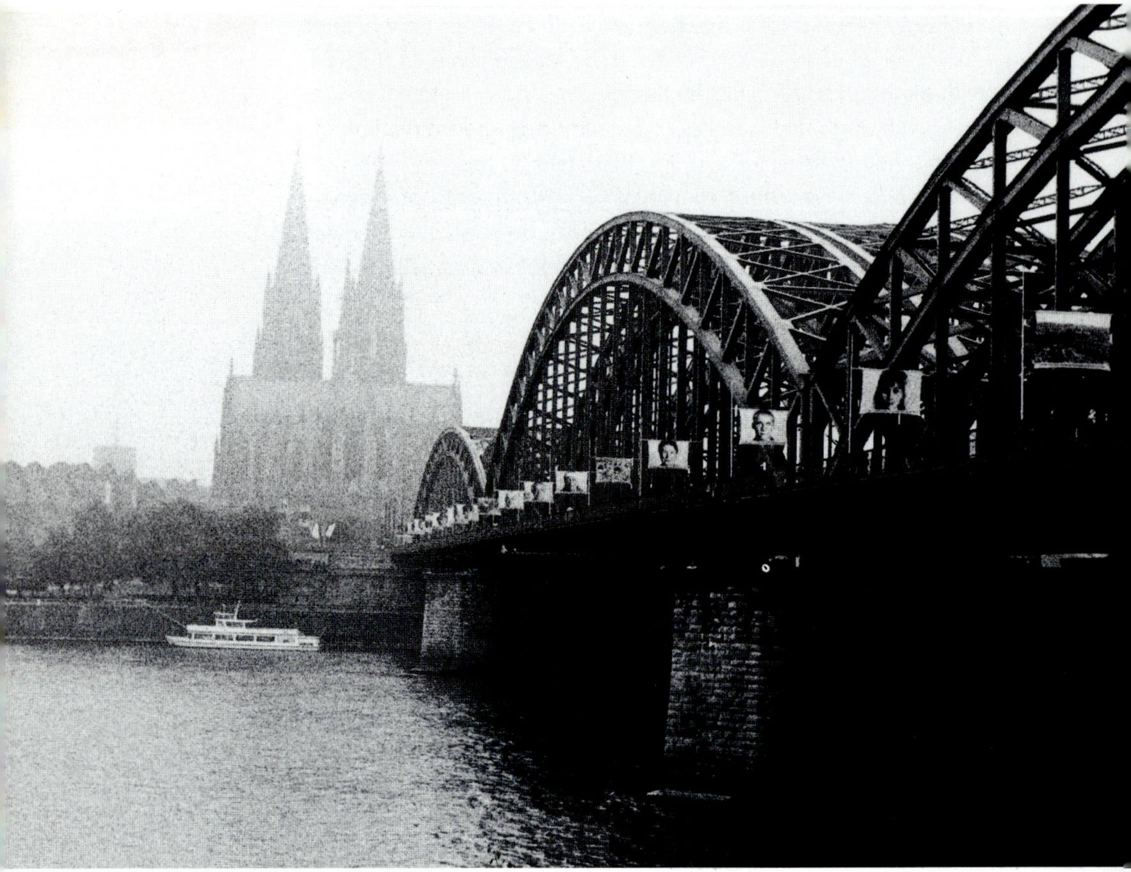

***Figure 1.8*** *Everyone shoots Cologne cathedral from this angle; it is the standard establishing shot for Photokina, the photographic fair. The weather is often poor, so the obvious thing was to turn this to advantage. In a sectional blow-up from a 35mm frame, the grain emphasizes the mistiness of the river; the bulk of the bridge on the right*

Of course, there are many ways of allocating your time. We tend to take a mixture of one-, two- and three-week trips, rarely staying on one project for more than a month: we have to get home to keep the business running. If we need much more than about three weeks, we make two (or more) trips. Others may spend two, three or four months on the road, or in one place. Obviously, a great deal depends both on your personality and on the project you are shooting.

We tend to mix domestically-based projects in with travel projects, and so do many others whom we know. The other work may be almost anything: we know photographers who work in reportage, celebrity photography, advertising and for that matter architecture as well as in travel. The truth is that travel photography rarely pays very well, simply because it is so popular, so many photographers mix more lucrative if less exciting work with their travel. Also, working in more than one field can cross-fertilize ideas, adding zest to the domestic work and providing new insights into travel photography.

## The bottom line

The bottom line is that you need to get your pictures in front of people – the right people, the ones with the budgets and the schedules and the publications that are hungry for pictures.

But before that, you need to shoot the right pictures of the right subjects. And before that, you need to get to the right places. And before that, you need to know what constitutes a good picture. And before that, you need to be able to operate a camera competently. There is an almost infinite regression of prerequisites, which goes back to your first Box Brownie or Instamatic. Ultimately, there's only one way to find out if you can make it as a travel photographer. Try it. This is a book about trying it.

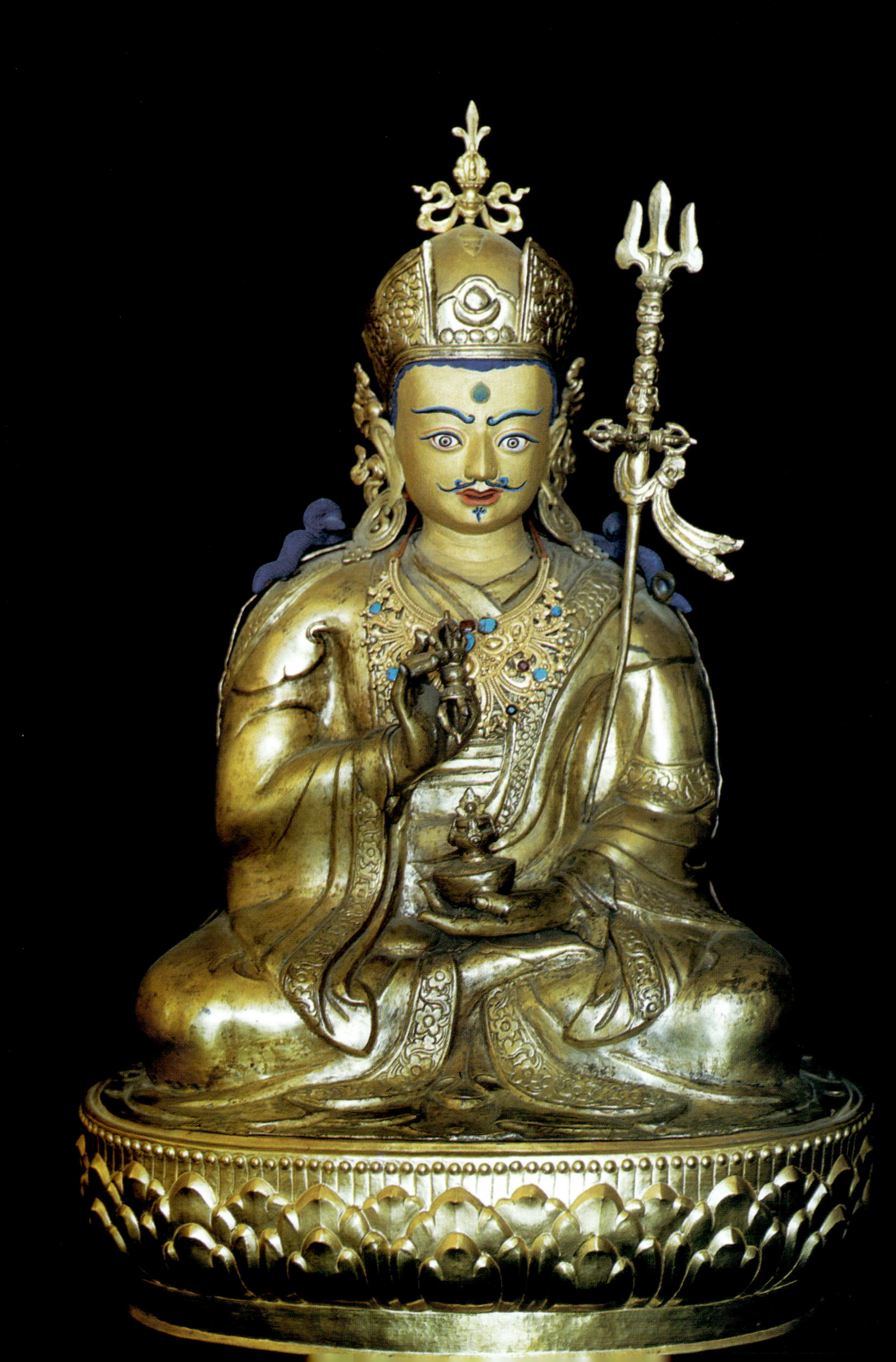

# 2 Equipment and materials

In one sense, equipment is irrelevant: any half-way decent camera should be capable of giving you the results you want, provided you know how to use it. In another sense, you need to pay very close attention to making sure that your equipment is suitable both for the rigours of travel and for producing the kind of final results that you want. You also need to be happy with the equipment you are using. Your principal concerns are reliability, portability and suitability for purpose. As well as cameras and lenses, of course, there are such accessories as tripods, filters, exposure meters and so forth: which of these you carry will depend very much on the kind of photography you have in mind.

When it comes to materials, there are again three considerations. The first (and arguably the most important) is that they should be able to deliver results which match your requirements. The second is that they should deliver the quality which the project demands. The third is that they should be able to stand up to the rigours of travel. Materials are covered towards the end of this chapter, after a closer look at equipment. The very last part of the chapter deals with non-photographic equipment, such as Swiss Army knives, Mag-Lite torches (flashlights) and the like.

## Reliability

Some cameras are inherently more reliable than others, and this must always be the first consideration. After this, a great deal depends on your budget; on where and how you are travelling; on how long you are going for; and on the opportunities for a re-shoot.

Reliability has several components. The first might be called 'normal' reliability, the ability to go on working for a very long time in normal use. The second is reliability under adverse conditions. The third is the nature of failure, and the fourth is ease of repair.

'Normal' reliability is one of the main things you pay for when you buy a professional camera. Some compact cameras apparently have a design life of under 100 rolls of film: they simply wear out. A professional camera should not wear out in anything like normal use, after thousands or even tens of thousands of rolls.

Reliability under adverse conditions is partly a question of how careful the photographer is, and partly a question of design. Underwater cameras or underwater housings can protect almost any camera, and you can greatly improve your camera's chances by taping over joins in the camera body and exercising considerable care in when and where you change film. Careful cleaning after use will also prolong the life of cameras and accessories,

***Figure 2.1*** *It is often possible to improvise studio conditions on location. This was shot against black velvet (bought from the bazaar in Lower Dharamsala) inside a 'tent' of cheap white cotton fabric (the bazaar again) supported on a framework of sticks cut to length with a Swiss Army knife and lashed together with string. Lighting was a Metz 45 CT-1 battery powered flash gun supplemented by two tiny Hanimex slave guns, also battery powered. Two of the four Hanimexes were still in use at the time of writing, having survived more than fifteen years. The camera was a 'baby' (6 × 9 cm) Linhof Super Technika IV. (RWH)*

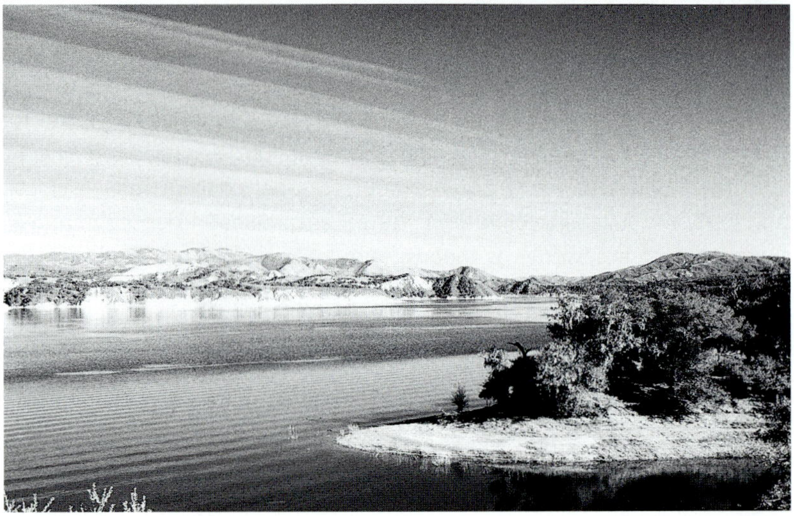

*Figure 2.2 We use quite a lot of Ilford SFX 200, a film with extended red sensitivity. With heavy red filtration, the results are akin to true infra-red and the haze-cutting effect is remarkable. Mono Lake in northern California is under threat from falling water levels, and dramatic pictures are often needed to accompany strongly-worded activist copy. The sky is what really makes this picture, though, and we have to admit that it was pure luck – though as the saying goes, fortune favours the prepared mind. (FES)*

but dust, humidity and (worst of all) salt spray will sooner or later wreck any equipment that is not fully protected. Kos, the well known yachting photographer, is as careful as she can reasonably be; but even so, she loses about a camera a year to corrosion.

The nature of failure is a little harder to explain, but it is easily illustrated. Old, mechanical cameras normally deteriorate patchily and with some warning: the meter may fail, the wind-on gets stiffer, and so forth, but the camera may well continue to work adequately. Modern electronic cameras, by contrast, normally work either perfectly, or not at all – and you get no warning of when they are going to stop.

Reparability can depend very much on where you are, and on what has gone wrong. If you are in a major city in an affluent country, repairs to any camera are rarely a problem, but the further you go from the beaten path, the more difficult repairs can be. Ordering spare parts from Tokyo may be a minor enough problem in New York or Paris, but if you have to contend with Third World customs and bureaucracy, your trip might end before you see the part, always assuming you can find someone to fit it. With a mechanical camera, you should be able to find someone who can repair it – even if you have to go to the local watch repairer. One of the legends of reliability, and indeed one which featured in the manufacturers' advertisements, was the story of the photographer whose Nikon Fs fell into a river. Rather than dry them out and lose the films in them, he carried them in a bucket to the nearest lab, many hours away; took out the films; had them processed; and then dried the cameras out while repeatedly working the wind-on and advance. After another few hours, they were ready for work again.

A specialized aspect of reliability, too, is battery dependency. There are four levels of risk here. The lowest (indeed, no risk at all) is to be battery-independent. This is possible with very few 35mm cameras today, and with a decreasing number of medium-format cameras. The next level is to rely on batteries only for metering, so that if they fail, you can still use all your equipment but you have to rely on guesswork (or experience, or a separate meter) to determine exposure. The third – which is the highest risk level we care to take – is to use equipment which uses readily-available batteries, principally AA and PP3. Such batteries are available in so many places that you would need to be travelling somewhere very remote indeed not to be able to get them within a day or two. The fourth level of risk is to use equipment which depends on exotic, hard-to-find battery sizes – though in all fairness, certain sizes are so widely used in cameras that even out-of-the-way kiosks may keep them. As well as camera batteries, do not forget batteries for flash guns, exposure meters, torches (flashlights) and in some locations even a small radio.

The argument that you can always carry spare batteries has some merit, but it is not unanswerable. Spare batteries are one more thing to remember and to carry, both when you are packing and when you are away from your base, and it is not unknown for 'fresh' batteries to have less life in them than you had hoped. As for always replacing batteries before a trip, if you are a professional travel photographer this could mean replacing surprisingly large numbers of almost new (and often expensive) batteries on an unrealistically frequent basis.

## Reliability and modernity

Modern, top-of-the-line cameras are very reliable and very versatile – but they are not necessarily any more inherently reliable than older and often cheaper cameras, provided those cameras are not actually worn out. Something like an old Nikkormat or Canon FTb has the potential to give results as good as any new camera available, and if you are likely to encounter the sort of conditions which could adversely affect any camera (again, such as dust or humidity or salt spray) you may choose to go for a semi-disposable approach.

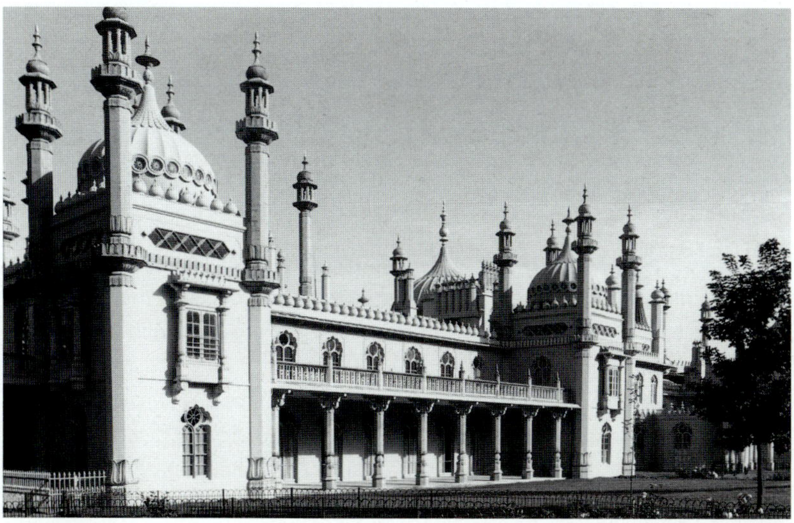

***Figure 2.3*** *The Royal Pavilion at Brighton is a most unexpected piece of Indo-Saracenic architecture at an English seaside resort. The tonality of Ilford Pan F Plus has however transformed weak British sunshine to the bright, hard light of India; you almost expect to see an ox-cart on the grass. Experimenting with different emulsions can give you a palette of different effects, even in monochrome. Of course, don't do your testing on important subjects, or if you do, make sure that you also capture them on familiar films where you can predict the results. (FES)*

Another point is that there are certain features which militate against reliability. In particular, very high top shutter speeds and high flash synch speeds for focal plane shutters are both inimical to long-term reliability, as shutter parts have to be made much thinner in order to be light enough to move at the required speeds. Top speeds of $^1/_{1000}$ second and synch speeds of $^1/_{60}$ second may be old hat, but if the shutter can be made to last halfway to forever, you may consider this a worth-while trade-off.

This is in fact the approach which we use. Both the original Nikon F and the M-series Leica are legendary for their reliability, and these are our favourite 35mm cameras for travel photography. With periodical servicing, these cameras can last a lifetime. Moving up to medium format, we use a 'baby' Linhof Technika IV, for much the same reasons; we actually wore out one 645 SLR body from another respected maker in a couple of years. By the time you get up to 4 × 5 inch cameras, most are pretty simple, solid and reliable, and they are also very easy to service.

This is however only one possibility, and plenty of top travel photographers use current state-of-the-art cameras: Heather Angel uses Nikons, while Kos goes for Canons.

## Portability

The most obvious constraint upon portability is that you must be able to carry your equipment. There is no point in taking every camera and lens you own, if you cannot carry them.

There is also a difference between what you can just about carry for moderate distances, and what you can easily carry all day. If you are travelling by car, and you rarely have to walk more than a few hundred yards from the car, you can carry whatever you like. This was the approach we adopted when working on the American Civil War book (Chapter 16); we had two hard-shell cases, three Leicas, a Visoflex, and a range of lenses from 21mm to 400mm. Equally, if you have to carry everything with you at all times, you may prefer to go for a much lighter outfit, even if you do not have to cover particularly great distances. In Rhodes, for example, we liked to spend the whole day in Rhodes Old Town. We probably walked only a few miles in any one day, but even when we sat down at a taverna for some restorative retsina or coffee, we still had to keep the cameras with us. This immediately introduces two further concerns, namely camera bags and security.

### Camera bags

We own ridiculous numbers of camera bags, partly because manufacturers give them to us for evaluation and partly because there is no such thing as the perfect camera bag.

For transport, hard-shell cases are excellent: we use Zero Halliburton, Doskocil and Pelican. If the bag is likely to be banged around by other people, such as porters or (worse still) airline handlers, hard-shells are the way to go.

If you are working out of a car, then hard-shells can still be suitable,

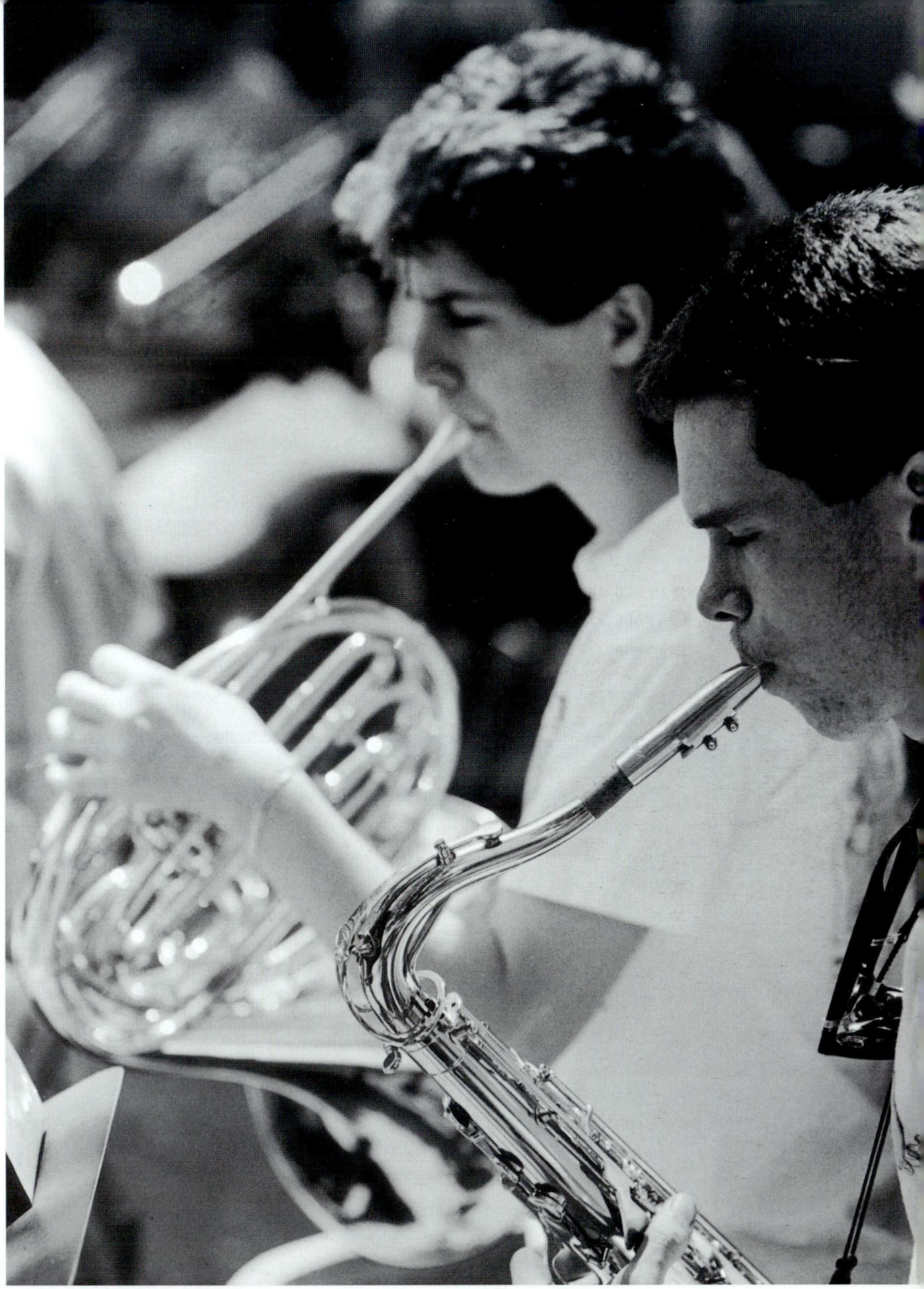

**Figure 2.4** *The sparkling tonality of the nearer instrument is what draws the eye in this picture; that, and the clear (though out-of-focus) shape of the more distant horn. The musicians' concentration is also very apparent. The film was Ilford XP-2, which is wonderfully forgiving of exposure variations: it can be rated from EI 50 to EI 800 on the same roll, with negligible loss of quality. XP-2 is our standard film for reportage. (FES)*

but if you have to carry the equipment any distance and work out of the bag on the move, they are all but useless. Even if you can set the bag down to work out of it, soft bags are usually more convenient; only if you are working out of a car is a hard-shell normally a realistic option.

Over-the-shoulder bags can still be surprisingly good for transport: a German magazine found that (soft) Billinghams offered the best protection of a number of bags they tried, including hard-shell, because the movement of the equipment and the deformation of the bag absorbed shocks rather than transmitting them.

Beyond a certain size, though, over-the-shoulder bags can become unwieldy even before they start to make your back hurt. Once, when we were snow-shoeing, Roger kept falling over because he was unbalanced by his over-the-shoulder bag.

What we prefer, therefore, is either backpacks (we use Tenba and Lastolite) or bags which have both shoulder and waist straps. Backpacks are the easiest to carry for long distances without fatigue, but access is more convenient with the sort of shoulder bag which has both shoulder and waist straps. The bag can be worn on the haunches or in the small of the back when walking, or swung round to the hip or front for working.

Another possibility is 'photographers' vests' or jerkins, those multi-pocketed garments which are based on the vests worn by enthusiastic fishermen. These vary enormously in quality, security and convenience. Roger lost a 21mm f/2.8 Elmarit-M out of the pocket of a cheap vest in Moscow, which made it a very expensive vest indeed. Also, a vest which is suitable for one outfit may be totally unsuitable for another: Roger has found his Billingham perfect for 35mm, but worthless for the baby Linhof outfit. Nor is price any great guide to convenience: Frances's 'no-name' vest was modestly priced in France, and is one of the best-designed vests we have ever encountered.

Some photographers use vests not for carrying, but merely as convenient storage space when working: they transfer the equipment they are actually using from bag to vest as they use it, then back to the bag when they are ready to move on.

## Protecting your equipment

Protecting your equipment has four separate aspects. The first is ensuring its survival when it is in use under adverse conditions. The second is protecting it from loss or damage when you are carrying it. The third is how secure it is in transit – in other words, whether it can withstand rough handling in the case. The fourth is how secure it is from theft.

Taking the four in reverse order, you can never fully protect yourself against theft. The best you can do is to reduce the probability. At the most basic, this means a secure bag or pockets; the cautionary tale of the 21mm has already been recounted. To this day, we do not know whether it was pickpocketed or dropped and then stolen. Keep zippers zipped and Velcro stuck, or at least keep flaps flapped over: a good pickpocket can lift

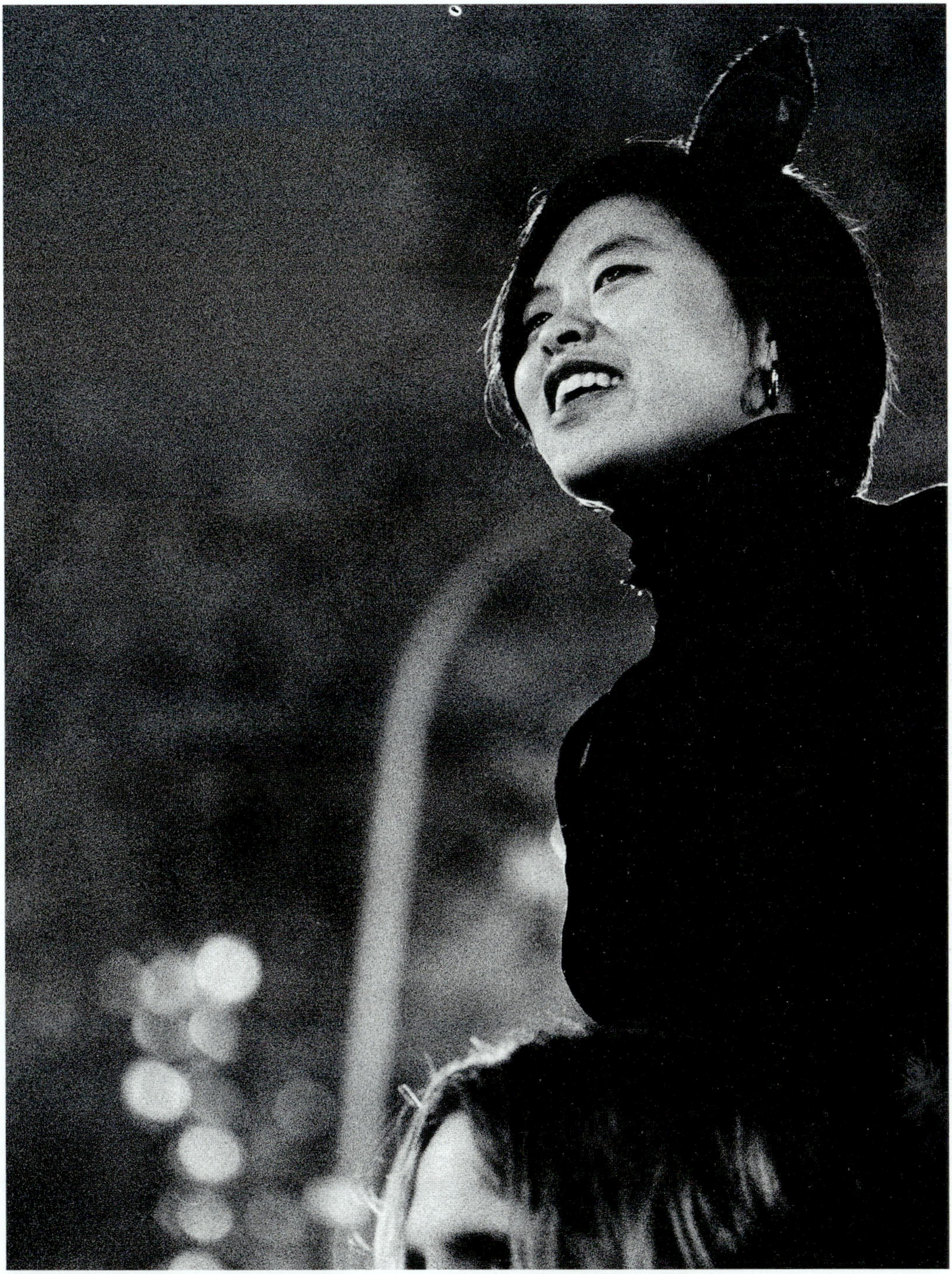

**Figure 2.5** *According to Kodak, their TMZ P3200 can be rated at up to EI 25,000. Of course, shadow detail has suffered long before that, but with the right picture, it doesn't matter. We find that we get the best results (or at least, the ones we like best) by rating the film at EI 12,500 and processing it in T-Max developer at the time recommended for EI 25,000. This was shot at a Halloween parade in New York City, using an M-series (rangefinder) Leica – arguably still the best camera for low-light reportage. (RWH)*

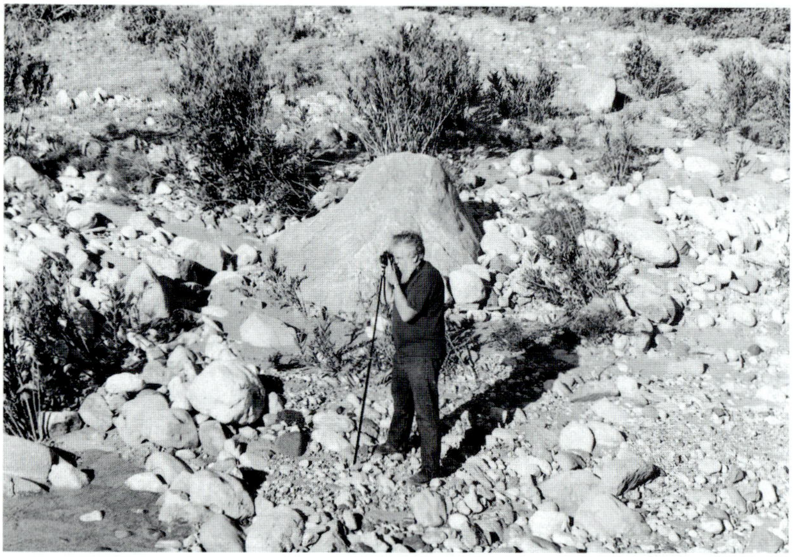

*Figure 2.6* One of the most useful camera supports we own is the CamCane. It weighs just 350 g (12 oz) and it extends from normal walking-stick size to a useful height for shooting. It can also be used as a conventional walking stick, either collapsed or extended, when negotiating awkward terrain. Best of all, we have never had anyone query its use, even where tripods and other camera supports are banned – and we carry our CamCanes on aircraft as permitted cabin baggage (you're allowed a walking stick by most airlines). (FES)

something out of an open bag without your realizing it. Velcro can be a nuisance, and it picks up debris, but the ripping sound of its parting can be an effective burglar alarm. One of Roger's favourite cases has a zip (which often gets left undone, in the nature of things) plus a shaped top-flap with a large Velcro seal. If the flap is simply pushed over, it seals automatically, but it is no hassle to open it again.

Also, protecting yourself from theft means never carelessly relinquishing control of your bag. Keep it with you at all times, preferably attached to your person with an over-the-shoulder strap running diagonally across your body and a waist strap. The only bag we have had stolen in fifteen years was when someone was 'helping' us into a train in Old Delhi railway station.

If you do voluntarily relinquish control of your bag, you want to make sure it is somewhere safe. Hotel rooms are for the most part surprisingly safe, and they are safer still if you chain a hard-shell case to something immovable such as a radiator: most theft is opportunist, and few hotel thieves carry bolt-cutters. We carry a small cable lock, intended for bicycles, with which we can secure hard-shell cases to things; we can also use it to wrap around wardrobes (or wardrobe handles) so that they cannot be opened. In some countries, hotel rooms have cupboards with a staple and hasp so that you can use your own padlock; some even have a staple and hasp on the room door.

The question of protecting your equipment in transit has already been addressed, though a point worth making is that high-density foam is best for absorbing blows while low-density foam is best for absorbing vibration. When we travel by motorcycle, we take great care to insulate the camera from vibration, ever since finding a Hasselblad back had unscrewed itself from its face-plate while being transported in a motorcycle top-box.

The risk of dropping the equipment out of a bag or vest is closely related to the risk of theft – guarding against the one will automatically guard against the other – while the risk of mechanical damage can be greatly reduced by taking a little care. We are constantly appalled by the number of people who sling their cameras over one shoulder, which is a sure recipe for banging them on doors and doorways.

If your equipment is knocked, though, it is much less likely to be damaged if it is of the highest quality. Our 35mm f/1.4 Summilux survived a six-foot fall onto granite cobbles in Prague (the lens shade took much of the force) and Geoffrey Crawley once lost his 35mm f/1.4 Summilux in the bilges of a boat for six months: he thought it had gone overboard, and was much surprised when he found it. He was still using it twenty years later. By contrast, a cheap lens which delivered excellent quality before a knock may be reduced to worthlessness afterwards.

Protecting your equipment while it is in use is a mixture of common prudence and (where necessary) special equipment or protective measures.

Common prudence includes sheltering the camera from rain, snow or blowing dust when reloading – this is where it is useful to have several camera bodies or backs, so that you do not have to reload as often – and cleaning the equipment each day after use. We carry a stiff 25mm paintbrush for cleaning the body, and a softer lens brush for cleaning the lens. Microfibre cloths from Luminex take care of cleaning optics when we are on the road, but a bottle of Paterson ProClens and a soft rag (an old T-shirt) will also travel with us if we have room. This can be used for cleaning both lenses and camera bodies.

In the most demanding conditions, special cameras (such as the Nikonos) or underwater housings may be necessary: after all, a camera which is waterproof is also dustproof. The Nikonos is also extremely rugged. An easier, cheaper and less demanding alternative is Ewa-Marine waterproof housings, which can stand less depth than rigid housings but are perfectly good for working in bad weather conditions. The cheapest options are taping the camera joints with low-tack draughtsman's tape (to avoid dust ingress) or simply protecting the whole camera with a large, clear plastic bag over the top: tape a hole in the bag around the lens hood, and operate the camera through the mouth of the bag. This is more suitable for wet weather than for dusty conditions, as dust can easily blow up into the bag.

Another option in hazardous conditions is to use 'disposable' cameras, by which we mean old, cheap, but still good cameras such as screw-mount Pentaxes, Canon FTbs, or even less common makes such as Konica and Topcon, both of which can be found with excellent lenses.

In conditions of extreme cold, you may do well to have your camera 'winterized' (cleaned, and all lubricants replaced with thinner lubricants) but if you use a 'winterized' camera in normal conditions it will feel very rough and it will wear more rapidly. Many modern cameras do not in any case need special lubricants, and with any camera you should only need 'winterizing' for prolonged use under seriously cold conditions, below –20°C or so. The biggest danger at this point is battery failure, and remote battery packs (which can be kept warm next to the body) are a good idea.

## SUITABILITY FOR PURPOSE

For the most part, like most photographers today, we use 35mm cameras: Leicas in Roger's case, Nikons for Frances. For the vast majority of editorial work, 35mm is all that is required. Which cameras you choose, and which lenses, are very much a matter of what sort of subject you are shooting and what sort of pictures you want to take. A bird photographer might want very long lenses; an architectural photographer might want shift (PC) lenses; and someone who liked traditional reportage might be influenced by sheer speed.

For what it is worth, Roger uses mostly a 35mm f/1.4, followed by 21mm, 90mm and 50mm, and occasionally a 135mm. Frances uses mostly a 35mm f/2.8 shift lens, closely followed by 90mm. After that, the next in line is probably the 15mm fish-eye or (where she wants speed) a 28mm f/1.9. Normally, we will also carry 14mm and 200mm lenses, along with a 2 × teleconverter. The fast lenses are ideal for reportage; the wide lenses are used mostly for interiors; the fish-eye adds novelty to familiar subjects; and the long lenses are mostly used for details.

There are however times when other formats are appropriate. The perennial cry of picture editors and picture libraries is that they want familiar subjects photographed in an unfamiliar way, or unfamiliar subjects photographed in an accessible way. Some kinds of commissioned work – annual reports, for example – may best be shot on medium or even large format, while for uncommissioned work it can be a case of the larger, the better.

We habitually bracket our exposures on 35mm, and for larger formats we normally shoot Polaroids: there is little sense in doing anything else, because if it is worth going somewhere and setting up a Linhof and shooting a decent-sized transparency, it is worth shooting a Polaroid as well. We use 4 × 5 inch single-sheet material; the slightly cheaper but considerably more compact 4 × 5 inch pack material; and the much cheaper, much more compact quarter-plate pack film.

### Library shots

Watch anyone going through pictures in a picture library, and you will notice that they look at the biggest images first. They may well stop once they have the big picture, but if they do continue to go through the files, they will look at roll-film next and at 35mm last, if at all. In all cases, a new picture has to be pretty good to knock the existing shot off its perch. Even if the smaller format picture is slightly superior aesthetically (or even technically) the bigger image will still have the edge because people assume that the bigger image is sharper and technically better. For many 'establishing shots', therefore, a 4 × 5 inch or 6 × 12 cm transparency will have the selling edge over a smaller origi-nal. Of course, you can always cheat and have smaller pictures duped up to the larger size...

There are however two arguments in favour of 35mm. One is that it is

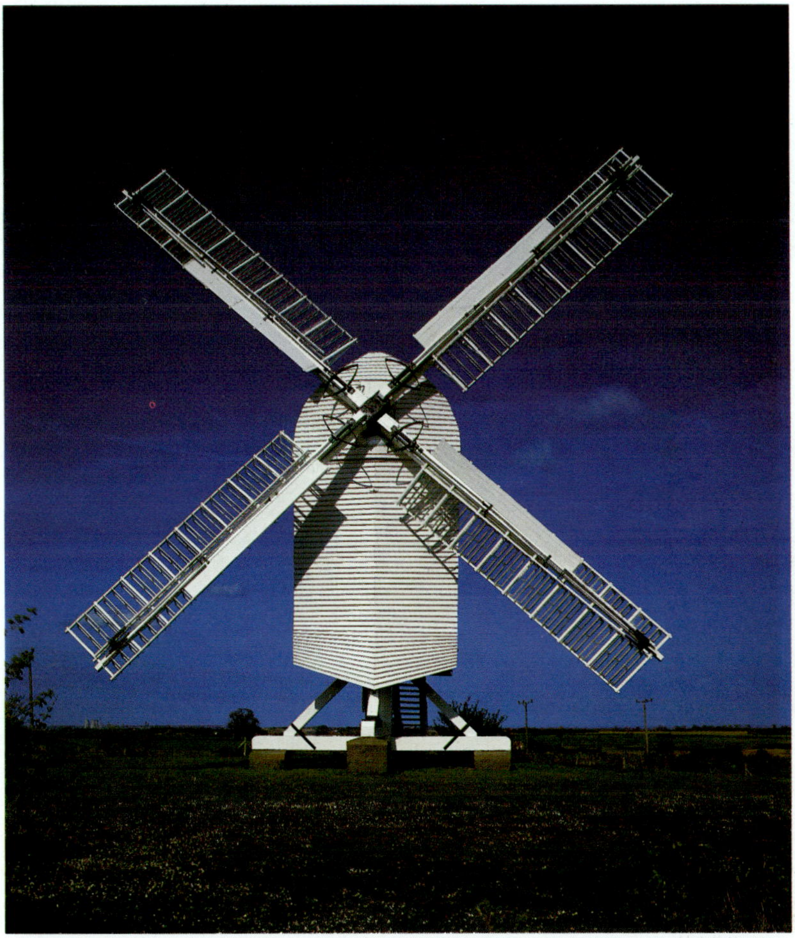

*Figure 2.7 A strictly literal picture of a relatively common subject will often be selected by a picture editor, and run very large, if it is graphically striking enough and technically perfect. This is not a particularly unusual picture, save for the fact that it is a very well-executed 4 × 5 inch transparency. (FES)*

a lot cheaper: each 35mm transparency is around one-half to one-quarter the price of a roll-film image, or one-twentieth the price of a 4 × 5 inch shot. The other point, easily overlooked, is that more and more libraries are sending out their catalogues on disk, and will scan a 35mm transparency in preference to a large one.

## Tripods, meters and accessories

We almost invariably carry at least one tripod between us, and we frequently carry one each. A tripod gives you sharper pictures, even at 'safe' hand-holding speeds, and by forcing you to slow down it also leads to a higher percentage of aesthetically successful pictures. At least, this is what we find. After many years' experience we have found no better tripod for travel photography than a mid-range Gitzo which weighs some 2.5 kg when fitted with a medium-sized (35mm ball) ball and socket head. We own numerous other tripods, some lighter, several heavier, many more versatile, and half a dozen different tripod heads, but the Gitzo is the best possible compromise when weight and

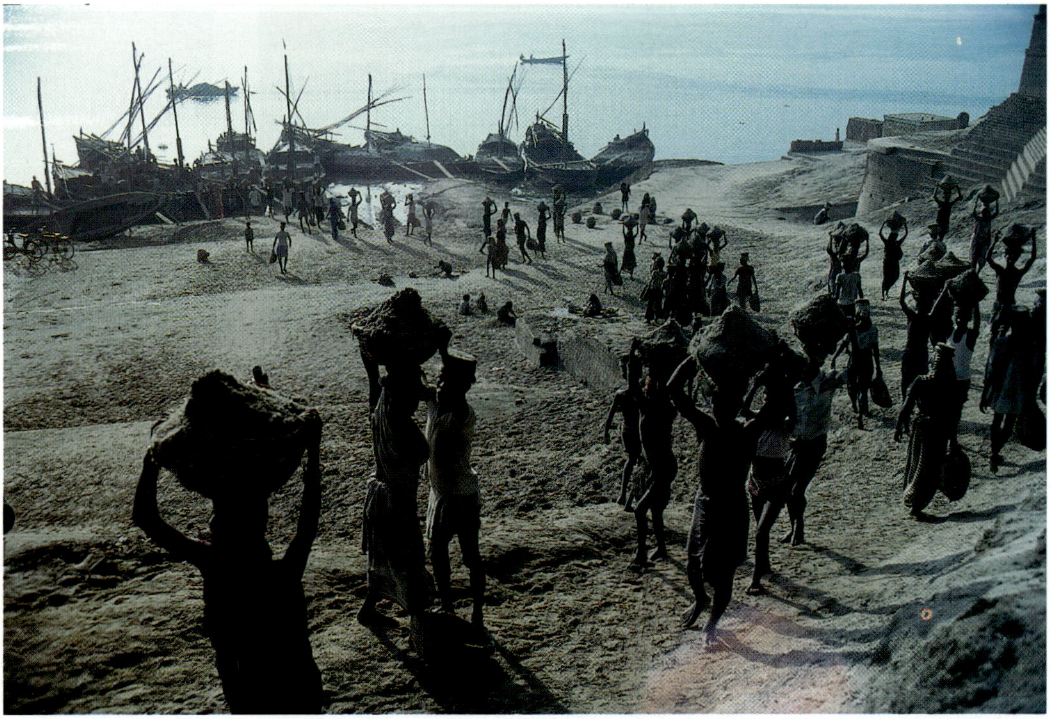

*Figure 2.8 Some pictures simply bypass all verbal description. It does not really matter what these people are doing. You can almost taste the dust in your mouth, feel the back-breaking weight of the baskets, weep at the bone-weary repetitiveness of it all. Unfortunately, the original colour transparency is let down by a patch of bright magenta flare on the lower right. Regardless of how such a picture may almost succeed, if it has technical faults, it is a failure. (RWH)*

bulk are a major consideration. If we are travelling by car, we may however use a Benbo tripod with an NPC ProHead.

Because we use ancient Nikons and Leicas, as well as medium- and large-format cameras which have no meters, we normally carry one Gossen each: a Variosix F for Roger and a Sixtomat Digital (LunaPro Digital in the United States) for Frances. If we have room, we also carry a spot meter, either a Gossen Spot Master 2 or a Minolta, and we will normally carry an old, non-battery-dependent Weston Master as a back-up. The Gossens have several major advantages over the old Westons, though: they are rugged, they are easy to read, they can read very low light levels, and they use readily-available batteries (PP3 for the Variosix and Spot Master, AA for the Sixtomat).

Other accessories include filters, lens shades, cable releases and so forth, but these are all pretty ordinary. The only one worth mentioning is perhaps a small pocket spirit level which fits into an accessory shoe or can simply be balanced on a flat surface. We carry one of these each, for levelling cameras.

## Redundancy and back-ups

It would be a brave (and indeed foolish) photographer who went anywhere with a single 35mm camera body: cameras can and do break, jam, and generally misbehave. We normally carry two 35mm bodies each, one for colour and one for mono but also in case of breakdown. Sometimes we will even carry a third Nikon F or Nikkormat body, just as a back-up, and very rarely we will carry a third Leica M-series body as well.

We have however met photographers who had two camera bodies go bad on them, or be stolen, or otherwise meet with misfortune. David Gibbon tells the story of using a Rollei 35 compact for almost an entire shoot, and still having plenty of publishable pictures at the end of it. Today, although the Rollei remains an excellent camera, a Contax G2 with its interchangeable lenses might be an even better choice for a back-up.

With larger formats, a lot depends on the camera. After all, there is not a great deal that can go wrong with a Linhof Super Technika, which is essentially a spacer between the film holder (of which we carry several) and the lenses; and what can go wrong is in most cases fairly easily repaired, though a spare ground-glass is a good idea. A Hasselblad body, on the other hand, may be superbly simple and reliable, but we'd still prefer to have two bodies, three backs, and two or more lenses.

What is rarely a good idea is to try to shoot with two formats simultaneously – 35mm and 4 × 5 inch, say. Normally, one will simply crowd the other out. Also, the weight rapidly becomes intolerable. By all means take two formats with you, but leave one at your base and carry just the other if at all possible. If we are shooting mainly 4 × 5, we normally carry 35mm only as a back-up or 'life-saver'.

## Materials

At the beginning of the chapter, we said that the three requirements for materials were that they should match your vision; that they should deliver adequate quality for the purpose in question; and that they should stand up to the rigours of travel.

The first point is quickly covered: only you know what will give the results you want, and your personal vision may be at variance with traditional views of quality. For example, we have done quite well with extremely grainy 35mm transparencies made on Scotch/3M 1000D and Agfa 1000, both now sadly discontinued. We have also illustrated numerous articles with Polaroid's excellent sepia material, and as we were writing this book we saw another book consisting entirely of infra-red photographs of ruins. When we get around to it, we want to try supplying some hand-coloured images to libraries, too.

The second point does not take long, either. For the vast majority of editorial use, and for increasing numbers of libraries, 35mm transparencies are perfectly adequate – though some films are preferred to others, particularly Kodachrome and Velvia, and slow films (ISO 100 or below) are almost invariably preferred to faster ones unless there is a compelling reason to use something faster. As described in the previous paragraph, this 'compelling reason' can be aesthetic as easily as technical. Similar considerations apply to larger transparencies.

Colour negative film is widely used for newspaper editorial work, but normally only by staff photographers; for freelance contributions, the norm is still colour transparencies. In other fields, colour negative film and colour prints are often rejected out of hand.

## The rigours of travel

The third consideration is more complex than the other two and demands a separate heading to itself. Heat degrades films; cold makes them brittle; and dust causes scratches.

If we are travelling in hot climates, we normally try to refrigerate films overnight, and to carry them in 'cool chests' during the day. This is feasible only if you are travelling by car in a country where hotel rooms are likely to have refrigerators or where you can persuade the hotel management to stick the films in their refrigerator.

Our preferred colour film for rigorous travel when we cannot do this is Kodachrome. Because this is a non-substantive film, i.e. the colour dyes are added during processing, it is more resistant to heat than other colour films. Our second choice is almost any slow substantive film – Kodak Elite, Agfa, Fuji Astia and so forth – but not Velvia, which seems particularly susceptible to colour shifts under adverse storage. Fast films normally suffer worst from colour shifts, but it is worth adding that for travel photography small colour shifts are rarely if ever as important as they normally are in studio photography.

Infra-red films are particularly vulnerable to hot weather, and particular care should be taken with them: put them in the coolest place you can find, and insulate them during the day with layers of clothing or anything else you can get. On the other hand, we have travelled with both monochrome and colour IR materials and have had no real problems.

In very cold conditions, the problems arise in two stages. One is an increased risk of static in cold, dry air, leading to static marks on 35mm film as it is pulled past the velvet lips of the cassette. Then, when it gets still colder, the film base itself is embrittled. Both problems can be minimized by advancing the film slowly and gently; motor drives present the greatest risk. Static, should it turn out to be a problem, can be eliminated by using all-metal reloadable cassettes such as those made by Nikon and Leica, though these are rare nowadays. As far as we know, all films are about equally vulnerable to the problems of cold weather.

## NON-PHOTOGRAPHIC EQUIPMENT

An essential tool for any travel photographer is a Swiss Army knife: as a general rule, the bigger, the better. Its uses are so numerous as to defy listing. A useful second tool is a Leatherman survival tool, though if you have a Swiss Army knife with pliers, it is less important. Buy the best quality you can afford: cheap imitations of both Swiss Army knives and Leathermans are available, but are not worth buying. You may care to carry either or both in belt pouches, where they are readily accessible and harder to lose. Frances carries hers on the belt of a waist pouch.

Almost as important as a Swiss Army knife is a small, high-quality torch (flashlight) and we use the California-made Mag-Lite, in the double AA cell fitting; the smaller AAA lights have a considerably shorter battery life. As

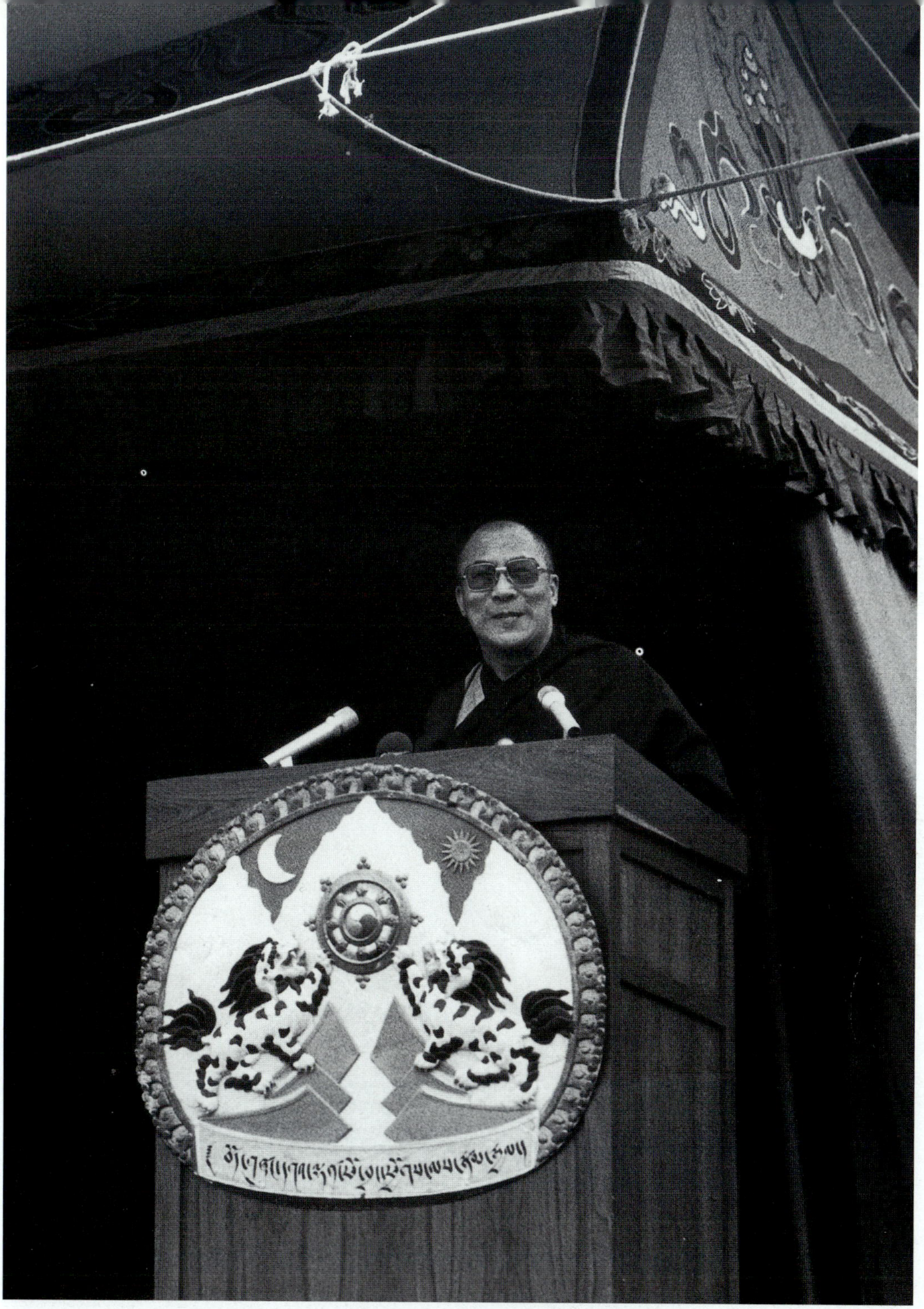

**Figure 2.9** His Holiness the Dalai Lama. *Although Roger favours Leica M-series rangefinder cameras, he emulates the photojournalists of the 1960s and carries an old Nikon F with a fast (f/3) 200mm lens and a 2 × teleconverter. Of course teleconverters cause a loss of image quality, but a good teleconverter (he uses a Tamron SP) and a good prime lens (Vivitar Series 1) will often give better quality than a sectional blow-up. Also, the teleconverter shot is much likelier to be used if you are shooting slides, simply because it is easier to see on the light table. (RWH)*

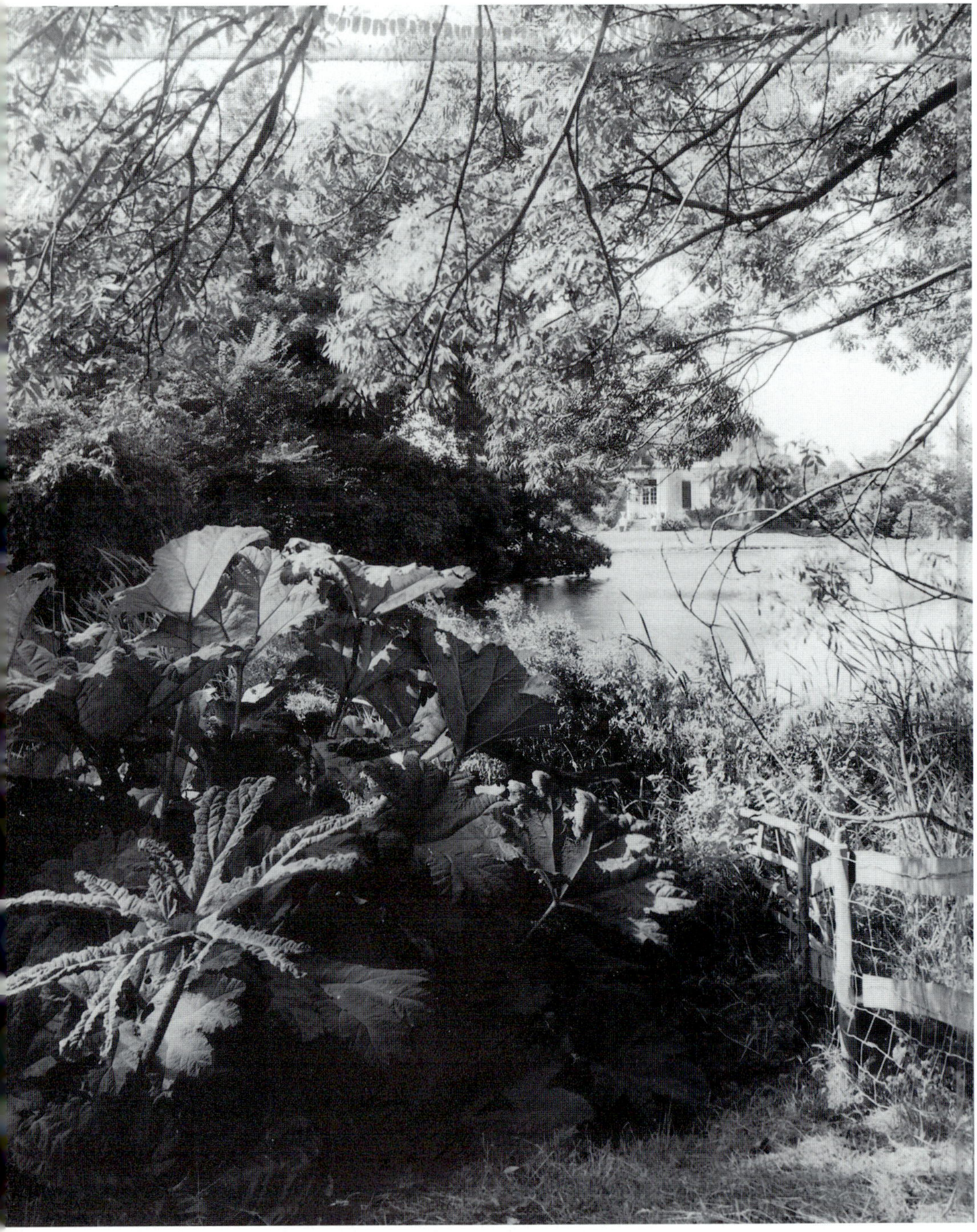

**Figure 2.10** *If you can stand the weight, and if you can afford the film, and if it is the way you like to shoot, by all means use 4 × 5 inch cameras and film – and remember, you can also use 6 × 7, 6 × 9 and 6 × 12 cm roll-film backs with 4 × 5 inch. Now that 35mm has all but conquered travel photography, there may well be room for a resurgence of the unique look obtainable with larger formats. (RWH)*

well as being focusing flashlights, Mag-Lites can be used as 'candles' if you unscrew the reflector.

After this, we find the following useful. A small compass, both for navigating and for determining where the sun rises. A small monocular or telescope, for checking distant scenes and reading distant signs; ours is a Russian-made 8 × 20. A map distance meter, either the familiar wheel type or the ingenious 'clicker' which we use (see Figure 7.8).

## Checklists

Given the amount of stuff we normally carry, it is alarmingly easy to forget some of it – though we have never done as badly as one assistant who packed everything his gaffer needed for a two-week glamour shoot in the Seychelles, except the film.

We therefore make extensive use of checklists. Normally, we use two for each trip. One covers the stuff we always need, such as film (and is subdivided into film types, so we don't forget monochrome film, or Polaroid, or whatever) and the other is an 'outfit' checklist for a particular camera or format. We even note the type of lens shade we need for particular cameras or lenses. The checklists live on the computer and are printed out when we are packing – often two or three copies, so one can go in the camera bag, one in a pocket, and one pinned to the studio wall.

We both go through them, and then go through them together: otherwise, there is always the danger of 'I thought you had packed it' – 'Well, I thought you had packed it...'

Such exhaustive use of checklists may sound a bit over the top, but they have two enormous advantages. One is that almost by definition, when you are about to set out on a long shoot, there's a good chance that you are fairly stressed and therefore likely to forget things. The other is that familiarity breeds if not contempt, then over-confidence. Pilots go through their pre-flight checks carefully, precisely because they have done them a hundred times or a thousand times before; when you have done something that often, it is very easy to forget whether you have actually done it this time, or whether you think you have, because you always do it.

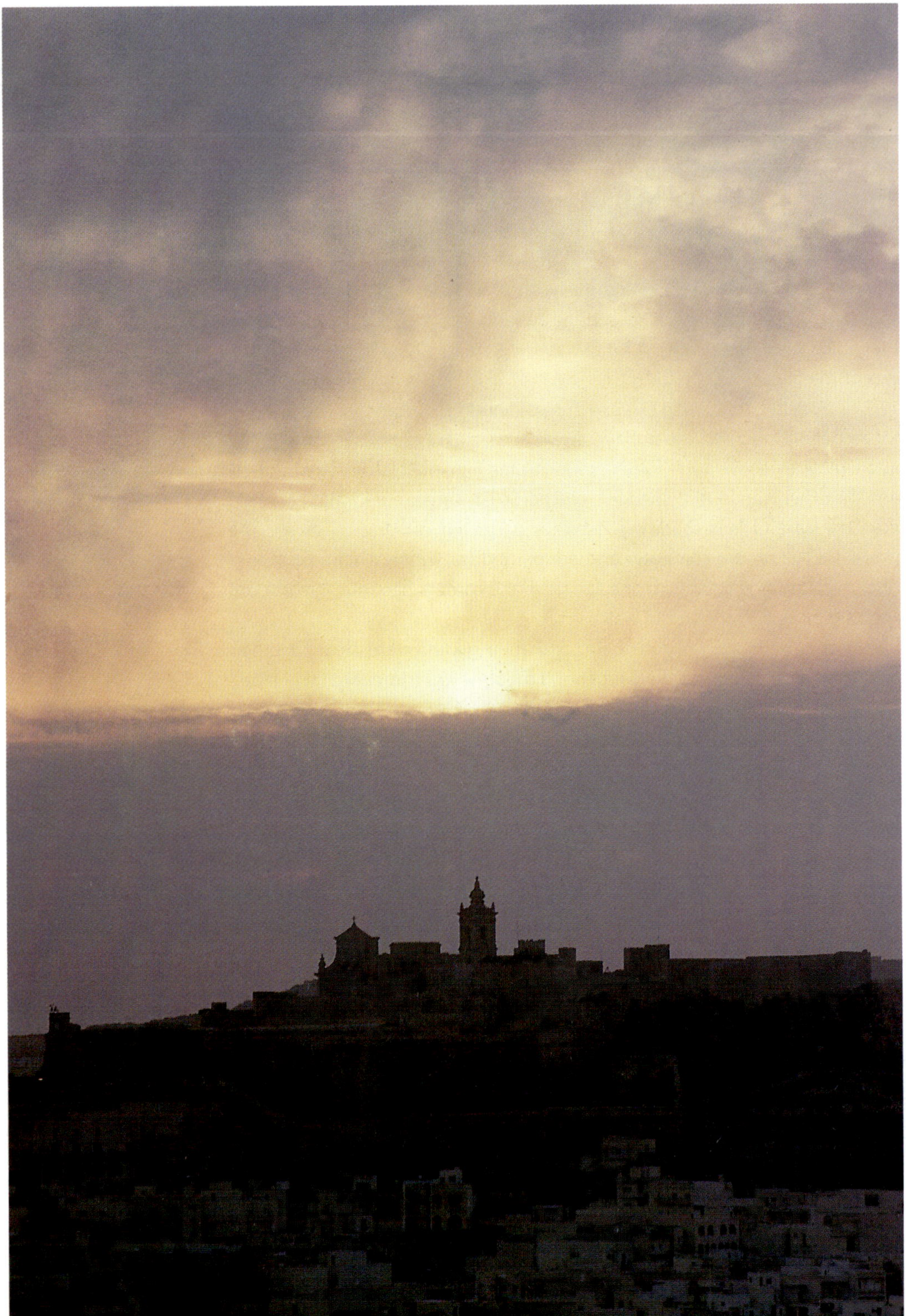

# 3 Keeping track: facts and pictures

A picture is often worthless unless it is properly and accurately captioned. In order to do this, you have first to know what you are photographing, and then to record it. This is true whether you are using a picture for a single article; filing it in your own collection; or submitting it to a picture library, as discussed in Chapter 9.

A counsel of perfection would be to make notes of every exposure, but in the real world, this just isn't going to happen. Write up your notes as soon as you can, on the spot or later that day – and remember that you don't necessarily need to write notes in a notebook. We write on maps and in guidebooks, and (sometimes) in brochures, though we try to avoid this as the ones with the important notes in are almost invariably the only ones that get lost.

All too often, though, the best you can do is to caption pictures as soon as possible, while the trip is still fresh in your mind, preferably with the same guide books, maps and other research material to hand as you used for your original research (see Chapter 7). Fortunately, most photographers report a sort of heightened awareness when they are shooting which makes it easier to recall things – and of course we work together, so there is always the possibility of cross-checking our memories.

The normal way to present a caption is hierarchically, with the broadest category first. Thus, for example, a caption might read 'Europe – Greece – Rhodes – Thari monastery – altar (crucifix) illuminated by sunbeam'. That way, it could readily be seen to refer to European monasteries (level one and level four) or Rhodes (level three) or Greek altars (levels two and five) or whatever.

Remember that the caption is as much for the publisher or other end user as it is for you, so make it as clear as possible: most people may be aware that Greece is in Europe, but would Malta be classified as Europe or Africa? What do you do about Central America? Exactly how you categorize your slides is up to you, but with our four-line labels we find that categorizing by continent, country, region, place and subject works best.

In addition to the descriptive caption, we have an accession number which is normally made up of the last two digits of the year (97, say, or 00 or whatever), the number of the month in that year, and the slide number itself. This gives a forbidding number but it does enable us to tell quite a lot about the slide. We have yet to shoot more than 9999 slides in one month, so the 8-digit maximum which our labels can accommodate is plenty. A separate label is used for copyright data, our address, and whether the slide is an original or a duplicate.

The only rational way to make these labels is with an

***Figure 3.1** The better you like a place, the easier it is to learn about it and to remember it. Rabat, the ancient capital of Malta's sister-island Gozo, is on a site which had long been inhabited when the Carthaginians came. The Romans fortified it, but the citadel of today is, despite its mediaeval appearance, surprisingly recent, dating from the early years of the seventeenth century. It is a wonderful place to wander in, a fascinating combination of ruins (partly the legacy of an earthquake in 1693) and restored buildings. The utterly wonderful Folklore Museum is in three houses inside the citadel, dating from about 1500. (RWH)*

appropriate computer program. We use Labelbase, which allows up to four lines of up to about 30 characters per line to be printed on a label about 11 × 45 mm (7/8 × 1 3/4 inch). Some word processing programs can be adapted to print small type-on labels, too, but a purpose-made program is easier and quicker and generally allows for better readability and more information.

## Keeping track of slides

A good labelling program such as Labelbase also allows you to set up a proper archive, so that you can find and re-file your slides quickly and easily. The system you use is up to you, but we have found from painful experience that for our purposes an accession number system is generally quicker than any other, despite the apparent logic of filing (say) all Greek slides together, and all Maltese slides together, and all Californian slides together.

This is only true because we are the only people who look through our files, and if we ran a proper picture library (see below) we would probably use an entirely different basis for filing, probably by country, region and city. On the other hand, a good database system allows you to search by topics. Usually, you can search singly or in combination.

Each caption can contain a number of key words – typically five – and for the slide described above these would probably be the ones underlined as follows: '<u>Europe</u> – <u>Greece</u> – <u>Rhodes</u> – Thari <u>monastery</u> – altar (crucifix) illuminated by <u>sunbeam</u>'. The more key words you enter, the smaller the group of slides that the system will select. In fact, with all of the five key words just described, there would be precisely one slide in that category for us, though (for example) 'sunbeam' on its own would bring up plenty more, from Monaco to the Himalayas.

You have to aim for two things if you want to use this sort of program, namely brevity and consistency: 'shaft of sunlight' and 'Jesus light' and 'Hand of God light' (the latter both deriving from the kind of sunbeam so often portrayed in religious paintings) must all be reduced to mere 'sunbeam' – and often just 'sunbeam', not even 'sunbeams' as well, unless the program recognizes plurals.

## Picture storage

We store 35mm slides in hanging files, each holding four rows of six slides, with the accession numbers marked along the top: 9606121 to 9606144, for example. Mostly, we mount the slides in GePe mounts, but sometimes we just stuff them into the slots unmounted, protected only by the sleeving in which they were returned from the lab. In those cases, we cut the labels mentioned above from the roll, leaving them on the backing paper, and put the label in the slot with the picture. Then, if we need the picture, we can just mount it and label it. Generally, though, if it's worth keeping and labelling, it's worth mounting as well.

One drawer of a filing cabinet can hold 100 to 200 hanging files,

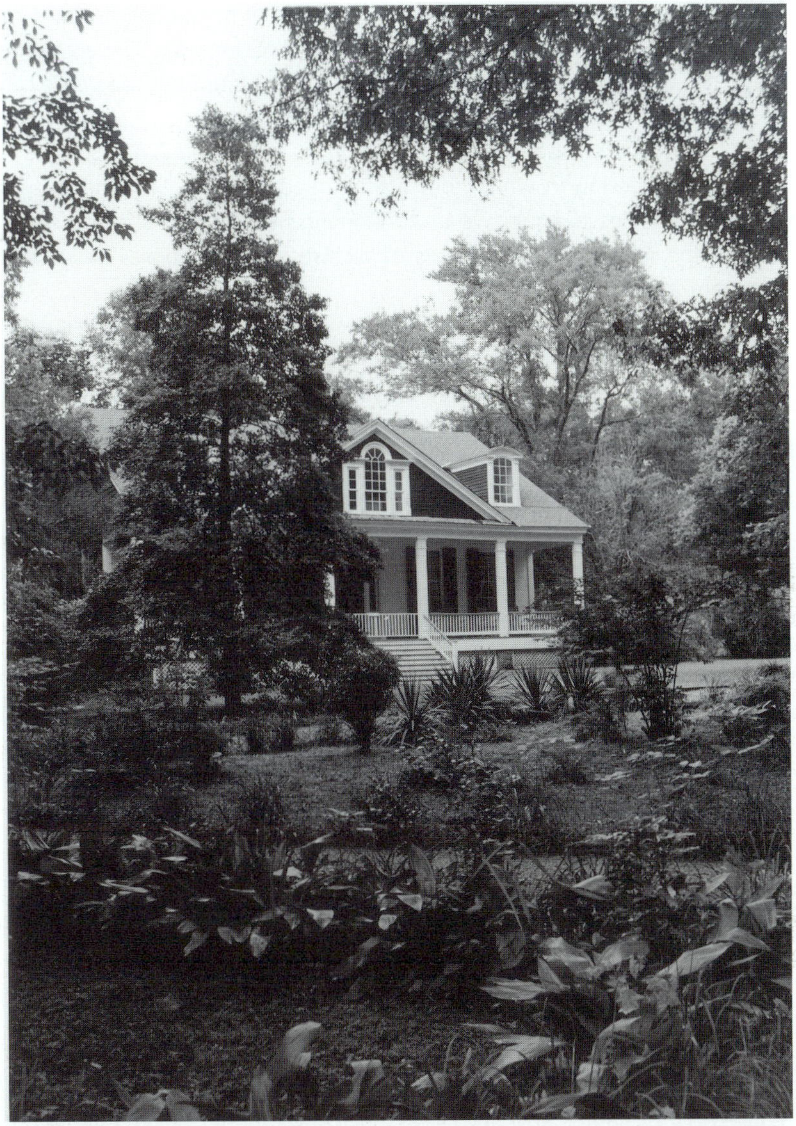

*Figure 3.2* *The plantation owned by Jefferson Finis Davis, only President of the Confederate States of America, has apparently fallen into ruin after being cut off by a change in the course of the Mississippi River; but his birthplace can be visited. Unless you are interested in this sort of thing, visiting historical sites can be rather tedious. People who are interested, however, are often obsessive, so you had better make sure that your captions are correct. If they are wrong, you can be sure that the editor will receive endless letters telling him so. (FES)*

which represents anything from 2000 slides upwards, so a three-drawer cabinet should keep you going for a while. When you pull a slide, you should ideally put a slip of paper in the slot saying what it was taken for, or alternatively log it in a book or file kept for the purpose, but even if you don't, you should be able to put it back when you get it back.

At the time of writing, most of our roll-film transparencies were stored in individual masked 4 × 5 inch sleeves in 4 × 5 boxes, though we were in the process of switching to hanging files for these too. The big advantages of masked sleeves are that they look very smart and that you can put two or three labels on the mask if you like (or one big one), but the drawbacks are that they are expensive and that they normally mask off quite a bit of the edge of the image. For instance, the '6 × 7' transparencies from our Linhof are 56 × 72 mm, but '6 × 7' masks can be as small as 52 × 65 mm. Stick labels to the mask, not the sleeve, as the picture is taped to the mount but the sleeve can be removed.

Cut film transparencies – all 4 × 5 inch – are stored in 4 × 5 boxes in the original sleeving in which they are returned from the lab. The label is stuck onto the sleeve. Again, we are considering switching to hanging sleeves, but for the relatively tiny numbers of pictures involved, boxes have been adequate so far.

Both 35mm and roll-film negatives are stored in archival sleeves in ring binders, and for this application they are divided by country as well as by date. If we want to find a particular negative, such as the lighthouse and mole of Chania harbour, this means we have to go to the file with GREECE on the spine and then look for the pages marked CRETE 1995. It takes a while, but it doesn't take long enough that we have ever really felt the need of setting up a database and accession numbers. You may feel differently; but we make this confession to illustrate the point that you do not need to be the kind of obsessive who is sometimes portrayed in books like this one, so perfectly organized and well advised and utterly in control that they may inspire dismay or disbelief, but never unqualified admiration.

As an aside here, an awful lot of people in an awful lot of fields fall short of the sort of perfection which is so often counselled in books on how to run your own business, yet still they survive and indeed in many cases prosper. There are certain things you have to do in order to stay in business, like delivering stuff on time, and there are certain things you have to do in order to stay out of jail, like paying your taxes; but you need a sense of proportion, or you can become so bogged down in minutiae and secondary considerations that you never actually take any pictures.

In the long run, you will almost certainly work out a *modus vivendi*, and while you may wish that you had organized yourself better at the outset, it is better to jump in and start work than it is to be frightened off by the nannyish advice which is so widespread. We do not follow our own advice, as given in this chapter, anything like as much as we should. So far, this has not got us into serious trouble. But each time we run into another hassle because of sloppy filing and captioning, we make a bit more of an effort to get better organized.

## Sending pictures out

Because most of our work is editorial, we tend to send original transparencies either on their own, or with articles (Chapter 11). We rarely feel the need to seal transparencies in their sleeves with stickers which say FEE PAYABLE IF BROKEN or something similar, but that is because we mostly deal with people we can trust. If you are supplying pictures 'on spec', on the other hand, you may find it advisable to take such measures.

The best system we have seen to date is made by DW Viewpacks, and consists of a mix-and-match menu of masks, sleeves, seals and an anti-use stripe. You choose the appropriate mask, and mount the transparency. Then you can, if you wish, sandwich it in the sleeve with a plain acetate mask which has a thin line down the middle – not enough to stop anyone seeing all they need of the image, but enough to make it very tedious indeed to remove the line in Photoshop or something similar. The mask and anti-use stripe are then placed in an acetate sleeve, and sealed with a sticker which says FEE PAYABLE IF BROKEN.

Admittedly, you always have to make a trade-off between recovering damages for lost or misused slides against the loss of goodwill that you may engender: unless it is an astonishingly good and irreplaceable picture, you do not want to lose a good client over the loss or misuse of one picture. On the other hand, good clients rarely lose pictures; they will normally only misuse them for dummies and presentations; and they will pay if there are disputes. It is the bad clients who cause the real problems, which is pretty much a matter of definition: the first time you have a problem with a client, look at their previous history and ask yourself if they are worth keeping.

## Dupes

An old and cynical saying is that there is only one way to make a perfect dupe. It is this: make two dupes, and throw the original transparency away.

There is however plenty of reason to be cynical. Clients will often demand originals – and a good choice of originals, at that – when they have no need of them. They may also hold on to them for an altogether unconscionable length of time, sometimes several months.

If pictures are to be reproduced small, or on newsprint at almost any

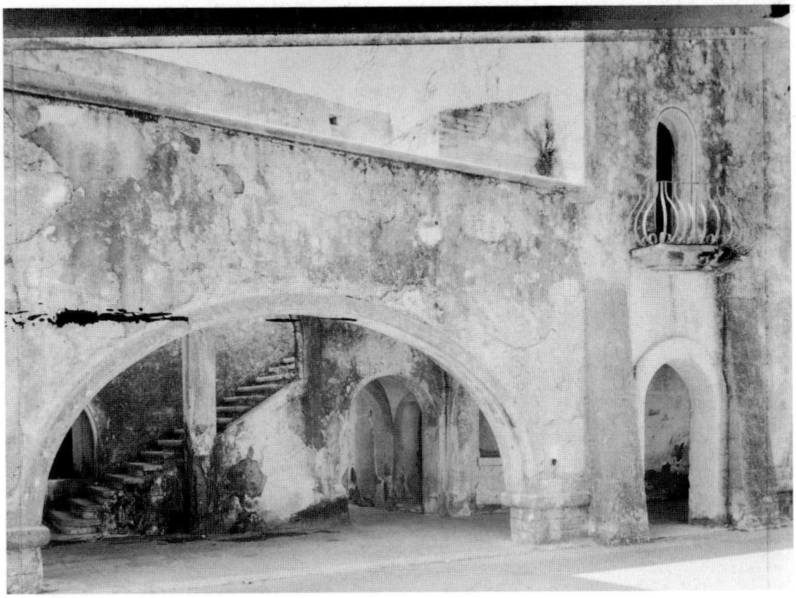

***Figure 3.3*** *Appearances can be deceptive. The intriguing thing about this ruin is that despite its antique appearance it was built in the 1920s for the Italian governor of Rhodes. The Italians had very romantic ideas about Rhodes, and did a great deal of excellent restoration (and a lot of over-restoration too), but they were understandably unpopular, and when Rhodes rejoined Greece this palace was simply allowed to decay. The scratch on the image was an accident, caused by use of an old-style Polaroid clearing tank; but when we printed the image, we decided that it worked well, giving the impression of a nineteenth-century negative that had suffered damage at some time in the past. (RWH)*

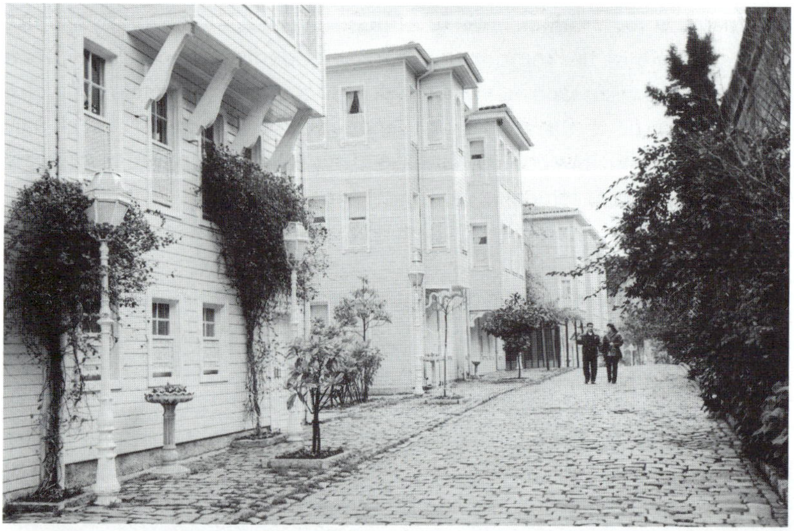

**Figure 3.4** *Behind Hagia Sophia in Istanbul – and both spellings are correct, Ayia/Hagia and Sofia/Sophia – there is a surprising and delightful street of affluent houses. If you caption it 'Street between Hagia Sophia and Topkapi Palace', this will probably be enough for most picture researchers. The catch is, if you are using a computerized database, what do you enter as the key words for your caption? When there are several alternative spellings, this can be a problem. (FES)*

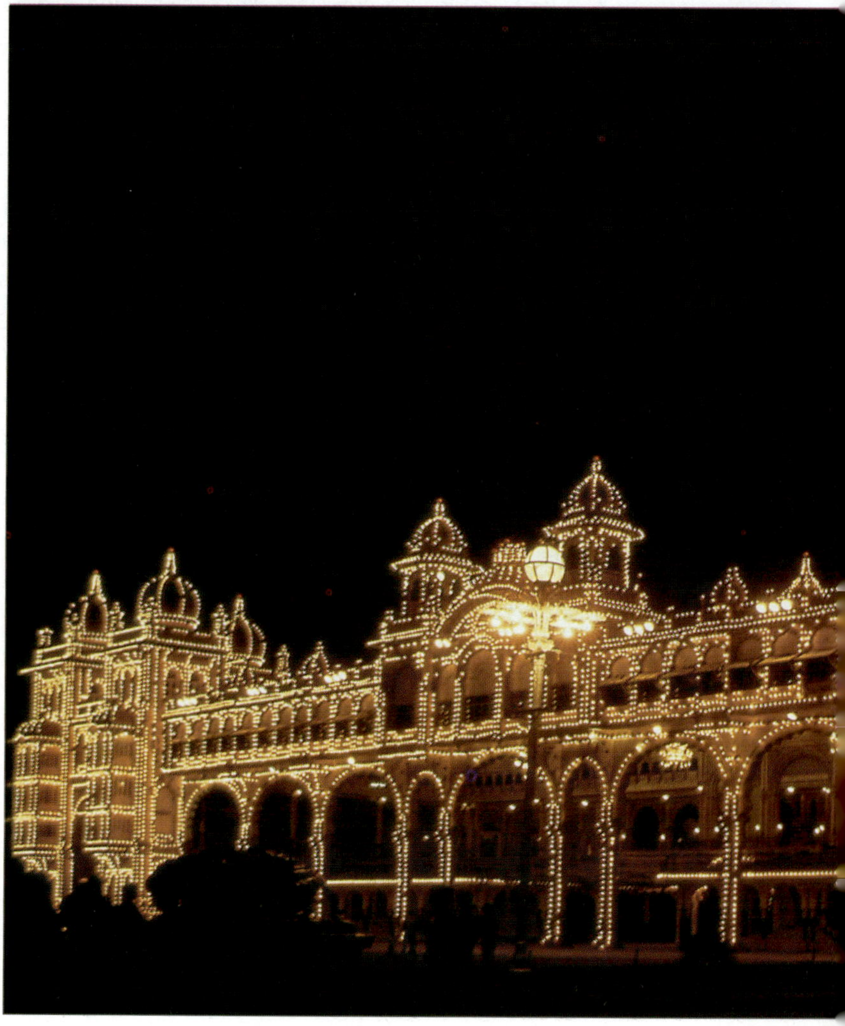

size, then a repro quality duplicate is perfectly adequate. We normally duplicate onto Kodak SO366 (balanced for short exposures), using a Bowens Illumitran, though tungsten-balance duping films are easier to find.

The important thing with dupes is to remove any evidence that they are dupes, in particular the tell-tale shadow which you will get around the edge of the image if you do not remove it from the mount for duping or do not crop in close enough to remove that shadow. This can play hob with images which are carefully framed to the edges, which is the principal reason we sometimes label slides as dupes: we just haven't disguised the fact adequately. Otherwise, depending on the client, you may prefer to pass off dupes as originals; or more honestly, simply to make no reference to the fact that they are dupes.

An alternative to dupes is to shoot originals on 6 × 9 cm negative film, then copy the neg using something like Kodak Vericolor 5072. If your original is of good quality, your copy trannies will be sharper than most

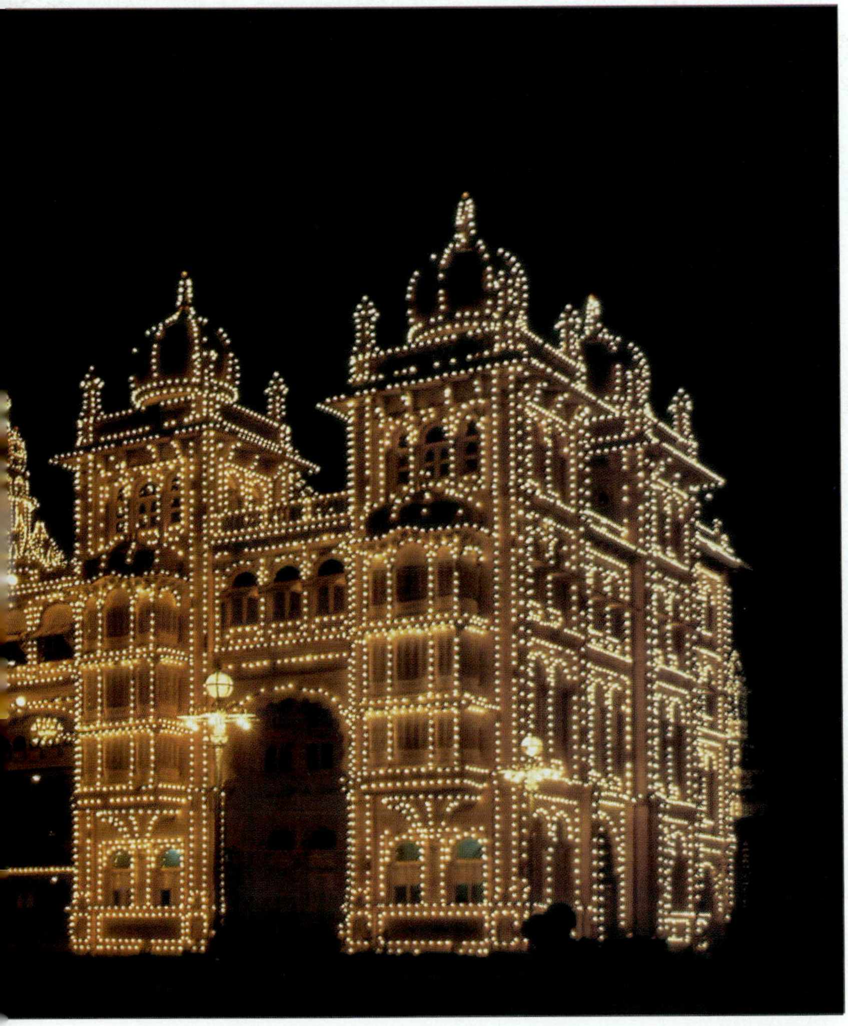

***Figure 3.5*** *The palace of the Maharajah of Mysore is (reputedly) lit by three* lakh *of bulbs (300 000), but we have never been able to get an authoritative figure. It is also (reputedly) lit between 7pm and 8pm on Sundays, and we have seen this; but given India's flexible attitude to time, and the fact that it might be lit more often for special occasions, there are always 'facts' which have to be treated with caution. What you can say with confidence, though, is that it is indeed the Maharajah's palace and that it is indeed in Mysore – and that it is a very impressive sight when illuminated. (FES)*

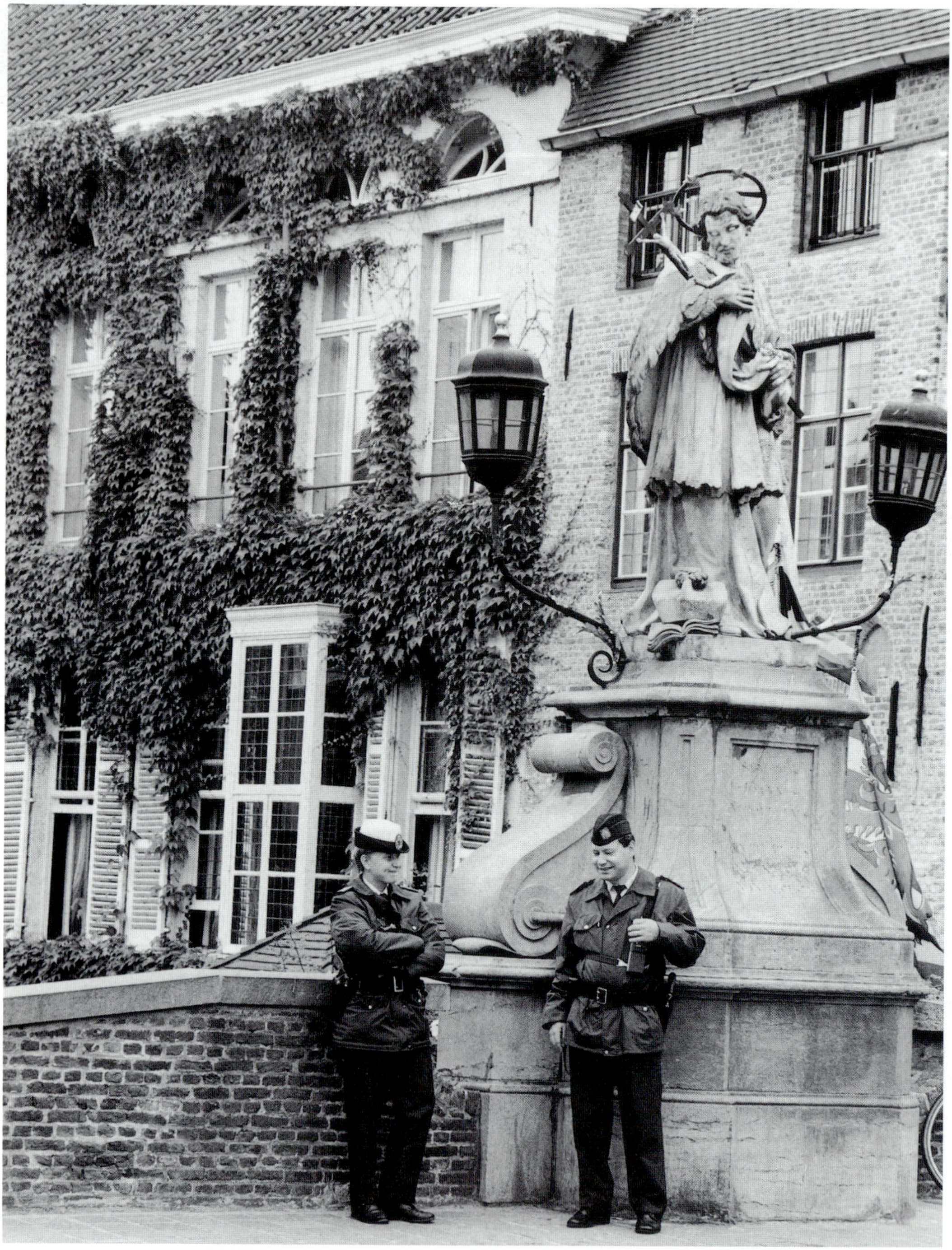

**Figure 3.6** *These are apparently two different varieties of police. What kind? The only easy way is to ask them, or to show the picture to a well-informed Belgian and ask him or her. Gathering accurate information can sometimes take longer than taking pictures. (FES)*

35mm originals, even after allowing for the degradation introduced by the duplicating process. The rebates are however clear instead of black, which tends to derange the more photographically aware clients. We have tried this, and it works, and we keep meaning to enlarge 6 × 7 cm negatives onto 4 × 5 inch Vericolor print film but we have not yet got around to it; it should work, though.

## Derivatives

Because the preferred medium for most repro is transparencies, it makes sense to convert things like hand-coloured prints, or toned black-and-whites, or even Polaroid sepias, to transparency formats. This has the additional advantage that you are only sending out dupes, which are replaceable. Ideally, you should only send out 4 × 5 transparencies of such derivatives, but in practice (especially for editorial work) you should find that 6 × 7 cm is no problem and that even 35mm is often perfectly adequate.

## Saving money on dupes

A good duping set-up will obviously enable you to shoot copies a lot cheaper than you could get them done by a lab, but we have also found that it can make sense to process your own E6 in a small hand-line, especially in the case of 4 × 5 inch. The big problem with E6 for most people is that the chemistry dies of old age before they have put the recommended number of films through it, but if you have a large batch of pictures to process, you can use an E6 kit to exhaustion. We use Nova hand-lines for both 4 × 5 inch (FP54) and roll-film and 35mm (FP4). A single Paterson kit allows us to process 4 × 5 inch film for about a quarter or a fifth of what a lab charges, and you can put up to 64 sheets through a 1200 ml kit.

Like the Fotospeed kit (which we have also used), the Paterson is a 4-bath kit (first developer, colour developer, bleach-fix and stabilizer) but, contrary to widespread belief, the principal advantages of 6-bath processes are for replenishment of working chemistry and disposal of used chemistry; a good 4-bath kit is capable of delivering quality which is comparable with a professional lab, provided you get the time and temperature right. The Nova hand-lines allow you to control temperature to within 0.25°C, and correct timing is easily achieved, even in the dark, with a tape recording of the times and stages required. Only the first developer and first wash steps need to be done in total darkness anyway: colour development and subsequent stages can be done in room light.

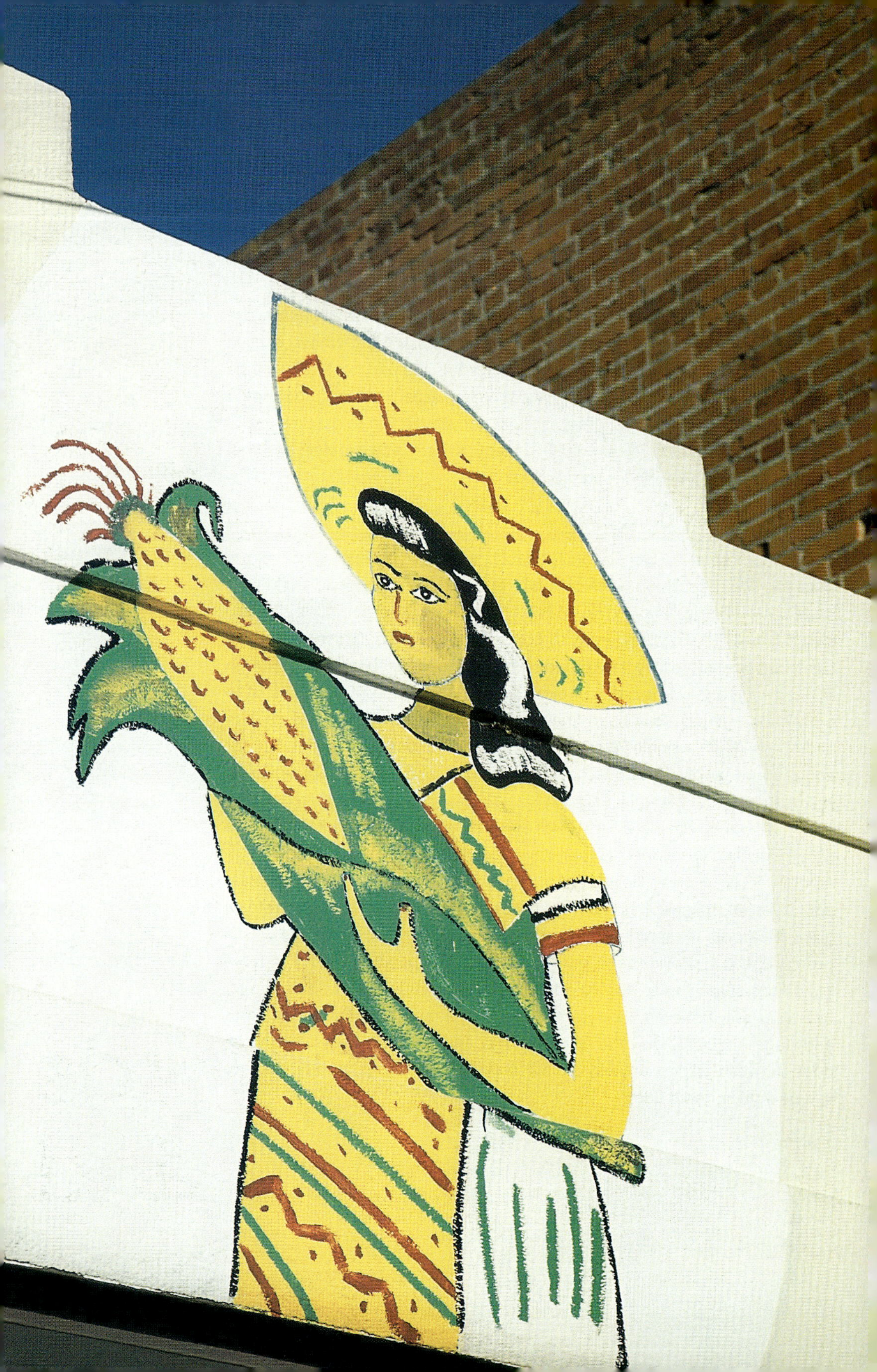

# 4 Words and pictures

Hard though some photographers may find it to accept, and despite the old saying that a picture is worth a thousand words, the truth is that the vast majority of pictures published today are intimately bound up with the words which are published alongside them.

Even in those publications which are in effect totally picture-driven, such as gossip magazines, words are typically used to add gravitas; and those publications which make few or no demands on the reader's intellect, such as British tabloid newspapers, continental European magazines dwelling on celebrities and royals, and the American supermarket sensationalist rags, use a good deal of text to supplement and indeed explain their pictures.

How else, after all, would we know that a presentable if unremarkable young woman was the Contessa of here or there, or that an unreadable smudge was a World War II bomber on the moon? And without verbal prompting, would we begin to look for, let alone see, the adventitious likeness of Mother Theresa of Calcutta in some product of the pastrycook's art?

Admittedly, there are a places – a very few – where travel pictures may stand alone. Mostly, such pictures are acquired from libraries. Record covers, book covers, advertising posters, backdrops to presenters in travel and other shows on TV, computer screen savers, and some types of advertisement provide examples, but it would be a rash photographer who planned on earning a living solely from this sort of thing unless he or she worked exclusively through a library or libraries.

There are rather more places where travel pictures are supported only by the briefest of captions. The most obvious are picture postcards and calendars, and while few photographers derive their entire income from these, they can be good earners. 'Coffee table' books of pictures also consist essentially of captioned pictures, but these are something that most photographers would be well advised to forget. Having a book of one's own travel pictures published is an enduring amateur fantasy, but indulging in such a fantasy (or at least, failing to recognize that it is almost certain to remain a fantasy) is normally a mark of extreme ignorance of the market-place.

Unless you work with a library, where your verbal liability is limited to the captions, the question therefore becomes one of making your pictures fit in with the words. How you do this depends on all sorts of things, such as whether the publication is 'text-led' or 'picture-led', and whether you are working with a writer on the spot; or subsequently; or to a brief.

## TEXT-LED AND PICTURE-LED PUBLICATIONS

Traditional text media are 'text-led'. In other words, people buy them for the words, and the pictures are there

***Figure 4.1*** *A picture can indeed be worth a thousand words, but often pictures are highly culturally specific. Anyone who has lived in Mexico or indeed much of California would recognize this as the symbol for a vendor of tortillas, but how much would it mean to someone without that experience? (RWH)*

merely to supplement those words – or, in extreme cases, merely to supply a bit of visual relief to a page which would otherwise consist of an awful lot of type, known as a 'grey page' in the publishing trade.

Since the 1860s or thereabouts, there has however been a meteoric rise in the number of publications which are 'picture-led'. These are periodicals (or increasingly often, books) which sell primarily on the strength of their pictures. The words are there merely to tell you what is going on in the pictures. Picture-led publications are (or should be) immediately attractive and eye-catching, but as pictures typically convey different things from words, they can (unless they are unusually well executed) prove curiously unsatisfying: when you have finished them, you may feel that you have a good overview of a subject, but precious little detail.

With the exception of works of fiction and academic or pseudo-academic treatises, even the most sturdily text-led publications today are likely to be more or less illustrated. Of illustrated books, the vast majority, except perhaps those which are written for small children, are likely to be illustrated with photographs. Travel photographs will appear in guide books and travel articles of all kinds; in some histories; in news reports and features about places near and far; and in all the other places described in this book.

In essence, you are reading a text-led book at the moment, though it is one in which pictures are more than usually important: a book about travel photography which contained no travel pictures would be somewhat unattractive, and would also beg the question, 'If the author knows anything at all about travel photography, why are there no travel shots here?' Similar considerations would also apply to those business supplements which appear from time to time inviting investment in far-away places: investors want to see what Transdanubia looks like, or Chile, just because it piques their interest, regardless of the financial details.

The ultimate picture-led publications were probably the great picture magazines such as *Life* and *Picture Post* and *Paris Match*, though their history can be traced back to things like *The Illustrated London News* – arguably the first major picture magazine to be illustrated (often indirectly) with photographs – or for that matter even the Victorian 'penny dreadfuls' or *Punch* and *Harper's*, though unlike the *Illustrated London* these were originally illustrated principally with engravings which owed little or nothing to antecedent photographs.

Today, many such magazines have either folded or are but shadows of their former selves, but the pictorial supplements to newspapers (especially Sunday newspapers) are in the same mould and for that matter the newspapers themselves are substantially picture-led at the lower end of the market. There are also large numbers of picture-led books, often in the 'how to' fields: cook-books, do-it-yourself and hobby books are increasingly often like this, though they range from the extremely informative (the very best cook-books) to mere fluff. Picture-led travel books are less common than they used to be in the 1970s and 1980s, and they are mostly cobbled together from library material, but they do exist.

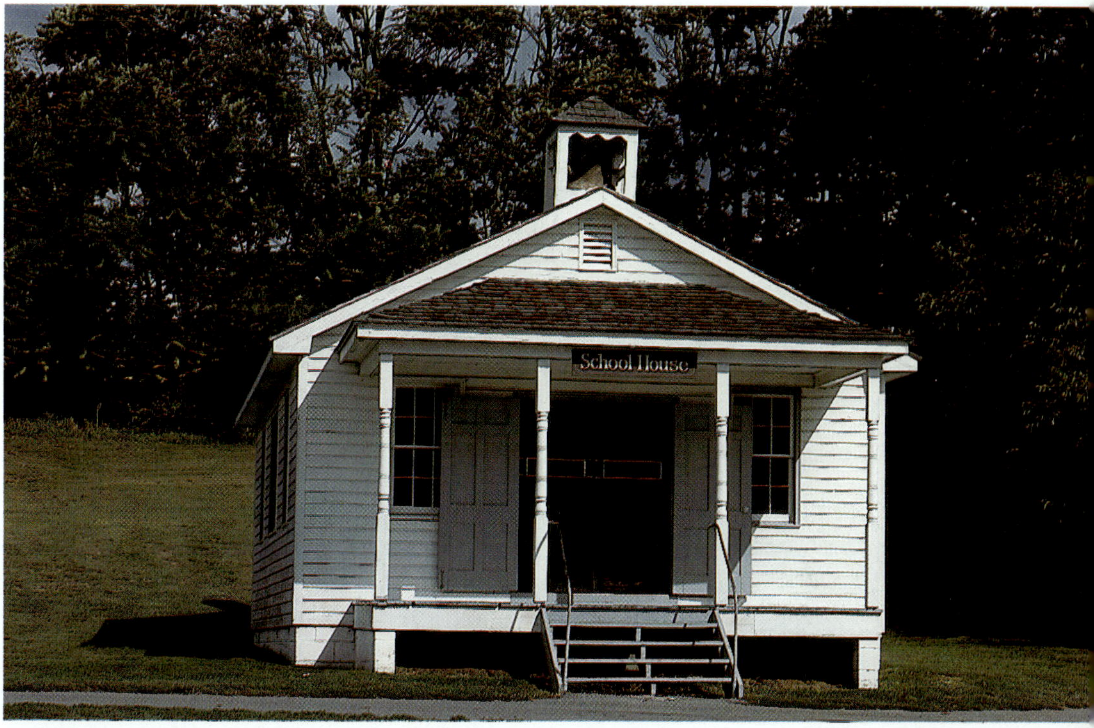


*Figure 4.2 This is a straightforward picture of a straightforward subject – and yet it will sell far better than a more attractive picture of a less culturally significant building. Colonial school-houses are a part of the mythology of America, and appear in travel articles, educational books, histories and more. (FES)*

## Hypertext

'Hypertext' is an electronic medium which allows people to jump about from one section of a publication to another, typically by putting an arrow or cursor over a particular word and clicking a mouse or trackball. It would be misleading to call hypertext either picture-led or text-led, as it clearly cannot exist without the linear, logical approach of text, but equally, it normally has little or no value without the pictures (and even sound and movie clips) which typically make up a substantial part of the medium. Thus far, there has been relatively little market for travel photography in hypertext, but this may and indeed presumably will change.

## WORKING WITH A WRITER ON THE SPOT

Collaborations of any kind tend either to be very, very easy or very, very difficult. It doesn't necessarily matter whether you like your collaborator very much: it is more a question of whether, in the 1990s vernacular, you are both singing from the same hymn-sheet. If you are, then you spark ideas off one another, and the result of the collaboration is better than either of you could have achieved alone. If you are not, the result is likely to look forced, strained, and cobbled together.

The easiest way to get good results when working with someone you dislike is to ignore them, and look at the project. Actually, that is probably the

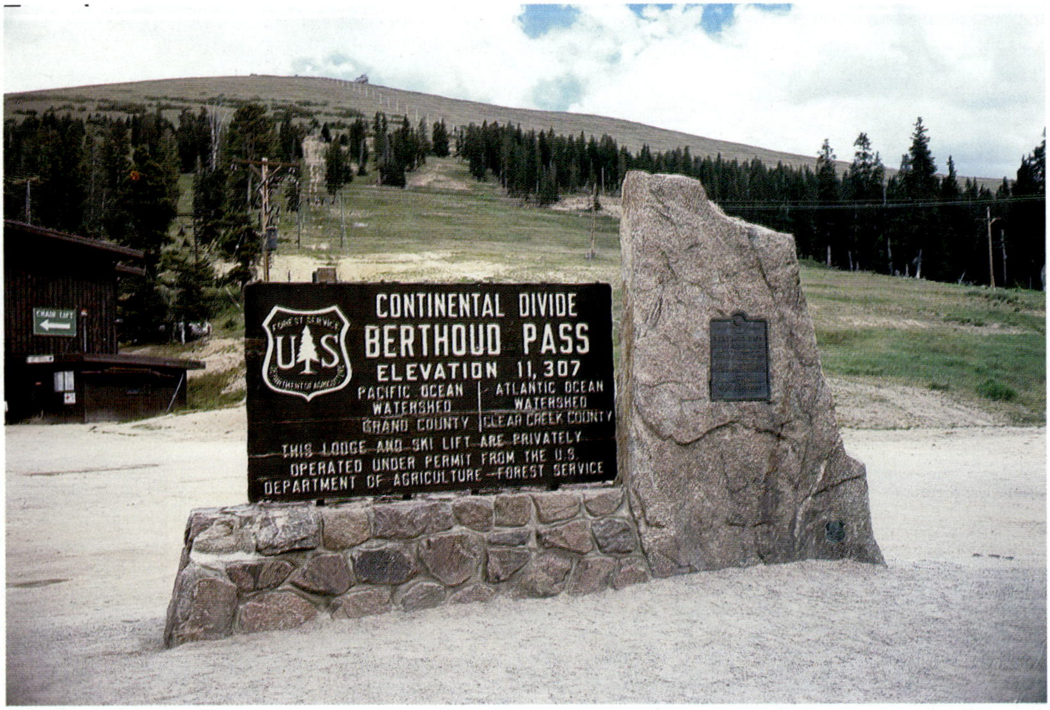


***Figure 4.3*** *There are times when a picture of a dull sign can tell you more than anything else. To be sure, you could try to show water running in different directions – but without this sign, or some other explanation, you would never know that the water which fell on one side drained eventually into the Pacific, while the water which fell on the other drained into the Atlantic. (RWH)*

easiest way to get good results when working with someone you like, too, because otherwise it is all too easy to get involved in what the Irish call 'the crack', with endless enjoyable but ultimately unprofitable conversations, divertimenti and (often) bottles of good wine or good whisky.

Constant feedback and reassurance are essential: 'Have you seen...?' and 'Mightn't it be a good idea if...?' are phrases which you should exchange as often as possible. Normally, the writer will impose the structure, because, after all, language is the linear, logical part of the package; but equally, the structure should not be set in stone if it turns out that there are better ways to present the material. The joke about how many writers you need to change a light-bulb may ease matters: the answer is of course none, because no writer will ever change anything voluntarily.

You must also have a good idea of not just the total numbers of words and pictures, but of how they can tie together. With this book, for example, there are some 65 000 words of text divided into twenty chapters, and there are about 120 pictures. There must therefore be just under two pictures per thousand words, and it doesn't take long to work out how many pictures are therefore needed for a chapter of a given length. It doesn't matter much if there are four pictures to a thousand words in one chapter, and one to a thousand words in another, but a chapter with no illustrations whatsoever would look rather odd.

With a magazine article, the problems are less pressing, but you still want to avoid concentrating too much on a particular subject, even if it is incredibly photogenic. In our coverage of Varanasi (Benares), for example, we have far too many pictures taken on the Ganges, especially in the early morning, and too few of the silk merchants, the bazaars and the monuments. Discipline is essential.

## Working with a writer later

Normally, this is the writer's problem: you are in effect functioning as a picture library. For instance, we once supplied a set of pictures to illustrate a Mexican cook-book: not the food shots, which were specially commissioned, but 'life-style' shots of Mexican shops, scenes, markets and so forth. At worst, all we had to do was read the text and make the pictures tie in as best we could, with appropriate captions based both on our own knowledge and on what the author said.

## Working to a brief

Instead of asking for pictures to accompany text which is already written, or instead of asking the writer and photographer to go somewhere together, a client may simultaneously commission words and pictures, without any expectation of the writer and photographer necessarily meeting; this is, in a sense, the reverse of the situation described above in which you are trying to illustrate existing material, in that your pictures may well exist before the text is begun, let alone completed.

Such a commission can range from the incredibly detailed to the equally incredibly veiled. Unless you know the client very well indeed, a bias towards the former is normally to be preferred. The perfect brief, from the photographer's point of view, is probably divided in half. One half consists of specified shots – a particular hotel, a particular bay, a particular kind of fishing boat – but takes account of the fact that you will not necessarily be able to get all of those pictures. In other words, the client wants 'at least twelve out of the following twenty', or whatever. The other half of the brief includes general directions

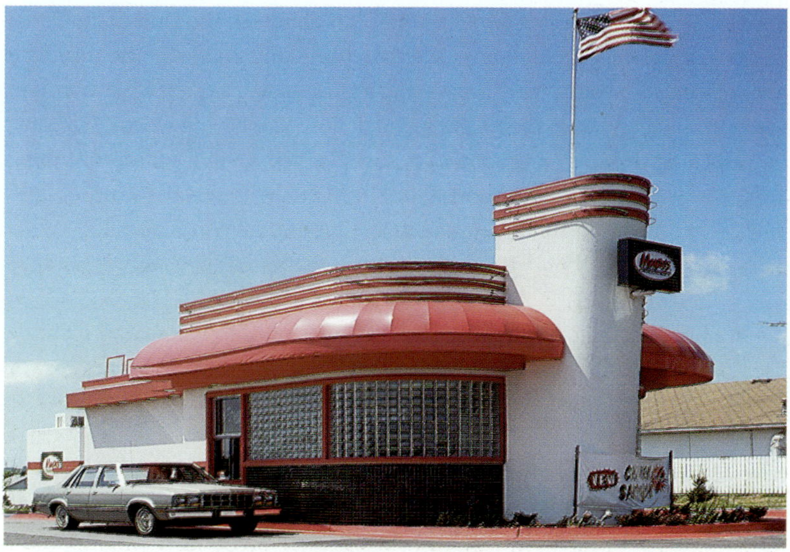

***Figure 4.4*** *A curious aspect of our increasingly visually oriented world culture is that certain highly specific cultural icons from individual countries have been incorporated into a general world picture. France has a monopoly on pavement cafés, for all that the Italians often do them better, so pavement cafés worldwide are modelled on the French style. Likewise, burger bars are (with rather more justification) a symbol of America – though rather less explicably, a sort of mythical 1950s America, rather than anything more modern. (RWH)*

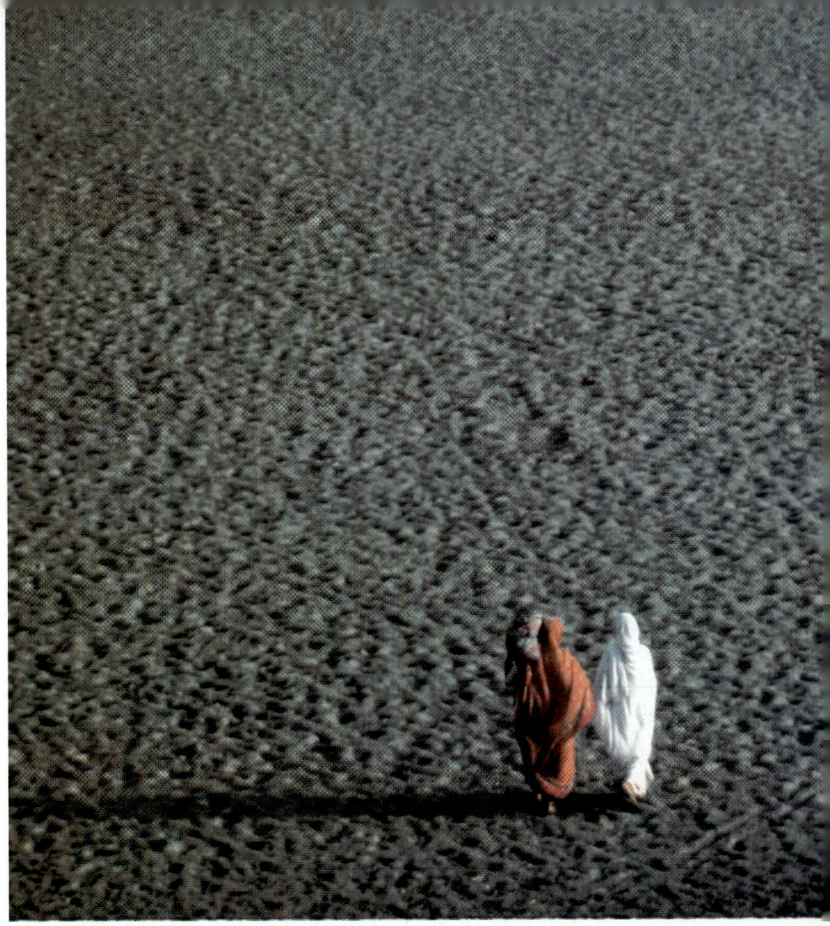

*__Figure 4.5__ Arguably, the best pictures are the ones on which the viewer can superimpose whatever he or she wants. Are these two women happy, enjoying a conversation as they walk along together? Miserable, trudging to collect water? Will the water be pure, from a spring, or dirty and polluted? Because their faces are invisible, and because thousands of women cover the same sort of route every day, they are anonymous; there is no need of a model release. This picture has been published several times, each time with a different interpretation, and each time with a rather different colour balance. (RWH)*

and key words – fishing shots, people eating, shops at night – but leaves it up to you what you actually shoot. Of course, most people would shoot the second half as well, even if they were only given the first half, and you may want to bring this up with the client.

Very vague briefs can be terrifying, and the only way to pin some clients down may be to ask them whether they can point out the kind of stuff they want, using existing guide books and brochures and anything else they have to hand. Few things are more depressing than showing a client what you think are great pictures, then seeing his face fall and hearing the words, 'Oh, that isn't the kind of thing I thought you'd be shooting at all...' Ultra-tight briefs are not a lot better: 'I want a sunrise shot from the Asian side of the Bosphorus' may be impossible if it is raining the whole time you are in Istanbul.

## The package: words and pictures

We are heavily biased towards selling packages of both words and pictures, because this is what we have found pays best. The rewards in both travel photography and travel writing are slender, and if the budget has to stretch to two travellers instead of just one, you need every penny you can get. We have sold packages of pictures alone, and we quite often sell packages of words alone, but the biggest single advantage of selling a package of both words and pictures together is that editors are for the most part word-ori-

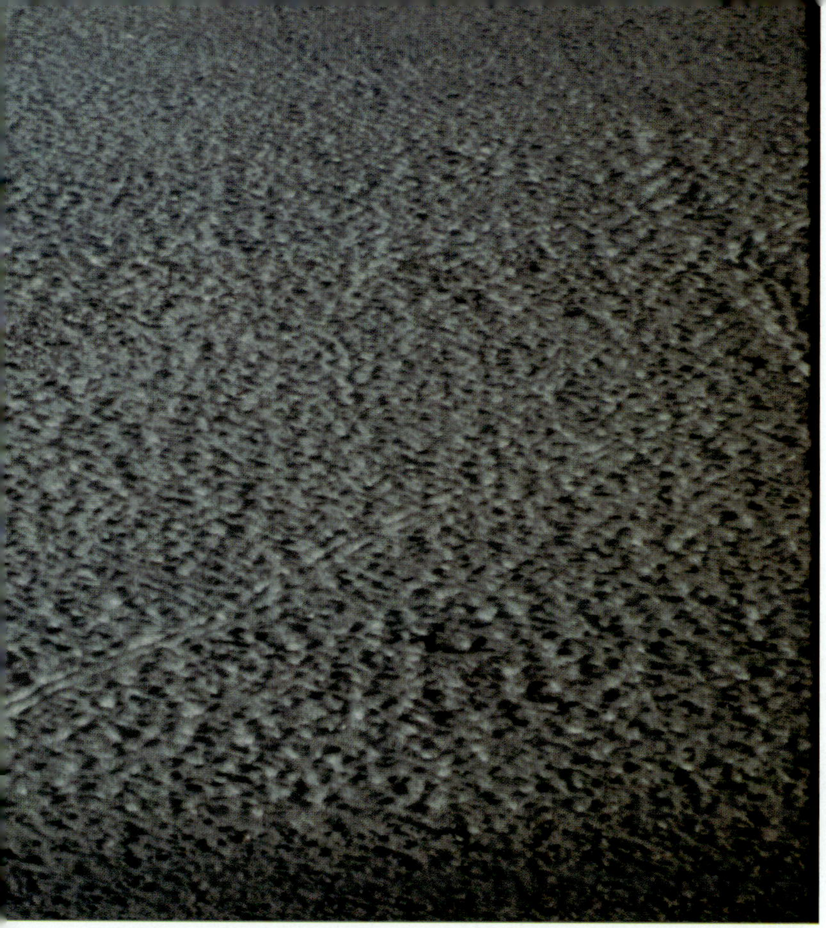

ented, for obvious reasons. In order to put a proposal together, you need words.

Believing that you can write competently because you studied English at school is about as realistic as believing that you are a photographer because you have a camera. Writing and photography are both crafts in their own right, and both repay study. There are books on the craft of writing – lots of them – just as there are books on the craft of photography. Read at least one or two of them, if you want to sell complete packages of words and pictures. Use the spell-check program on your computer, and read what you have written out loud: if you stumble in your reading, or if what you have said does not sound right, then ask yourself why. Ask around to see if there are any writers' groups in your neighbourhood: these cater mostly to aspiring fiction writers, but they can also be useful for constructive criticism of travel articles and even proposals.

Finally, there is an old editors' saying: opinions are cheap, facts are expensive. When in doubt, use Rudyard Kipling's advice:

> I keep six honest serving-men
> They taught me all I knew
> Their names are how and what and when
> And where and why and who.

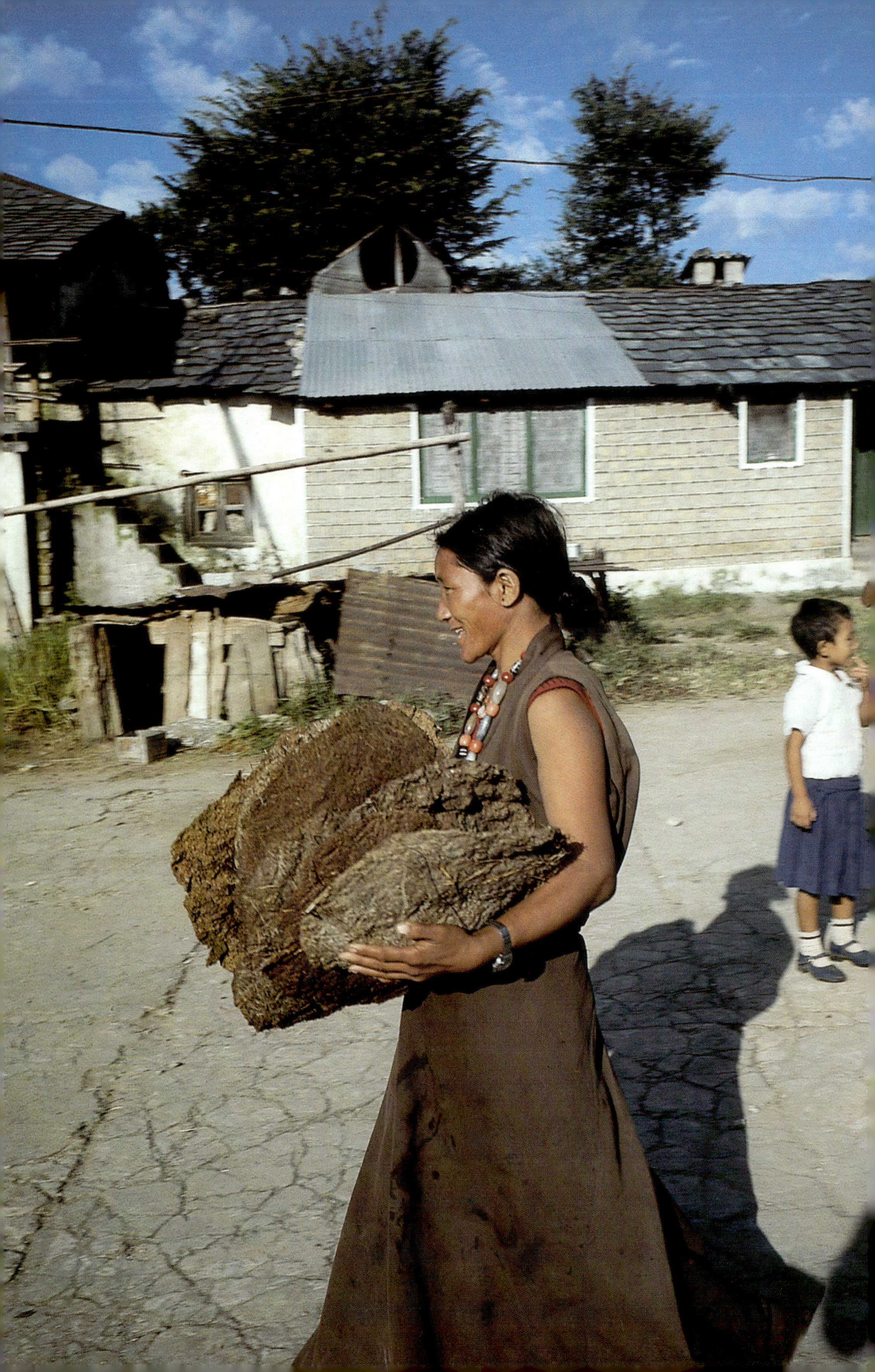

# 5 Financial realities

Just as the power-to-weight ratio of a racing car can be improved either by adding power or by decreasing weight, so can the financial feasibility of earning a living by travel photography be improved either by increasing earnings or by decreasing outgoings. At least at first, and possibly for many years afterwards, decreased outgoings are likely to make the difference between success (or at least survival) and failure.

Where you live will have a considerable influence on how much you can afford to travel. We live in a big old Victorian house on the Kent coast, some 20 km from Canterbury; not exactly the centre of the universe. It needs a lot doing to it. For example, we really could do with a new ceiling in the drawing room, to say nothing of a lot of new carpets. But a new ceiling would cost the same as another trip to Greece, and new carpets would cost the same as a month in India. Our car is elderly and slightly rusty at some of the corners; but a new car would cost as much as a year's travel budget.

When we bought the house in 1992 we made a conscious decision to buy somewhere big where we could imagine spending the rest of our lives and where we would have adequate room for a small studio and a well-equipped darkroom. The alternative would have been to buy somewhere much smaller, and concentrate more on travel photography: from 1987 to 1992 we had effectively been living and working in two rooms, and travelling up to seven months a year. Since then, we have been able to afford less time to travel – the transition from two rooms to nine implies a significant financial burden, and other work often pays better than travel photography – and it may be that we have over-reacted slightly to our previous situation; but either balance was pretty good, and we greatly prefer living in Britain to living in California, which is where we were before.

A good-sized part of the improvement comes from the fact that it costs far less to go to most places from the UK than from the USA, and that fares comprise a smaller part of our budget. When we lived in California, we tended to stay away for long periods at a time. This was because when you spend $1000 or $1500 on fares alone, you have to spend a fair while working in a cheap country in order to recover. From the UK, on the other hand, that same $1000 or $1500 can pay for an entire two-week trip, fares and accommodation and maybe even car hire as well. We therefore tend to travel in shorter, more frequent 'hits' of a couple of weeks at a time.

As well as living in modest houses, and running elderly cars (and motorcycles, in our case), and not spending much on decoration or non-essential maintenance, there are all kinds of other ways you can save money. For example, neither of us is a great clothes-horse; by most people's standards, our clothes

***Figure 5.1*** *Despite what is said elsewhere in this chapter about the desirability of living as comfortably as possible when you are working, it is also essential that you do not allow cultural prejudices to stand in the way too much. Buffalo dung makes a good fuel, and if you cannot handle being offered food that has been cooked over a buffalo-dung fire, you may have a problem in some places. (RWH)*

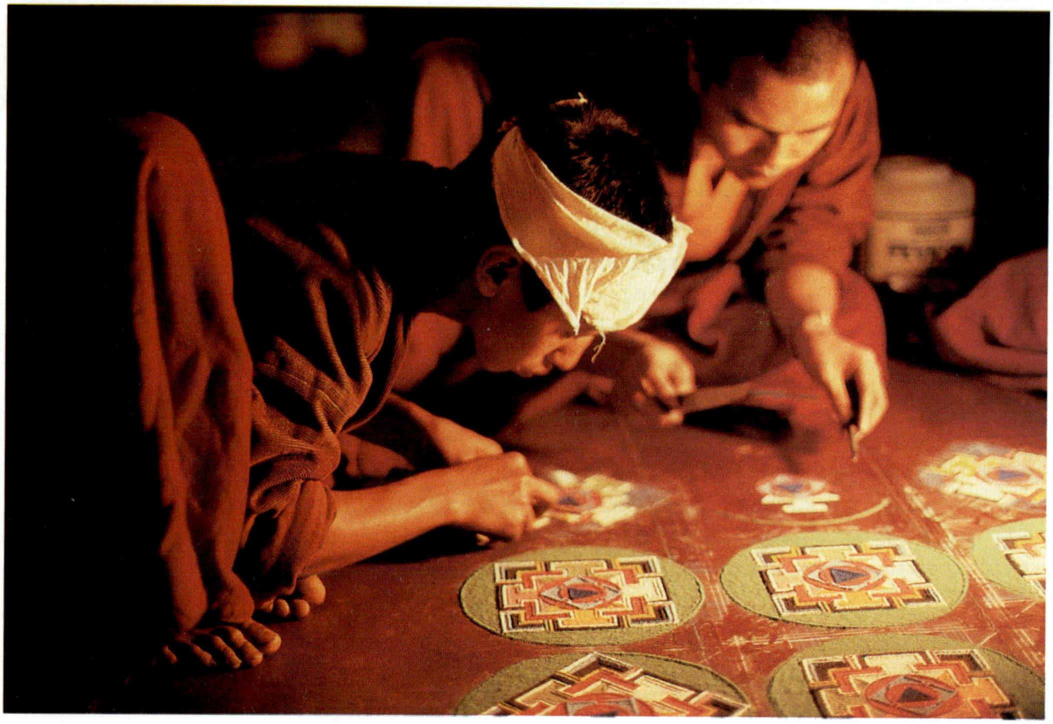

*Figure 5.2 Sometimes, money can't buy you anything; all you can rely on is goodwill and (let's be honest) influence. Roger shot a series of pictures of making a chalk-dust mandala at a monastery in the heavily Tibetan Clement Town area of Dehra Dun, staying at the monastery for five days. He gained access by virtue of a letter from the Office of His Holiness the Dalai Lama, saying that he was working for them. (RHW)*

budgets are laughably low, though we do buy good shoes and boots and good foul-weather gear. We do not eat out a great deal in the UK, just for the fun of it; as we have to eat out when we are travelling, and as we often eat better and cheaper than we could in England, there seems little point. We don't buy much in the way of consumer toys, though we do have something of a weakness for cameras. In fact, eating and drinking well at home is our principal indulgence – apart from the way we earn our living. Both of us could earn more money if we had stuck to the conventional jobs for which we were once well qualified, though now, after years of self-employment, it is doubtful that either of us could ever return to a nine-to-five job.

We are not unique in this. Although we know a few well-to-do photographers who either specialize in travel or whose work involves a lot of travel, we know many more who keep their outgoings to a minimum, both at home and on the road. Tim Page, for example, is a brilliant photographer. He made his name in the Vietnam War, and today he still spends a lot of time in South East Asia. We don't know how he lives on the road, but his house in the UK is surprisingly small and modest. As he says, it's a base, that's all.

Another example is Hiroki Fujita: another brilliant photographer, the author of a number of superb and shatteringly expensive coffee table books. He shoots (or shot – we have not seen him since the early 1980s) with Hasselblad and Linhof. We met him in a cheap hotel in Dharamsala, almost 2000 metres (well over 6000 feet) up in the Himalayas; he was staying in an unheated room, with cold water only, at (from memory) $2 or $3 a night. 'Take what you want, and pay for it, sayeth the Lord'; this is the proverb we live by, and so do most other travel photographers we know.

## When you're away

An inevitable consequence of earning all or part of your living from travel photography, no matter how you slice it, is that you are going to have to spend quite a lot of time away from home. At this point, security and insurance raise their heads.

Our house is protected by a serious burglar alarm, which dials a central station if it is activated. Our insurance covers us for up to eight weeks' absence at a stretch, and for as many trips away as we may make; many policies may place unacceptable limits on the number of trips you can make, or on their duration.

This is only one possible solution, and a middle-aged one at that. Young photographers, if they and their parents can stand it, may do well to maintain a base at their parents' home where someone will be on the premises for some or most of the time, or they may prefer to come to an arrangement with a flatmate whereby they may pay a slightly lower share of the rent in return for not being there very often. You need a base somewhere, though, to store your pictures and the equipment you are not using, as well as to write captions and to stay when you are looking for work and so forth; the option of crashing at friends' and relatives' houses whenever you're not on the road can wear your welcome thin, and make it difficult to organize your life properly, though some people apparently manage it.

Another solution which we know can work – Heather Angel manages it very well, for instance – is to leave your spouse or partner at home to get on with his or her job as you get on with yours.

Choosing an appropriate base can also make a considerable difference to your insurance premiums. You need to insure your equipment, which is often cheapest as an add-on to a domestic policy. You would also be very well advised indeed to take out an annual travel insurance policy against medical expenses and cancellations and loss of baggage and all the other ills which can befall the traveller, and the insurer will insist that you have a fixed abode in order to do this. The insurance premium can be quite a wedge out of your budget, but it is important to put it in context: for excellent annual cover, world-wide, we each pay about 50 per cent more than a typical package tour operator charges for two weeks' holiday cover.

An aside on travel insurance is that many policies cover you for delays, missed flights, etc., only if you go to the airport by scheduled public transport. This is why we normally take a train to the airport: delays due to a derailment or a station closed because of a bomb threat will trigger the insurance, but a taxi stuck in a jam on the M25 will not. Always read all your insurance policies very carefully, especially the travel policies. For example, we travel a lot by motorcycle, but some policies exclude all injuries resulting from motorcycle riding; some exclude injuries arising from riding motorcycles *under* a specified capacity, in order to avoid liability for people who hire putt-putts at holiday destinations and cannot ride; and some don't allow you to ride motorcycles *over* a certain capacity, presumably because they haven't thought it through very carefully.

## CHEAP TRAVEL

*Figure 5.3 The confluence of the Little Rangit and the Tista is described in the Darjeeling district gazetteer of 1907 as follows: 'Here there is a great difference in the colour of the two rivers, the Tista being turgid and milky white, the Rangit dark green and very clear. The waters preserve their colour for some hundred yards...'*

*The only easy way to get to see this is to hire a Land Rover (and driver) in Darjeeling. There are plenty available, and prices are low. What is really surprising is that waiting charges are minimal. We hired a car from Darjeeling to Kalimpong, stayed overnight in Kalimpong, and returned the next day. The cost was very little more than for a day trip. It is important not to see costs in familiar, Western terms. (RWH)*

There is no such thing as a free lunch. Although 'freebies' or 'comps' abound in the travel business, they are mostly of two kinds. One is the sort that is offered to a publication, rather than to an individual, and the other is the sort where a travel company wants your pictures for its brochures.

The first kind is only of much use once you are well established, and once you are well established with a particular publication at that. Rather than handing out free trips to freelances, no matter how good those freelances may be, most publications understandably keep the goodies for themselves and distribute them among their full-time staff or their friends. If you can cultivate a good relationship with an appropriate publication, you may in time be in line for these; but they are hard to come by.

Also, the vast majority of travel articles are text-driven (see page 43), so the free tickets tend to go to writers rather than to photographers. Pictures come from tourist boards, travel companies, and picture libraries – though many publications are unwilling to pay for the last, and will instead publish the most appalling holiday snaps taken by their writers, devoid of either technical quality or artistic merit.

As for 'brochure' pictures, the drawbacks here tend to be two-fold. First, you are often handed a punishing list of 'must-have' pictures, which will leave you little time to shoot the sort of thing that you want, and second, you are normally given the worst room in the hotel (over the disco, next to the lift) at the beginning or end of the season, when the weather is 'iffy' and you may have extreme difficulty in getting even such dull pictures of hotel interiors and exteriors, and crowded beaches, as the client expects.

If at all possible, it is therefore desirable to travel at your own expense. This gives you much more freedom, and besides, many leading and influential publications – the *Los Angeles Times*, for example – will only accept material from people who paid their own way; they reckon, not unrealistically, that anyone who has been 'comped' will praise their sponsor to the skies and gloss over any disadvantages. This is not so much a question of gratitude as of forward planning: if you can show another potential sponsor an effusive article and say, 'Look what I can do for you', you can get another freebie from them. The net result is a sort of vicious circle, where the readers are misled more and more mercilessly in order to keep the travel correspondent in free trips.

### Cheap tickets

We said earlier that one of the reasons we moved back to the UK from California was that travel from the UK is much cheaper, and it is time to qualify this.

From California, we could of course get to other American destinations

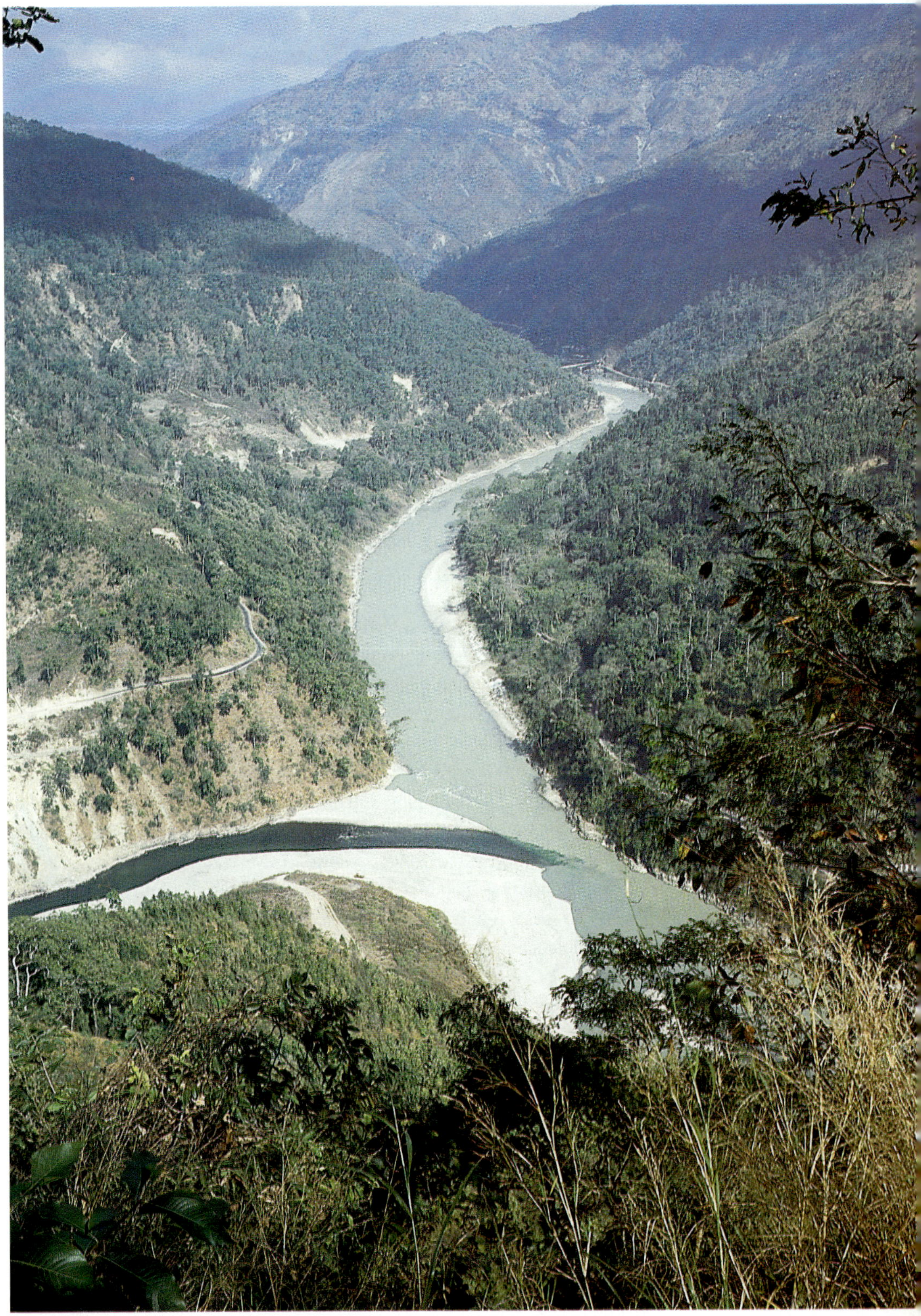

(including Canada and Mexico) much more cheaply than would be possible from Europe. On the other hand, we greatly prefer the cultural diversity of Europe, and the simple truth is that Europe is where people go. Europeans in general devote far more time and money to travel than Americans, not least because American vacation times are ridiculously restricted by European standards, and Europe is a favoured destination for Europeans as well as Americans.

Because Europeans are so much more oriented towards leisure travel, the travel industry is better organized, more competitive, and has a much greater variety of considerably better bargains. To be sure, from California there were plenty of cheap fares and packages to Hawaii and Las Vegas, but that was about it. From London, there are cheap fares and packages all over the world. Endless 'bucket shops' or consolidators advertise in mainstream media, and as long as you see one or more of the magic acronyms ATOL, IATA and ABTA, they are likely to be 'safe' – in other words, they won't take your money and run. As a further safeguard, always pay with a credit card, as this normally means that if anything does go wrong and you have no other redress, the credit card company will reimburse you. Check with your credit card company to make sure that they offer this protection, though most do.

## Packages

In the UK in particular, you can often pick up package holidays at ridiculously low prices, especially at the beginning and end of the season.

These exist for two variations on the same reason, which is that fixed costs have to be met. If a company's fixed costs are (say) £100 per room per week, it is better to run at a loss and let that room for £50 than it is to leave it unfilled and lose the whole £100. This means that many resorts offer very cheap packages at the beginning and end of the season, when they know that room occupancy will be down, and it also means that there are often particularly good prices on 'short dated' travel packages. Travel companies block-buy tickets and accommodation, and a package holiday has an absolute sell-by date: if there are any seats unfilled when the aeroplane takes off, they are wasted, and the pre-paid accommodation at the other end is also wasted. Again, it is better to sell the package at half price, and lose all of the profit and some of the out-of-pocket expense, than it is to lose all of the profit and all of the out-of-pocket expense.

We have bought cheap packages a number of times, and while they have their disadvantages, they can be ridiculously cheap. We have paid as little as £150 to £160 ($230 to $250) each for two weeks in Greece, flight and accommodation included.

The principal disadvantages are that the flights are normally on crowded, uncomfortable charter flights; that they often depart or arrive at unsocial hours, and are frequently delayed at that; that the accommodation can be pretty basic; and that you would not necessarily choose your travelling companions. On the other hand, you are not on the flight (or in the company of the others)

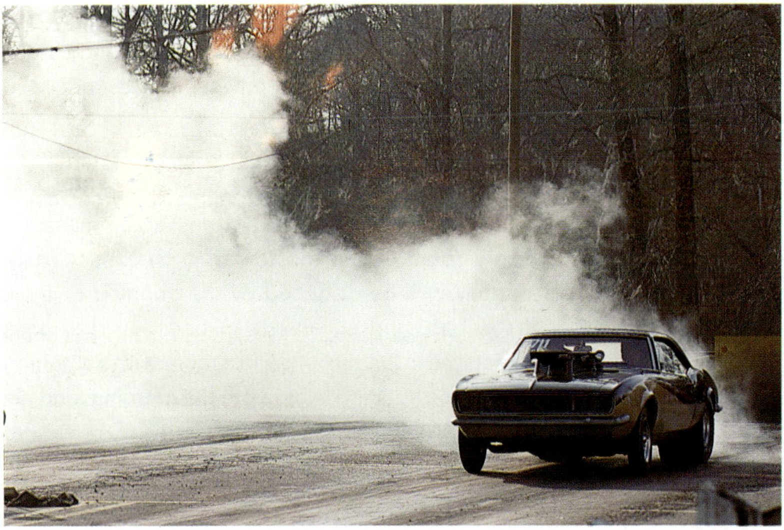

*Figure 5.4 The best things in life may be free, and it may go against the grain to spend good money on going to a redneck drag race in Alabama; but a lot of people are interested in this sort of thing, and if you reckon there is a market you will do well to consider whether first, you want to spend the money, and second, whether you can take pictures which will sell. It is rarely a good idea to try to shoot subjects which really do not interest you, as there is too great a risk that your indifference will show in the pictures. (RWH)*

for long; a good night's sleep soon cures the disadvantages of awkward hours; and the whole package is frequently so ridiculously cheap, often less than the cheapest scheduled air fare, that while you are away you can afford to stay somewhere else for part or all of the time. We typically crash out at the pre-paid accommodation for the first night, but after that, we use it or not as we feel inclined.

Given the choice of one-week or two-week trips, we almost always go for the longer one. This is a matter of simple logic: with a one-week trip, you spend a disproportionate amount of time on recovering from the journey, packing and unpacking, and getting to know the place. On the other hand, if it is a destination we are unsure about, we may take a week or even a long week-end, just to see whether we like it or not, and whether we want to go back. We once bought a very cheap six-day package to Istanbul, for example, and we were glad we were not there for longer. The hotel and the food were not too bad but we had virtually no sympathy for the place. The fact that the immigration officials stole £10 from us on the way in did nothing to improve our temper either.

## Accommodation

If you haven't pre-booked accommodation, or if you want to stay somewhere other than your booked accommodation, it is usually pretty easy to find somewhere. In many years' travelling, we have only had to sleep in the car once (in Florida) and the second-worst time was when we arrived late one night in Paris and ended up sharing a single room over a sauerkraut factory on the rue Monsieur le Prince – but as it was only £4 ($6) in about 1983, and as it was reasonably clean, even that wasn't too great a hardship.

In general, we prefer country inns and guest houses, and although we prefer private facilities, we'll put up with a bathroom down the hall if the price

is right. In France, for example, it was still possible in the late 1990s to find perfectly acceptable double rooms for FF125 (£13–15 or $20–25) and even in Germany there are plenty of excellent rooms with private facilities for DM70 (under £30, $45).

There is more about rooms and room prices in Chapter 7 (Planning a trip), but a point worth making here is that you have to get enough sleep to work efficiently, so there is a certain standard below which your accommodation should not fall. Don't take a room at the foot of a hill by a busy road, for example, or your sleep may well be disturbed by the grinding of truck gears, and remember that what is an advantage in one way may be a disadvantage in another. We stayed in Prague, once, in a room with a stunning view but no curtains. The sun came flooding in at five in the morning, and we just couldn't get enough sleep. When we got back to Germany, in a quiet room well off the main road and equipped with totally light-tight shutters, we slept for 18 hours straight.

Even when we are economizing to the hilt, we try to stay in at least one really nice room every few days, generally with a bath-tub instead of a shower (far more relaxing), just to recharge our batteries for the next part of the trip.

## Food and drink

As with getting enough sleep, so with getting enough nutrition. By all means rely on picnics and snacks, but not all the time; eat a decent meal sometimes. Also, remember that food (and pictures of restaurants, and so forth) may be an important dimension in many accounts of travel.

## Car hire

In general, we have found it cheaper and better to reserve cars in advance. You typically get a better rate; in countries where maintenance is casual, you will generally get a safer car; and you are more likely to know what you are paying, though you need to be very careful and to get a copy of the rental agreement in writing. American car hire companies in particular can behave appallingly: we have been told flat lies, such as that insurance is not pre-paid (when it is, and we have it in writing), and that there is an extra charge for both of us to drive (when we have it in writing that there is no extra charge for a spouse). Again, there is more about planning car hire in Chapter 7.

## Film and processing

An old figure from *Life* magazine was that on average, across a trip, their photographers shot eight rolls of 36-exposure, 35mm film every day. We find that we shoot roughly that much between us, but then, we are normally travelling as writers as well as in the role of photographers.

Although it is a good general rule to be as generous with film as possible, it is all too easy to overdo it when you are faced with something

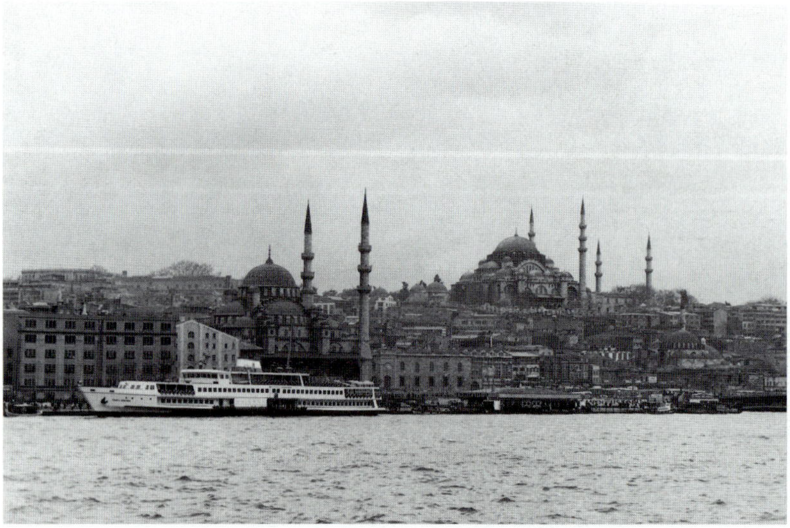

***Figure 5.5*** *The classic picture of Istanbul from the Asian side of the Bosphorus means that you will need to take either a tour boat or a ferry. The ferries are working boats for the local populace, and make very few concessions to English speakers, but they can afford excellent vantage points and they cost next to nothing. Much the same could be said about the Staten Island ferries in New York; you are expected to know how they operate, because everyone else does. You can learn a certain amount from guide books, but beyond a certain point you have to put your coins in the slot or go up to the cash window and hope that you are doing it right. (FES)*

hopelessly photogenic, and it is also very easy to overdo it when you are desperate for pictures in a place where the weather is against you or where you have little sympathy with the place, both of which applied to us in Istanbul. At the end of each day, mentally review what you have shot, and ask yourself how good it is, and how it fits into your overall needs.

It will never be possible to get your shooting balance precisely right, but both of the scenarios in the previous paragraph are controllable. With a 'perfect' subject, all you can do is to say to yourself, 'Well, I must have what I need somewhere in those 20 rolls, so I'd better stop now.' When either the weather or the mood is against you, concentrate on shooting a relatively small number of pictures. Ask yourself what the 'must have' material is, and try to cover that, but don't just shoot for the sake of shooting. We have found that the latter is a very good way to waste time, film, money and energy: you just feel bad when you realize how horribly little you have to show for four days and forty rolls of film, when you could have got the 'must haves' in ten rolls.

As for processing, we almost invariably wait until we are home to have our films processed; we have had too many bad experiences with so-called 'professional' labs, especially in the United States, where anywhere that processes E-6 calls itself 'professional' even if it has a 24-hour turnaround time (a good pro lab should do it in two hours) and zero process control. The only way we have found to ensure professional treatment in a strange place is to call a local professional, explain our predicament to them, and ask for their help; so far, this approach has always worked, while simply relying on the local

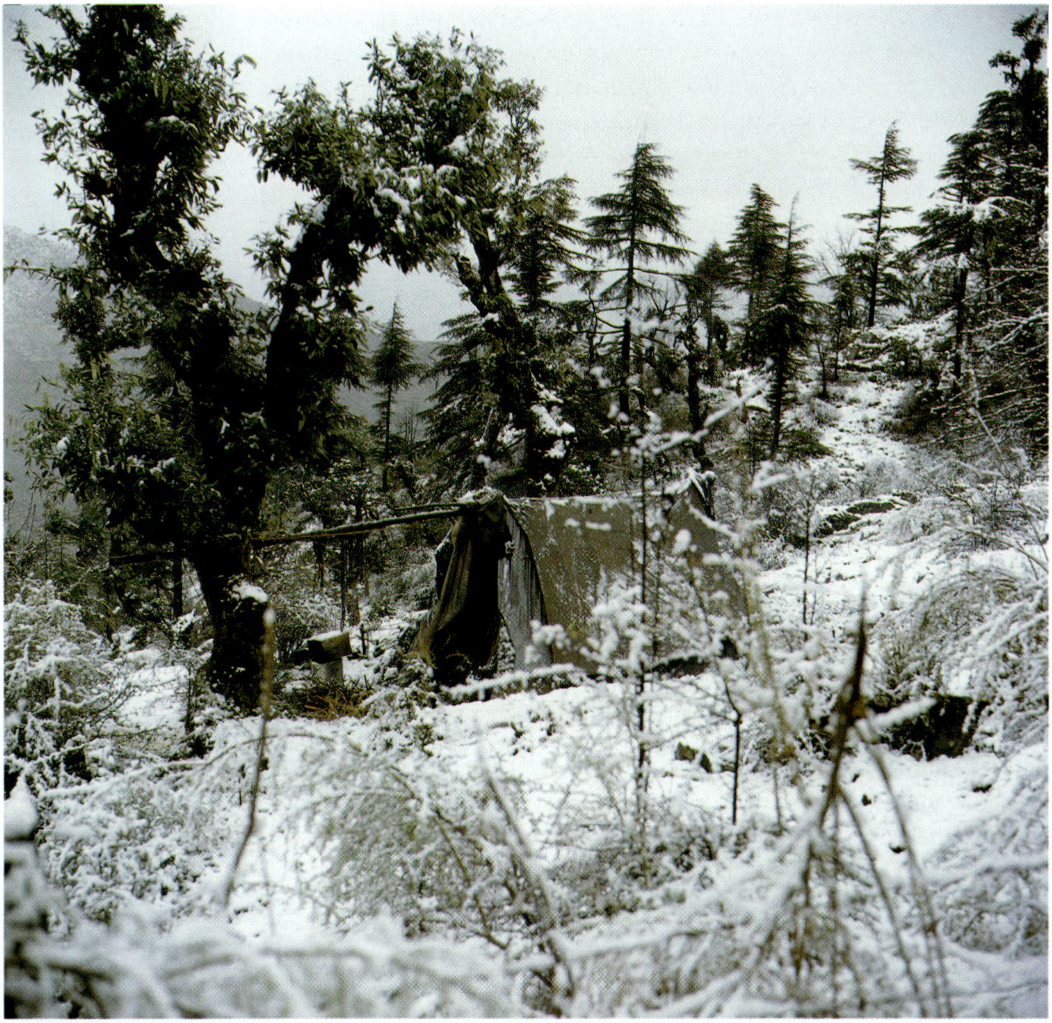

**Figure 5.6** *While you might not care to live in quite such basic accommodation as this bivouac at Dharamsala, it is a reminder that in adverse conditions you need warm, secure quarters if you are to work effectively. There are some people who reckon that enduring hardships and privations makes them better photographers, and indeed there are times when you have to live pretty rough; but whenever possible, it is easier to work from a comfortable base. Also, to be cynical, this will bring you closer to the people who will ultimately be looking at your pictures, who are for the most part voyeurs. (RWH)*

*Yellow Pages* has given us as many disasters as good labs. We have never tried sending film home by registered, insured post, simply because we feel more secure carrying it ourselves.

## COSTS AND RETURNS

In a perfect world, publication of your pictures would be guaranteed and you would have had a decent-sized advance to cover your costs. In the real world, this is very rare indeed. Even a guaranteed commission can go wrong – the magazine can fold, the editor can change, or they may just dislike your pictures – and the number of people who are willing to pay 'up front' before you go on the trip is very small indeed.

You will therefore need a 'float' which is sufficient to cover all your expenses: tickets, accommodation, film, processing, and the time between returning home and getting paid. Although it is tempting to use credit cards for the float, this is a risky strategy. We know; we used to do it. An overdraft is also risky, but there are times when it is your only realistic option; cash flow, as much as income, is one of the major problems of a freelance's life.

When you have worked out what a trip is going to cost, you also need to work out how it will pay for itself, and when the money will come in. Multiple use from the pictures from a single trip is all but essential, and you have to be careful to avoid overlap. If you sell to one travel magazine, you can hardly sell to another in the same market (or if you do, you will never sell to either again), so you have to diversify. We try, whenever possible, to use pictures from any one trip in both British and American travel articles; in both British and American photo magazines; and in books.

Estimates of income will always be just that – estimates – and the best you can do is to work in round numbers, to the nearest $100 or so; anything which brings in less than $100 must be treated as a secondary bonus, because it just isn't worth the effort of trying to sell someone something, corresponding with them, sending them pictures in padded sleeves and envelopes and so forth, for under $100.

Finally, remember that money isn't the only thing you are working for. If it is, you are in the wrong business. You have to earn enough money to live on – you can't afford to run at a loss, at least for long, unless you are independently wealthy – but you are earning that money in a way which most people would regard as something they have to pay to do. You are visiting attractive or interesting places, eating in restaurants, and taking pictures. Most people regard all of these activities as luxuries, so it's not unreasonable that there's a trade-off between your lifestyle and the money you earn.

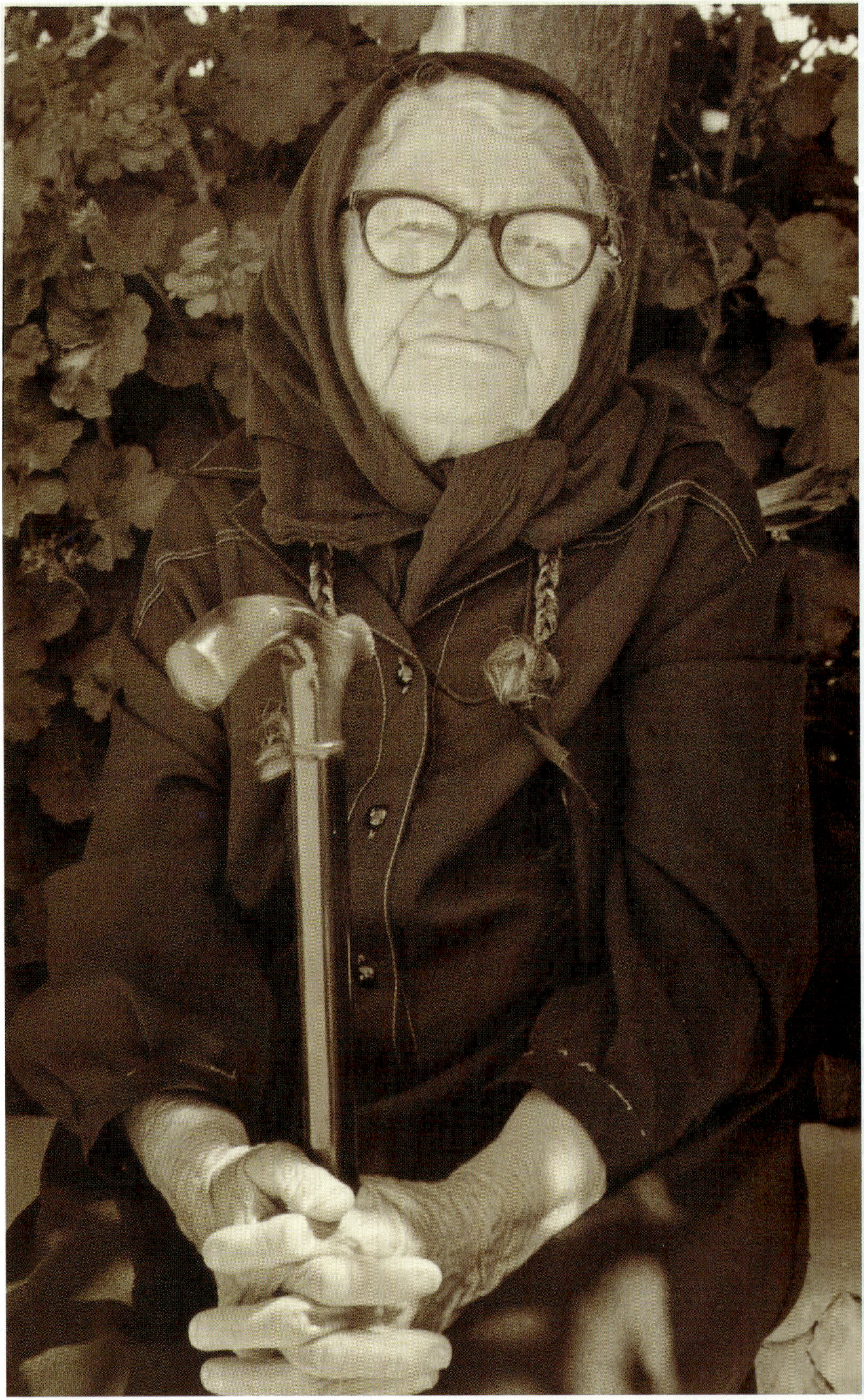

# 6 Women and travel

There are still many places where women are not taken seriously, or where the very expression 'women's rights' evokes either incomprehension or outright derision. Nor are these places necessarily in Islamic theocracies: a Glasgow pub, or a redneck bar in Orange County, California, might not be the ideal place for a woman photographer on her own. At least until recently, and quite possibly to this day (we do not care to inquire) a Moose Lodge in the United States was a place where women were admitted only on the say-so of a male friend or relative, and the same was true of many English cricket and golf clubs.

For that matter, no less a photographer than Kos has been denied access to a boat, when one of the crew said, 'If she comes on board, I go.' If one of the world's leading boat photographers can be turned away like this, there are many places where men have a lot to learn.

On the other hand, if a woman cares to take advantage of her sex rather than fighting its disadvantages, there are a number of things she can do more easily than a man. Just as there are places which are not open to women, there are places which are not open to men, especially where religion rears its ugly head, and it is often easier for women to gain the confidence of women and (especially) children than it is for a man to do so. There are plenty of societies where a woman may feel that she cannot be alone with a man – it is only since World War II that the notion of being 'compromised' has begun to decline in Britain – but where another woman, regardless of her nationality or cultural background, will be afforded a sisterly welcome.

Admittedly, this can have its drawbacks: you may be expected to take an altogether greater interest in babies or clothes or other 'women's things' than you might normally do, but you may also be surprised at the interest which cloistered women may take in you. Pretty much throughout the world, even in the most repressive societies, women in purdah are increasingly aware that things do not have to be like this, and the intrusion of a non-threatening potential role model may be extremely welcome.

You may also find that, if properly treated, men will respond very well to women photographers. Look at how Margaret Bourke White managed to photograph both Stalin and Gandhi. Neither came from cultures which were noted for women's rights, but both responded positively to a woman, perhaps because they did not feel threatened by her. For that matter, she once found that the Twelve Lions of Babylon, the Lion of Judah, His Highness Haile Selassie, Emperor of Ethiopia, carried her cameras for her!

A separate but related issue is sexual harassment when you are not among women. This is more complex than is immediately obvious to some people.

*Figure 6.1 There is not much that a man can photograph which cannot be photographed by a sufficiently determined woman, as Margaret Bourke White repeatedly demonstrated; but it can be easier for a woman to relate to another woman, and even the most traditional and old-fashioned women may be surprisingly taken with the idea of a woman photographer. (FES)*

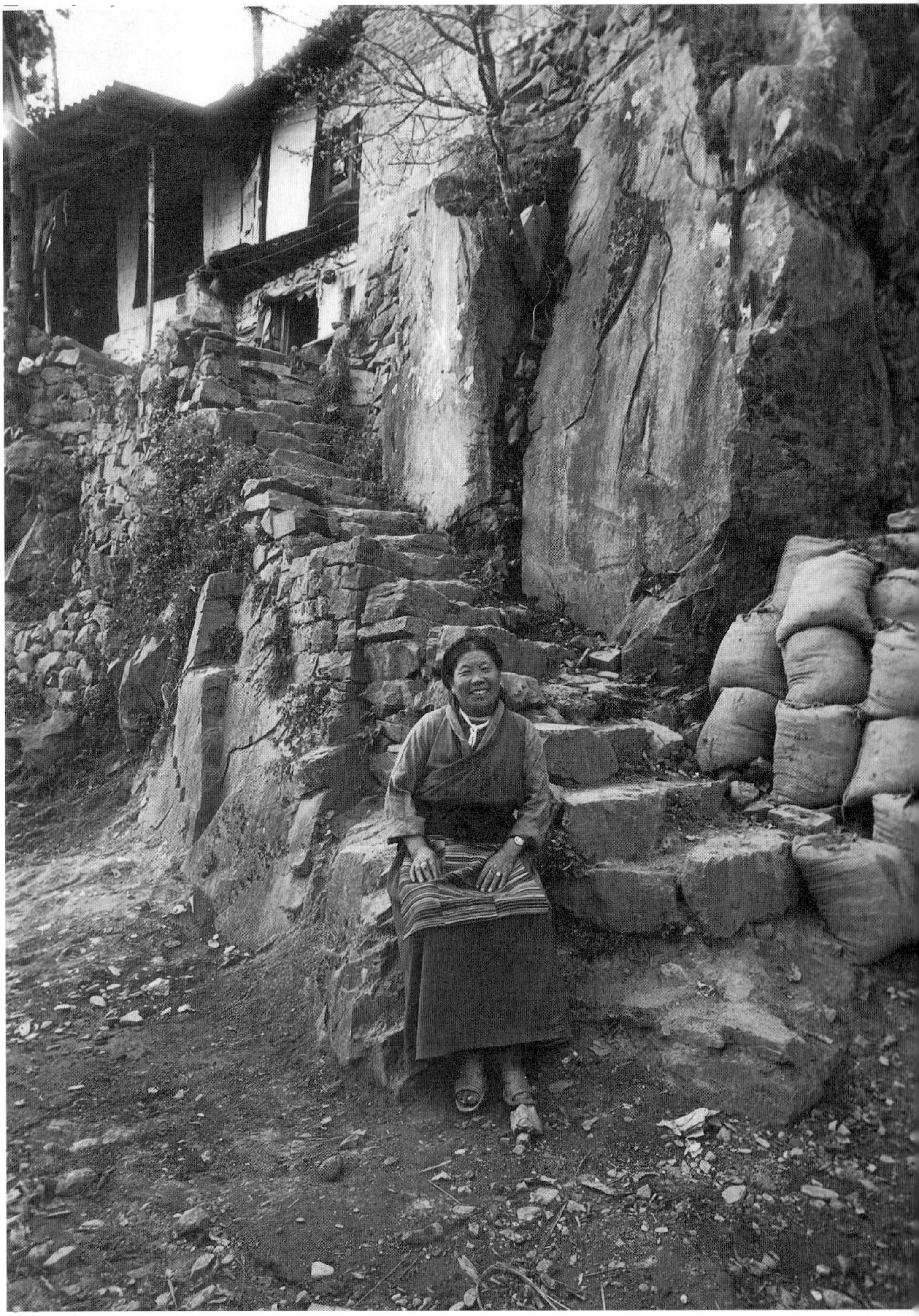

First, you have to accept that you are not going to change the entire culture of a country, single-handed, at once. The old cliché which appears so often in historical novels, 'I like a girl with spirit', reflects a mood which is still widespread. 'Spirit', seen as a masculine characteristic, means that the woman has invited herself into the world of men and may therefore be treated without the respect which is due to the world of women. Being combative or aggressive can exacerbate a problem rather than ameliorating it.

Second – and this may sound like the exact opposite of the above – an awful lot of harassment is in the nature of a 'try on'. In many countries, 'everyone knows' that foreign girls are easy; and it has to be said that in some resorts, some girls do nothing to discourage this belief. A firm rejection of unwelcome advances can switch you from the category of 'easy foreigner' to 'respectable woman', at least with that particular person. The reason that this is not in direct conflict with the above piece of advice is that you should only react like this when the occasion demands. In other words, use aggression (or at least firmness) when it is called for, but otherwise behave towards men in much the same way as you would at home.

Third, it helps if you have a reasonable awareness of the cultural norms of a particular society. In many places, for example, women normally dress very conservatively. If you wear jeans, you may attract disapproval, but you will not automatically be thought of as a hussy. Wear a mini-skirt or shorts, or a halter top, and the cultural message is that you are a strumpet. You may object to this; you may feel that you have the right to wear whatever you like; but if you cannot handle the fact that some cultures have different norms from your own, and you try to fight those norms, you can hardly be surprised when someone fights back.

It is not just a question of dress, either. In the United States, and to a lesser extent in most of northern Europe, a woman is expected to meet a man's eyes, just as another man would. But in many other cultures, the norm is to look away – usually down – if you catch a man's eye. Again, you may not approve, but there are times when it is easier and safer to accept that this is the way the world is, rather than trying to change things.

Likewise, body language is important. You want to project confidence, but not brazenness. This can be as important in 'Western' cultures as anywhere else. If you look like you know where you are going, and as if you are alert and ready to stand up for yourself, you are significantly less likely to be mugged than if you are visibly nervous, and you are less likely to be sexually assaulted than if you dress and walk provocatively on the one hand or look excessively gentle and vulnerable on the other.

A third aspect of being a woman photographer – and this applies everywhere – is that a ridiculous number of people assume that you cannot possibly be serious, because women cannot handle anything as technical as photography; it makes their brains overheat. This prejudice can manifest itself in several ways. Men may give you 'helpful' but unwanted and frequently



***Figure 6.2*** *In Dharamsala, Frances became friendly with Yuchen, Ama-la's daughter. She was invited to Ama-la's house on several occasions, and was presented with a traditional* ponggye *neck-warmer to wear with her* chuba. *The friendships and acquaintances which men and women make are likely to be different. (RWH)*

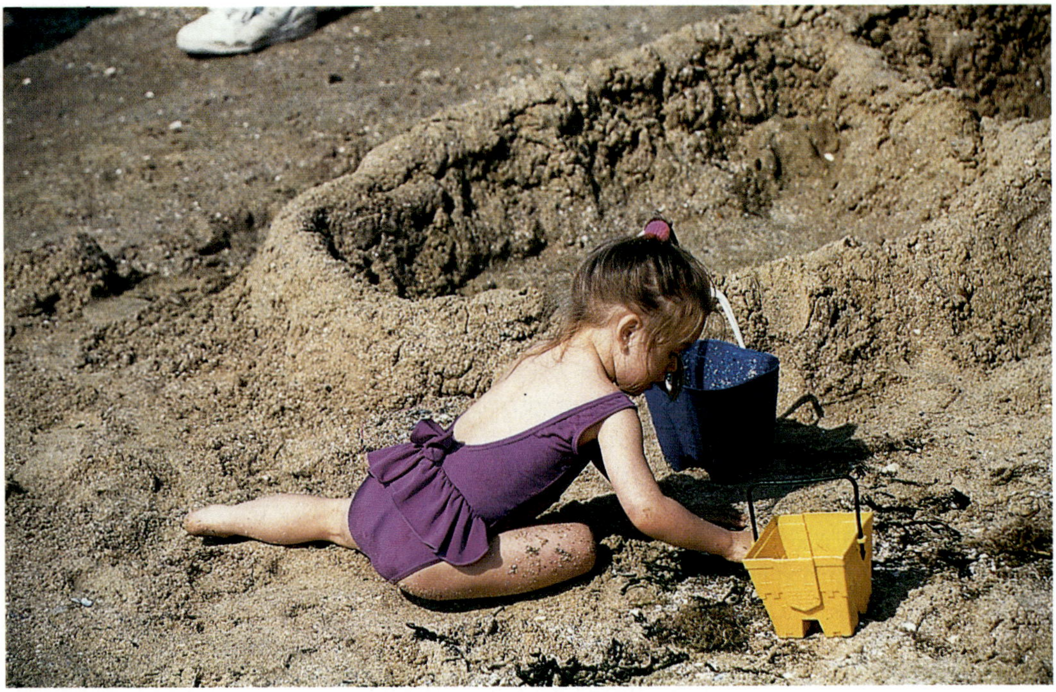

**Figure 6.3**
*Photographing children is increasingly fraught with problems in the paranoid West. Roger has been asked not to take pictures of children playing in the street in New York, in case we were planning on kidnapping them, and such was public hysteria in Britain in 1997 that a (male) photographer was arrested and detained until his films had been developed because he was taking pictures on a beach. A woman is however less likely to be suspected of paedophilia. (FES)*

useless advice on photography; shop assistants may ignore you, or try to tell you that you don't know what you are talking about; and subjects may refuse to cooperate, even if you have been commissioned by head office and they have had a fax warning them of your arrival.

Sometimes, this can just be funny. Frances went into a camera store in Stockton, California, to get a quarter-to-three-eighths adapter for her camera's tripod socket. She asked for 'a tripod socket adapter, please.' The girl behind the counter said, 'What size?' and Frances replied, 'There is only one size.' The girl was unconvinced. 'Oh, no, I don't know about that. I think you'd better wait until one of the men comes back, and he can tell you what size you need.' Frances could only persuade her to part with the adapter by telling her that she would take personal responsibility for the purchase, and that as it was only seventy-five cents, she didn't really mind if it was the wrong size; she would take it on the chance that it would fit.

Sometimes, too, there can be advantages to not being taken seriously. Many times – far more often than Roger – Frances has been asked by groups of women or families if she would mind taking their picture: she is 'just' a woman, albeit one who knows how to use a camera, and can be interrupted with impunity, whereas Roger is clearly a Professional Photographer. These requests can lead to interesting conversations which reveal a lot more about a place or a culture than you might otherwise learn.

You may also find that traditional feminine attributes and clothes may be more practical than you had thought, if you normally dress and behave in a typically Western style. In particular, a shawl has many uses. It is an attractive antidote to jeans, a reminder that just because you are wearing men's trousers, you are not a man. It is one of the best ways of keeping warm when the chill of the evening sets in. It can be used to cover the head, if necessary. This is all but compulsory in some churches and mosques, but quite apart from that, there are many situations where a covered head is a signal that you are a respectable, modest woman. And it even provides a useful shelter when changing films!

Finally, remember that you don't have to be an ice maiden. There are plenty of cultures where flirting is still perfectly acceptable, though it is an art which has almost completely vanished in many parts of the United States and which has always been a somewhat fragile plant in the Anglo-Saxon world in general. As long as you are confident that you are safe from genuine assault, a little fluttering of eyelashes, a smile and accepting a kiss on the hand may not be entirely a bad thing.

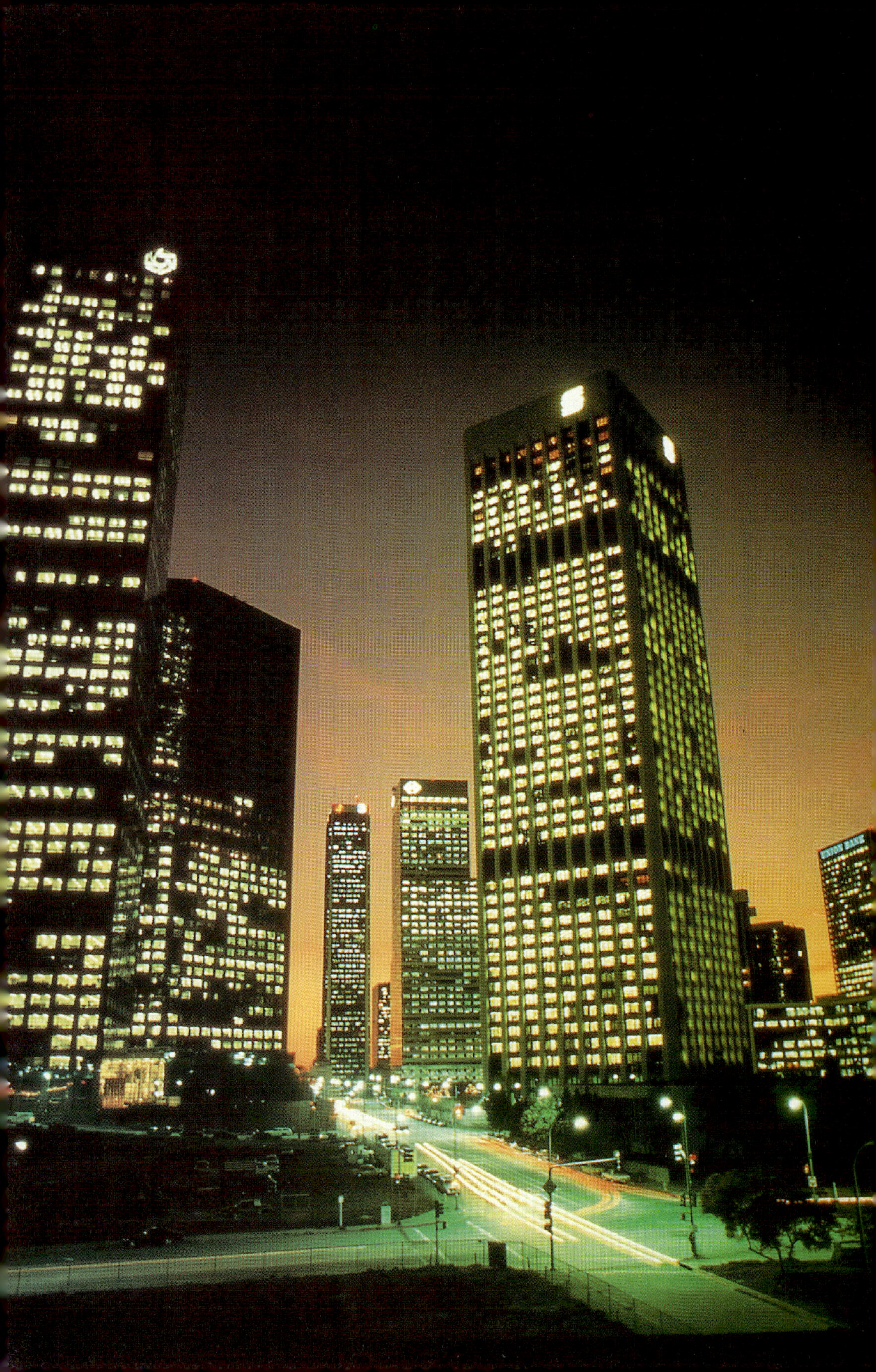
UNION BANK

# 7 Planning a trip

The very first question to ask about any trip is whether you can afford it. For instance, we have long wanted to go to the South Seas, but given the costs of doing so, we never have. We don't know if we could make it pay or not; we simply can't afford to risk the up-front investment which would be necessary to do it, and even a commissioned trip normally requires up-front expenditure out of your own pocket.

Ideally, you should know in advance that the trip is going to pay for itself, because it has been commissioned. There are two ways to get commissions. One is to come up with an idea and sell it, and the other is to agree to realize someone else's idea. A third route is uncommissioned or speculative work, where you don't sell it before you go: you may have specific markets in mind, or you may simply be shooting for a stock library.

The second question is whether it is feasible to go there. There are always plenty of war zones which are theoretically accessible, but which would only attract war photographers. Yes, you may be able to make your name there, as Tim Page did in Vietnam; but you may also die there, as Tim Page nearly did. He is the only person we know who has twice been pronounced dead on arrival at a hospital, and the second time was in Vietnam.

Even if the country is not too dangerous, it may be unwilling to grant you a visa, or it may let you in and then give you a good deal of grief once you are there. As running-dog lackeys of the reactionary Dalai Lama regime, we might have some difficulty in getting into China, or indeed in getting out again, and Frances's American passport (to say nothing of the fact that a good deal of our work is published in the United States) means that we would be very rash to go to, for example, Iraq, Iran or Libya.

Then of course there are the places which your own country may ban you from visiting: most non-Americans find it astonishing that the original bastion of freedom, the arsenal of democracy, should even dream of forbidding its citizens to go to Cuba.

Even if the above hurdles are surmountable, there is still the hassle factor. At the time of writing, we had not been to India in seven years, purely because of the hassle of getting visas. Regardless of the fact that we have been there many times, and regardless of the fact that we have in the past published a number of articles extolling its virtues, India takes an extra ten days and charges an extra fee to issue a visa to anyone who might be a writer, photographer, author, journalist or anyone else who gets anything published. For that matter, the US Visa Waiver Program specifically excludes

***Figure 7.1*** *This is one of those pictures that everyone intends to take when they go to Los Angeles, but finding the right vantage point can be surprisingly difficult, even if you know L.A. – and Frances lived there for almost twenty years. Many of the best viewpoints are closed to pedestrians, and the California Highway Patrol takes a dim view of people who pull over to take pictures. The only possibility is to reconnoitre when you get there. (RWH)*

'representatives of the foreign media'; the sight of the richest and most powerful country in the world behaving like a paranoid Third World dictatorship is more than a little unsettling.

With the financial and political considerations out of the way, you start looking at whether you can make the trip pay. The simple truth is that if you keep the cost down far enough, you can make almost any trip pay, but the more it costs, the greater the risk. The other side of this coin is that some topics and some places are a lot likelier to sell than others. The example of the South Seas comes back: we are not looking at typical destinations for mass tourism, and indeed we are not looking at destinations which could even handle large numbers of tourists. Paris, on the other hand, for all that it is done to death, is a destination which interests everyone. Chapters 9 to 20 are pretty much about making travel pay, so there is no need to go into greater depth here.

## When to go

Let's assume that a trip is feasible: you can afford the investment, and the payback looks reasonable. The next question is when to go.

Most tourist brochures, and many guide books, tend to skate over the details of climate. They either give the impression that the destination is paradise all year round, or they assume that you will be there in 'the season', while taking care not to specify when that might be. An invaluable book here is the *World Weather Guide* (Times Books, a division of Random House, ISBN 0-8129-1881-9), which gives temperatures and rainfall figures, together with the number of days with more than 1 mm of precipitation, on a monthly basis. It will enable you to avoid the monsoons in India, or blocked passes in the Alps, or the sweltering unpleasantness of Chicago in summer.

Any weather guide must however be used with some intelligence, and preferably with some additional information. For instance, we once met a couple in Darjeeling in February who had no real winter clothing with them. They had bought the trip as an add-on to a trip to Calcutta, and when they had asked their travel agent what sort of clothes to take, he had said, 'Well, it's not very far from Calcutta, so the climate is probably much the same.' If either they or he had exercised their minds in the slightest, they would have realized that Darjeeling is well over two kilometres from Calcutta in a vertical plane, regardless of the horizontal distance, and that the temperature at that altitude might well be a little different.

## Guide books

As well as a bare collection of weather statistics, you will need guide books. The choice is immense, and there are numerous specialist publications which are first-class on particular regions, but there are three series of guide books which we have found particularly useful. Each has its strengths and weaknesses, and we will often buy all three before we go somewhere.

The first and most basic (in more than one sense) is the Lonely Planet series. These are uneven in quality and often slapdash in the extent to which

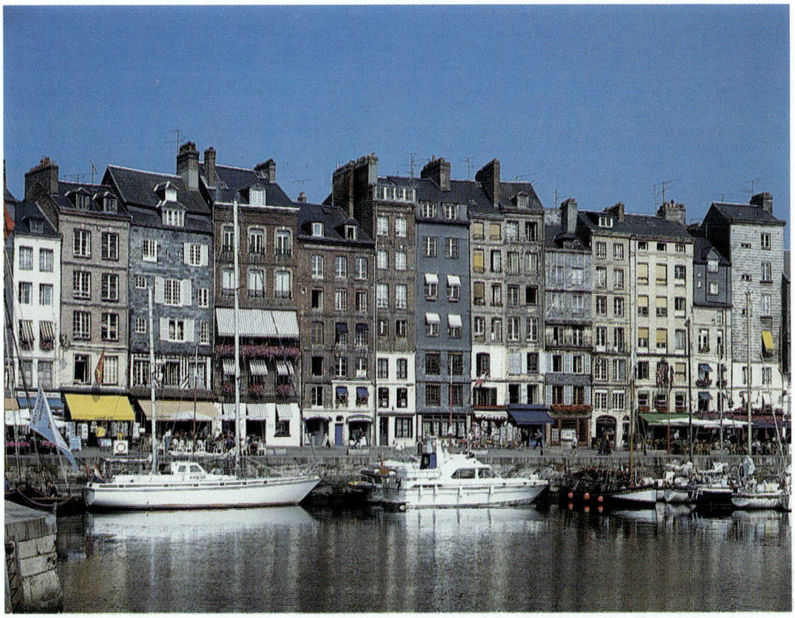

*Figure 7.2 For many travellers, Honfleur in Normandy is pretty much defined by this picture – but you very rarely see any other view. When you get there, you soon realize why. Although it is a charming and picturesque place, this is so far and away the easiest, good shot that you can practically place your tripod-legs in the worn hollows. Also, if a client wants shorthand for Honfleur, this is the shot they want. Whenever a place is represented by just the one picture, ask yourself why. (RWH)*

they are updated, but of the budget guides they are incomparably the best. They give you an excellent idea of costs and facilities, and if you ignore their bottom-end recommendations (which are often out-and-out flea-pits) they will generally enable you to find decent accommodation at a reasonable price, along with adequate food and how to handle the local transport. The original Lonely Planet Guides were aimed very much at hippies, and it shows. Those hippies have however grown fat and prospered, and this too shows in some current editions. We used to aim to stay and eat at the top end of their 'mid range' recommendations, or at the lower end of their 'splurge' or 'expensive' recommendations, and with some books, this is still what we do; but with their recommendations in Paris, for example, we find that we know better places, at cheaper prices.

Next come the Blue Guides. Although at first sight they may seem stuffy and visually unattractive, they are nevertheless chock-full of information about what to see and what it means. They assume that you have a good reason for going somewhere, and that you know the sort of thing that interests you; they make very little effort either to extol a place, or to point out its defects. For captioning your pictures, there is no finer general resource.

Finally, there are the APA Insight Guides. The big attraction of these is their illustrations, which give you an excellent idea of the 'must shoot' pictures which you should look for, but they also have the kind of running text which actually makes you want to go and see a place, instead of the relentless negativity and 'hassles, man' approach of Lonely Planet. They are however quite poor on specific information on where to stay, what to eat and how to travel.

Depending on the market for which we are working, we may also buy a guide book from a series aimed at that market. For an insight into the concerns

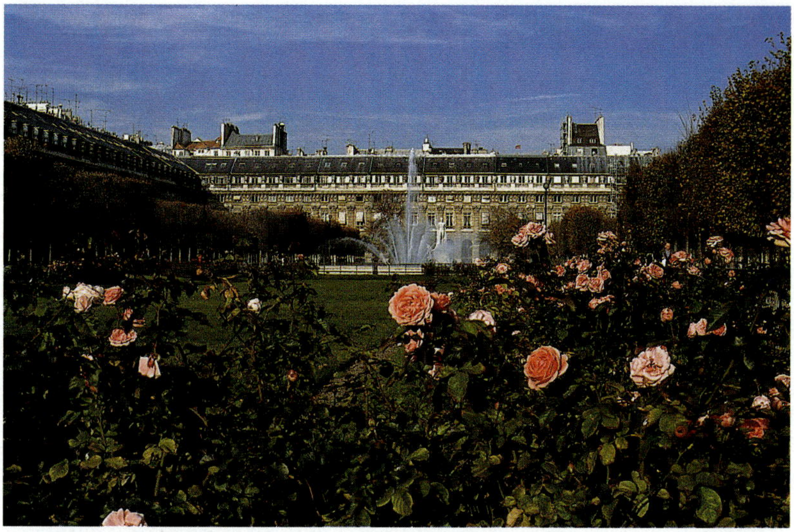

*Figure 7.3* *A great advantage of travelling in spring and early summer is that you can often use flowers to fill unattractive or difficult foregrounds such as this one at the Jardin du Palais-Royal, Paris. We used to know one photographer who worked for a national tourist board and habitually carried bunches of flowers to use as out-of-focus foregrounds. He eventually reconciled his employers to the idea that his daily flower bill was an essential part of his expenses. (FES)*

and priorities of Middle America, the Frommer guides are pretty good. For young European professionals, you could do worse than the Rough Guides. But there are also guide books which we avoid like the plague, either because they show absolutely no awareness of any culture other than that of the authors; or because they cater only to people who want to do nothing more than shop and sunbathe; or simply because they have next to no genuine information, but are highly personal and often rather vague.

With books which give specific information on accommodation, restaurants, tourist attractions and so forth, it is a good idea to buy the most recent edition you can: a book which is more than two or three years old may be so outdated on prices as to be useless. By contrast, the information in Blue Guides dates much more slowly and you can often learn a lot from travel classics which are decades or even centuries old. For example, we find that Samuel Puffendorf's *Introduction to the History of the Principal Kingdoms and States of Europe* (we have the ninth edition, 1728) still provides useful insights today. The Engifh, for example, 'are fomewhat proud, and Lovers of Eafe, and fpend every Day fome hours in walking and fmoaking Tobacco, which is the Reafon that they do not fo much work as otherwife they might; and yet they expect to be paid for their idle Hours as well as the reft ... they have always been inclined to Rebellion and inteftine Commotions.'

Remember that the principal purpose of guide books is to sell guide books, not to help travellers. 'Always knowingly oversold' might well be their motto. Many more times than once, we have eagerly gone somewhere that sounds wonderful, only to find – substantially nothing, at least from a visual point of view. This is where APA Insight Guides and the like are so useful. If there are no pictures of somewhere; or if the pictures are dull; or if there is only one shot of a place, which occurs again and again, like the Lion Gate at Mycaenae, then you can draw your own conclusions about how photogenic the destination in question may be.

Remember too that the very fact of inclusion in a guide book will most likely lead a place to increase its prices and to have more bookings, so you will often do better to go to a hotel or restaurant recommended by a guide book, and then look at its nearby competitors. A basic rule of economics is that in a city at least, competitors tend to congregate so that customers can more easily compare and be lured from one shop to another, and you can turn this to your advantage.

## MAPS

Maps are a vexed question. In general, we have found that detailed maps are usually cheaper and almost invariably better when bought in the country you are visiting, but there are exceptions. In particular, there are some countries or areas where good maps are all but unobtainable, either as a matter of deliberate policy (try buying maps of Indian border areas, for example) or because no-one has got around to updating older maps (as in Malta). You may have to hunt around the second-hand shops, or put up with the indifferent cartography of tourist maps.

Britons, used to the incomparable Ordnance Survey, may be surprised at the casualness with which maps are treated in other countries, and of course there is always the argument that getting moderately lost can be an essential part of exploring a place: as long as you can get back onto the main road before nightfall, and get to your hotel, what is the problem?

In Britain, an excellent source for maps and guide books and the like is Stanford's, near Victoria Station, London, while in the United States there are a number of travel bookshops which have reasonable map holdings. It is also worth knowing that if you buy a lot of United States Geological Survey (USGS) maps from the headquarters in Reston, Virginia, you will get a substantial discount. In the 1980s, we were very annoyed indeed after spending $350 there without a discount, when we found a few days later that if we had bought another $150 worth, we would have got a 50 per cent discount on a $500 purchase and thereby saved $100.

## TOURIST OFFICES

It may seem strange to have left tourist offices so late, but with few exceptions, national tourist office information is both extremely patchy and understandably somewhat biased. Of course it is a good idea to send for whatever they have got, or better still to go in and pick it up for yourself, but with few exceptions, tourist office material is no substitute for a good guide book or two (or three).

Local tourist offices are another matter, but by definition, you don't go to them until you have already got to the country. Again, the range of material on offer is extremely variable and may bear relatively little information which is relevant to the real world, but equally, this is the way to find out about local attractions which are far less known than they ought to be. Less than a mile from where we live in Kent, for example, is Quex House. Hardly anyone has

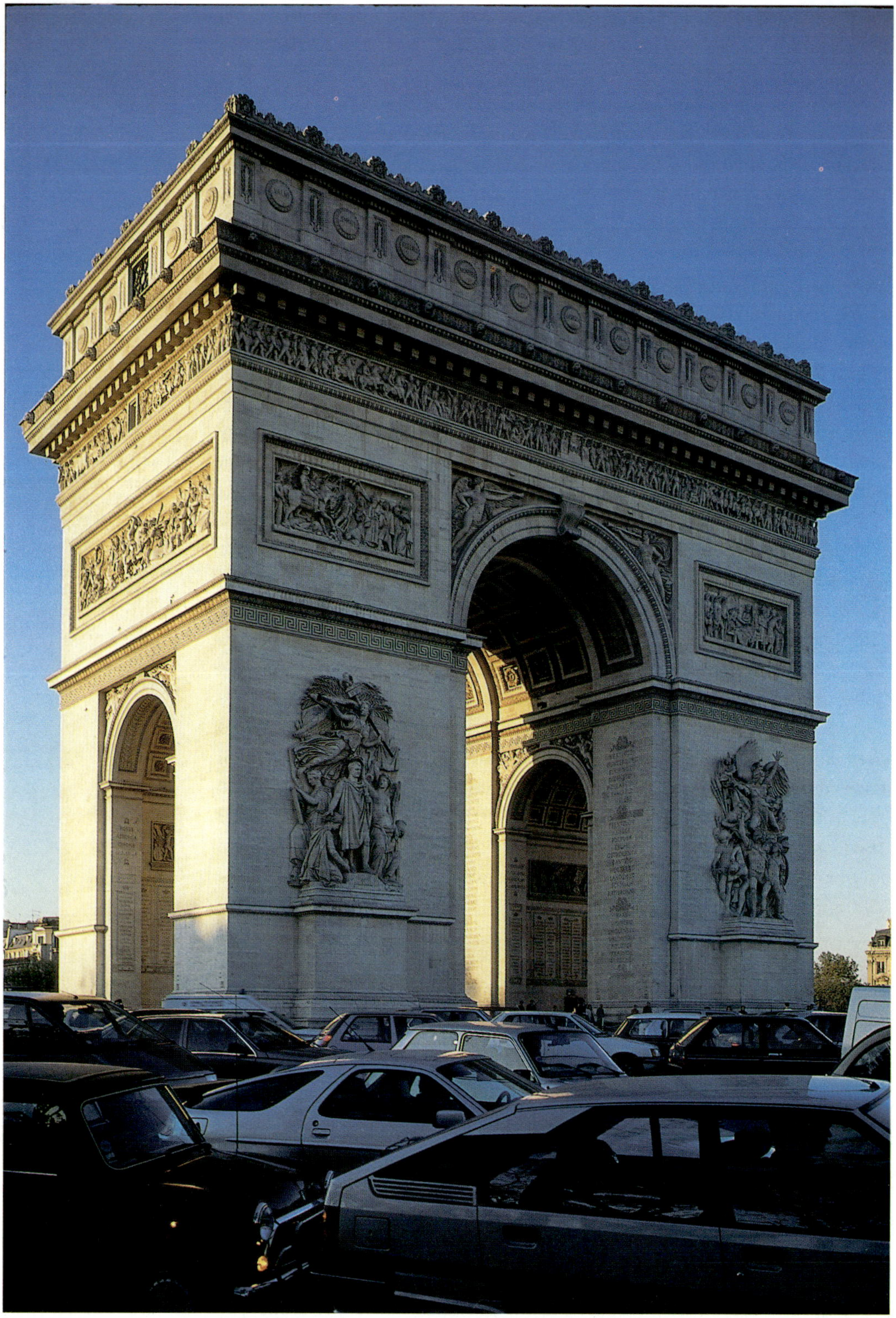

heard of it – but once you go there, it is remarkable. Among museum-keepers, it is justly famous as one of the best of the numerous small museums in Britain.

## Accommodation

We have already touched on accommodation more than once, but this is the place to reinforce the point that you need certain minimum standards of comfort and security if you are to work efficiently. Yes, you can put your cameras at the foot of your sleeping-bag and use your backpack for a pillow, and we have done it on Indian trains; but a good night's sleep behind a securely locked door is something of considerable value.

Another point worth making is that sometimes you may have to pay more than you would like in order to get a good location. If you want to shoot a place at sunrise, for instance (and many of the best shots are obtainable at sunrise) then it makes sense to sleep within walking distance of that place. It's safer, quicker and easier, and by the time you have figured in a taxi fare it may well be cheaper too.

## Dietary requirements

If you are fussy about what you eat, an awful lot of destinations will either be closed to you or will be less than enjoyable. Vegetarians, in particular, will find that in many countries they are regarded as simpletons – though they may be in for surprises, as we were at the extraordinary range of superb vegetarian food in Crete – and vegans might as well stay at home, because the concept of avoiding meat, eggs, milk and cheese will be all but impossible to get across in a language you do not speak well. Much the same is true in many countries (especially in Eastern Europe) if you want to keep kosher or halal.

## Clothing

The world is far less formal than it used to be, so smart casual clothing is more than adequate for the vast majority of destinations. There are however a number of points which are worth remembering.

The first is that local sensibilities must be respected. This affects women more often than it affects men, but there are places where one sex or the other, or both, will require covered (or bare) heads, bare or at least stockinged feet, covered legs (and in some cases arms) and so forth. It is all very well to object to Arab repression of women, but if you want to take pictures in one of the more repressive Islamic states, you are going to have to put up with the rules. Otherwise, don't go. Remember, too, that there are still pockets of old-fashioned stuffiness, such as some of the Raj-era clubs which survive in India. Men may not need a collar and tie, but they are likely to need shoes and socks rather than thongs or even trainers, and a well-cut bush shirt or possibly a *kurta* instead of a T-shirt.

The second is that something which is comfortable for an air-conditioned lifestyle in California may well be unsuitable for life on the road in India – and vice versa. Climate, terrain, the sort of subjects you want to shoot:

***Figure 7.4*** *The Parisian rush-hour is inimitable, and the Etoile epitomizes it; but you will do well to pick a time of year when the setting sun coincides with the worst of the traffic. In the winter, everything can be too dark; in the summer, too light. Of course, you can shoot it at any time, but some pictures are more effective than others. This was shot with a shift lens to avoid the 'falling over backwards' effect with the Arc de Triomphe itself. (RWH)*

all will affect your choice of dress. If you have to walk, you will need good walking shoes; if you are going through snake country, then high boots or gaiters are a good idea. Fashion clothes are rarely designed for an active lifestyle, even if the marketing people suggest differently. A polyester safari shirt, for example, will soon get sweaty and sticky and smelly and uncomfortable, where a cotton one will not: natural fabrics, comfortable (and generous) cuts and well-finished seams are more important than looks.

A third point is laundry. Clothes which can be washed and dried quickly are at a premium, and if they need no ironing, that is a bonus. 'Perma-wrinkle' dresses are ideal for women, and the same fabric can make good, light sun-shirts for both sexes. Some countries are very much better than others when it comes to laundry: in India, for example, laundry is typically done overnight, to a very high standard at a very modest price, and returned to your room beautifully ironed, even the underpants – though clothes need to be well-made to withstand the pounding that the dhobi-wallahs will give them. Last time we were in Moscow, by contrast, laundries and laundromats were almost unknown, though things may have improved since.

A fourth point is that for photographers, clothing can be as much a tool as a means of keeping warm and staying decent. Photographers' vests are an obvious example, but there are many others. We both wear Billingham waterproof jackets made of Ventile cotton, a near-miraculous fabric which is, in Billingham products, allied to specific design for the photographer. Roger habitually wears fisherman's smocks, which have two large (150 cm/6 inch square) patch pockets on the front: these can be invaluable for storing meters, films, dark slides and so forth as you are working.

You may even decide to have some of your clothes specially made: Roger has in the past had moleskin trousers made with extra pockets, and Kos has her oilskins specially made oversize, so that she can keep her cameras dry underneath. For a motorcycle tour in India, Frances made a denim top to go with jeans, thereby creating in effect a denim *salwar-kamiz* outfit. On the one hand, it was quite unlike any other *salwar-kamiz* you ever saw, but on the other, it was sufficiently familiar-looking that many people probably never even realized she was wearing Levi 501s.

A perennial question is whether or not local clothes are appropriate. There is an inevitable temptation to try the local clothing, and to assume that doing so will be accepted by the locals. You must however be aware of the full implications of what you wear. Often, 'ethnic' clothing is worn either by the poor (in which case people will wonder why a rich photographer is wearing such funny clothes) or as 'best' on high days and holy days, in which case even the locals feel faintly ridiculous and over-dressed when they wear it.

Women can often get away with more than men in this respect, but even then, you need a fairly keen eye for what is proper. Frances won many approving glances and comments for her Tibetan *chuba*, but (as two or three women said) this was partly because she dressed as a well-to-do Tibetan would dress, with bright silk blouses and a proper apron in (to borrow T. E.'s phrase) 'nine primary colours'. Most *Inji* (Westerners) apparently wear dull, drab versions of Tibetan clothing because they think it is more appropriate, and in Tibetan eyes, they are wrong. Another point is that aprons are worn by married women, not single girls.

All in all, fashion is less important than style. Wear what you like, because you like it, and you are likely to look good and to be accepted for yourself. Worry too much about fashion (as distinct from comfort, practicality, and local mores) and you will look like a tourist.

## Medical kits

As you get older, you take health and safety less and less for granted. This is not necessarily because you are hopelessly enfeebled, but because you see more of the things that can go wrong. Some of them happen to you, while of others you think, 'There but for the grace of God go I.'

It is well worth carrying a small medical kit in some countries, including a couple of sterile, disposable syringes – the ones in the hospital may or may not be sterile, or sharp – but it has to be clear that this is medical, not recreational, equipment: carry it in a pack with a big red cross on it, and no unidentified drugs. Talk to your doctor before you go, and ask what vaccinations you need (US doctors are sometimes alarmingly ill informed on this one) and whether you need anti-malarial prophylactic drugs. For any prescription drugs you do carry, get a doctor's letter confirming that you need them, and remember that some drugs (prescription or non-prescription) may be banned in one place even if they are readily and entirely legally available in another: Codeine is a good example, and we hate to think what an American customs official would make of good old 'Mist Kaol et Morph', aka mixture of kaolin and morphine, the traditional remedy for diarrhoea known in the Royal Navy as 'hard stoppers'.

Nor should you think only of emergency treatments or of prescription drugs for medical conditions when considering a medical kit. Women, in

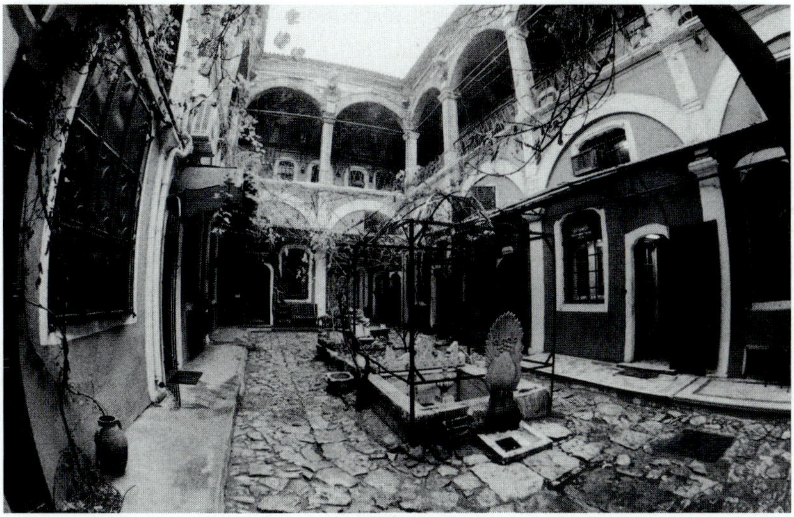

***Figure 7.5*** *If you know you are likely to be photographing confined spaces like this* han *near the Grand Bazaar in Istanbul, you may care to consider a fish-eye lens. They have to be used with discretion, but more adventurous clients may welcome the different viewpoint which they make possible. (FES)*

particular, should carry enough sanitary supplies and (if appropriate) birth control pills. You may also wish to carry condoms.

## Insurance

*Figure 7.6 You can't plan for everything. The walk from the road-head at Sougia to the long-ruined theatre at Lissos goes up one of Crete's famous gorges, across the top of the island, and down to another. It takes well over an hour each way, before you set aside picture-taking time. The path is barely more than a goat-track, and when we walked it, we had to clamber over fallen trees. We really had very little idea of what we were getting into: we knew there was a theatre, and we knew there was a walk, but the guide books told us little more than that. (RWH)*

We now carry annual travel insurance, which covers us for health, lost tickets, cancellations, missed connections and a good deal more. Read the policy carefully, though. For example, we habitually take the train to the airport, rather than a taxi. Why? Because, as mentioned elsewhere, our policy covers us for failure of scheduled public transport, but not for taxis which arrive late.

When you consider that it is easy to run up a thousand-dollar bill in a few hours in an American hospital, while an air ambulance from somewhere you would prefer not to be treated will cost considerably more, a good travel insurance plan is essential and (at least in the UK) astonishingly cheap; at the time of writing, around £90–120 (US $150–200) for one person for a year, and surprisingly little more for a couple travelling together.

The cover which travel insurance gives for cameras and other possessions is however laughably small in most cases, so you will also need some other kind of insurance. There are specialist insurers dealing in this sort of risk; check the professional photographic press for their advertisements, and again, check carefully what cover they offer and where.

Again as previously mentioned, insurance is in our experience easier and cheaper to get in Britain than in the United States. In general, though, you must be ordinarily resident in a place to get insurance, so a US resident may find it difficult or impossible to buy insurance in Britain.

One last point on insurance is that many credit card purchases are automatically protected. Many years ago, we lost several hundred dollars on an airline ticket when the airline went bankrupt. Today, we always buy our airline tickets by credit card for precisely this reason: if the airline fails, the credit card company will either refund the money or get us out of trouble. The most useful card world-wide is almost certainly Visa, though Mastercard is beginning to catch up. Despite its self-promotion, American Express is likely to prove a poor third in many destinations.

## Packing

There are some trips when you never have to carry your luggage, except perhaps to and from the airport at home. For example, you may always be able to engage porters, or you may be based in a car, or better still in a motor home, and never venture far from it.

Far more often, though, you are going to have to carry your luggage at least some of the time, and quite possibly most of the time. It therefore makes sense to carry the bare minimum possible. This means relying on local laundry facilities, and it may mean carrying less of a wardrobe than you might like; but after you have been through a single trip where you regularly dreaded having to move from one place to another, or where your back was constantly aching from what you had to carry, you may be amazed at how much you can

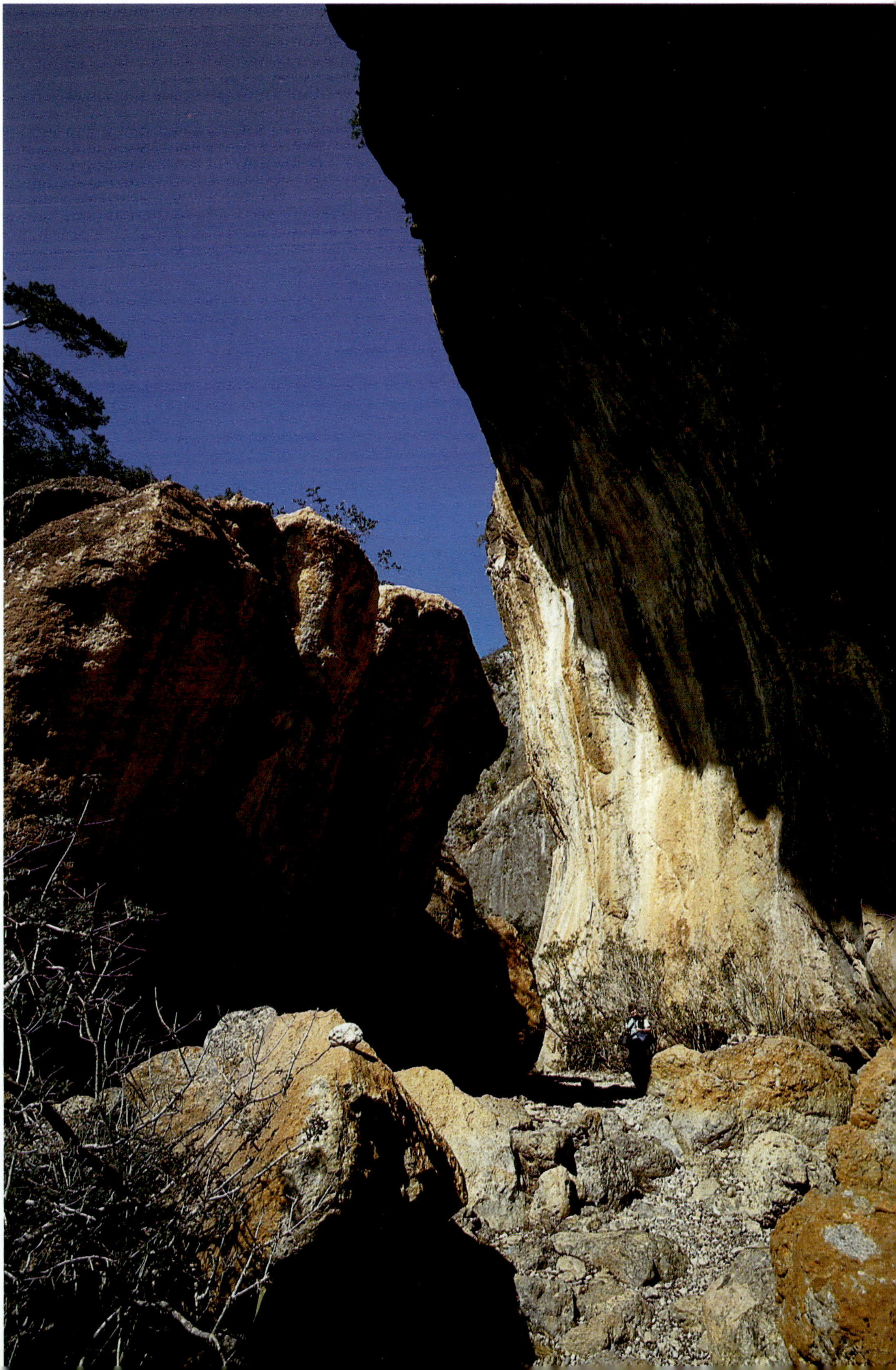

cut down on your luggage. It comes down, as so often in this book, to the oft-repeated point that you are not on holiday: you are working.

In general, you need two sets of clothes – jeans, dresses, whatever – one to wear and one in the wash. You need more smalls than that: socks, underpants, T-shirts. If you are wearing heavy boots, it is often a good idea to carry a second pair of shoes or sandals, to give your feet a rest (or an airing), and a lightweight kimono can come in handy in all sorts of situations, and packs away to very little. You'll need a sponge-bag of toiletries, too. For the basics, that's about it. You will have more than enough camera kit to carry, before you start on clothes as well.

If you know you are going to need clothes for particular occasions, as described above, then obviously you will have to pack those too. What you should not pack, however, is 'just in case' clothes. Losses or damage can usually be made good locally, so why carry a spare pair of jeans or two extra bras 'just in case'?

As for what you should carry your luggage in, we use three kinds of bags. One is a hard-shell Zero Halliburton light alloy case. Enormously strong, this affords excellent protection to anything inside it. It is not the ultra-expensive

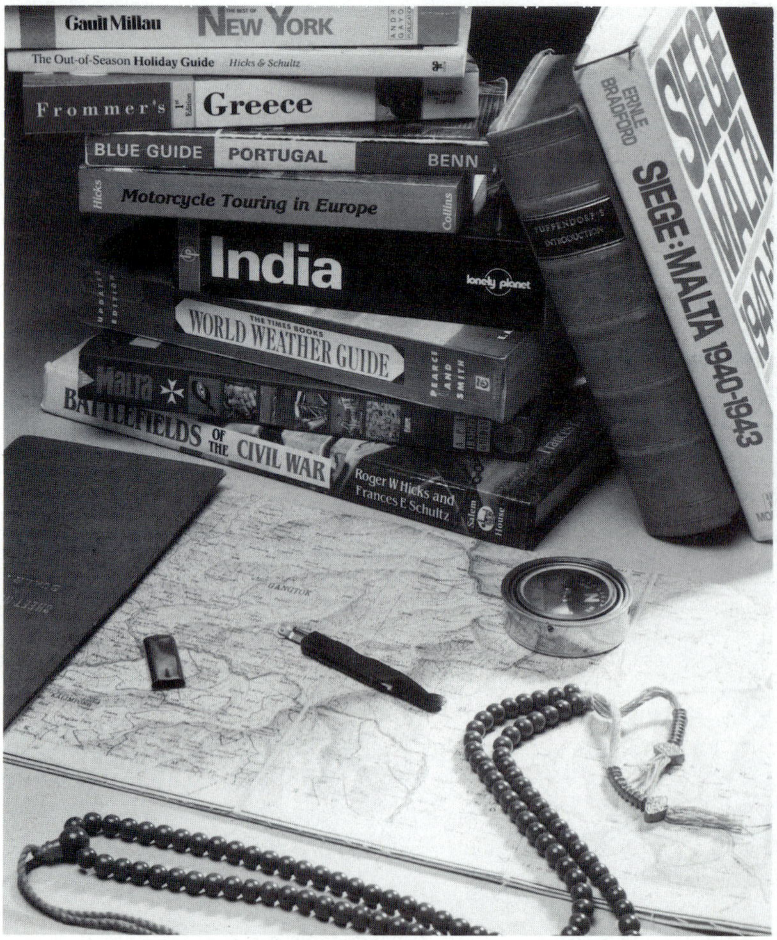


**Figure 7.7** If you are travelling for fun, you will often do better if you do not rely too heavily on guide books, which try to impose the writers' view of their destinations on you. If you are travelling on business, to take pictures, you need all the information you can get. Reading different types of travel book will give you a good idea of what interests different people, and collateral material such as Puffendorf's *Introduction* or Ernle Bradford's account of the second great siege of Malta can give you unexpected insights.

The map is an India Survey edition from the 1920s, 1/2 inch to the mile (253,440:1, approximately 1 cm = 2.5 km) and the pen-like instrument is a 'clicker' which you roll along the map; it clicks every 1/2 inch, equal to 1 mile on this map. The compass is probably Edwardian, and cost less than a modern equivalent.

suitcase version of the case: rather, it is a camera case (which is still pretty expensive!) with all the foam taken out, so it consists only of a light, thin, strong alloy shell. The second kind of cases are high-quality soft-sides, originally made for shipping computer equipment. We bought them at a going-out-of-business sale. The third is Tenba bags, which roll up to a very small size but can carry an enormous amount of non-fragile goods such as clothes, guide books, tourist office information and so forth. Because we normally acquire things on our travels, we typically carry at least one Tenba bag inside either the Halliburton or one of the soft-sides.

The important thing about all of these is that they are very, very strong and resistant to abusive handling. We typically make at least three or four trips per year by air, often more, and usually when we are waiting at the carousel to collect our luggage we will see the sad results of poor quality luggage, most notably burst zips. Nowadays, we rarely use back-packs any more, but when we do, we use high-quality internal-frame bags with a minimum of pockets and straps: external frames do not mix well with airline baggage handling, and nor do too many straps or external pockets.

In general, when we leave home we try to have no more than one main (checked) bag each, and one cabin bag (containing the cameras), though we sometimes compromise and have a third checked bag between us. On the way back, one of the Tenbas almost invariably comes into play. One person cannot easily carry more than three bags, one in each hand and one on a shoulder strap, so this is our absolute limit. When we put them down, or when we pick them up, we recite in the sing-song voice of an Indian porter (where we first encountered this trick), 'One, two, three, four, five piece...' (or whatever) and look at one another for confirmation. Even though this sounds funny, like most rituals, it has a purpose. When you are really tired, or ill, or generally groggy, a ritual can be a life-saver. We also use a light, flexible cable-lock, of the sort sold for securing bicycles, to lock the bags together at an airport or station, or on a train.

Normally, too, we will carry at least one small, high-quality padlock, both for securing zipped cases (far more thieves will unzip a case than will slash it open) and for securing hotel doors, cupboards, etc., in those countries which provide staples and hasps for this purpose – an excellent amenity, which we wish would catch on in affluent Europe and the United States.

## Documents

Strictly, passports are far less often a legal requirement than border police would have you believe. In practice, even though they may not in theory be essential, they are one of the most useful forms of identification you can carry, which is why so many officials love them so much.

There is not much to say about passports – if you need information that basic, you need to read other books than this one – except to say that you should guard them as closely as possible, either keeping them on your per-

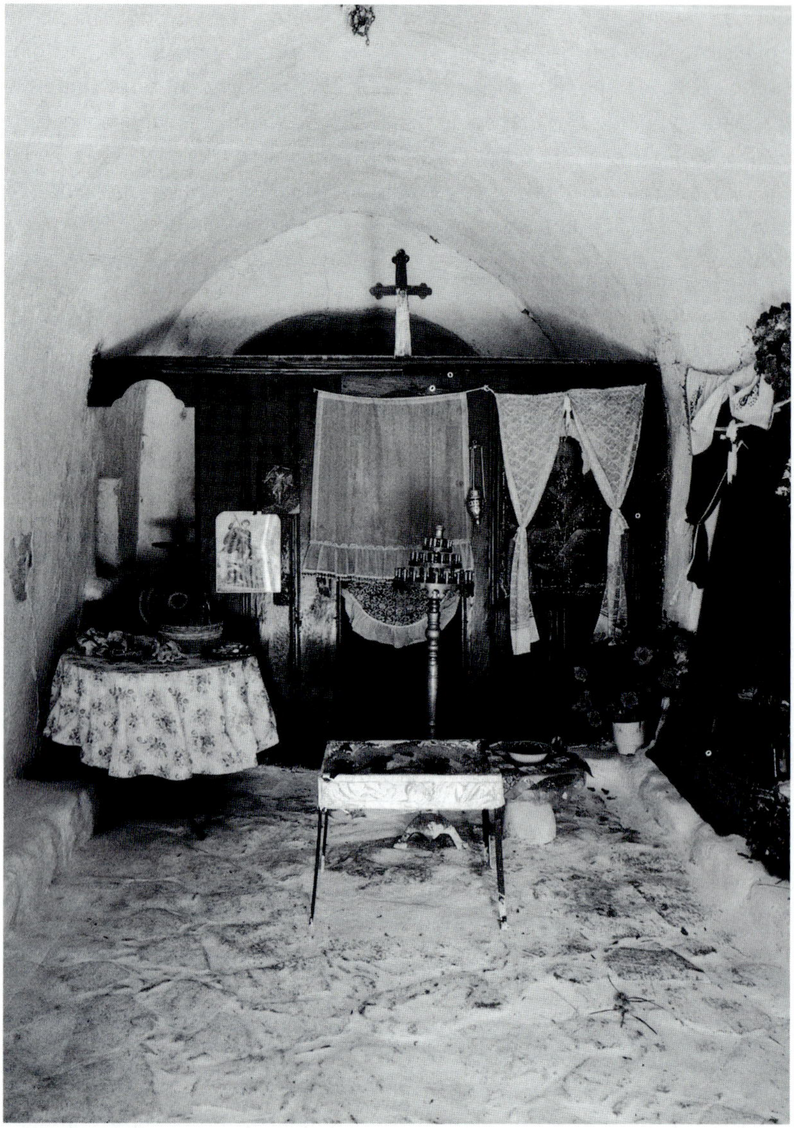

*Figure 7.8* *Tiny, whitewashed churches appear in countless photographs of Greece – but what are the interiors like? If you are interested, the chances are that someone else is, too. Such a picture may not have the mass appeal of the exterior shot, but equally, it is not up against the same competition. This was shot with a 21mm lens. (RWH)*

son or putting them in a hotel safe or similar safe storage. Bear in mind that in many countries, unless you can produce some form of identification you may be committing a criminal offence and even if you are not, nasty things can happen. We read in the *Los Angeles Times* of an Indian (from the sub-continent, that is) who was picked up by *la migra* (the Immigration and Naturalization Service) and dumped deep in Mexico without money or papers, and without a word of Spanish. Well, he looked like a Mexican, didn't he, and he had a funny accent.

## Visas

There are however a number of things to say about visas. The first is that it is totally unpredictable who needs them; the only way to find out is to check, preferably several times from several different sources. The second is that most immigration officers have an extraordinarily high opinion both of their own importance and of the desirability of settling in their country. Even in a place where no-one in their right mind would want to stay, you may be in for a grilling if the immigration officer thinks you might overstay your visa, or if your visa is not precisely in order. The third is that you may, in some countries, choose to lie about your occupation and call yourself a student or a school-teacher or a company director or just about anything rather than a photographer. The fourth – almost the mirror image of the third – is that if you have a specific project in mind, you may find it easiest to canvass the help of the visa department, rather than concealing your activities from them.

What other documents do you need? Your driving licence is essential, if you want to hire a car or motorcycle; most places will accept your ordinary licence, but some insist on an IDP (International Driving Permit), usually obtainable for a small fee from the principal automobile club in your country or state. For some countries, you may need certificates of vaccination against certain diseases: if you don't have one, you may be forcibly injected at the airport, with a needle of uncertain provenance, cleanliness and sharpness. The usefulness of a letter from your doctor about any prescription drugs has already been mentioned, and it's a good idea to carry several copies of your travel insurance policy to reassure hospitals, etc., that they really will get paid.

A curious one which we carry is a small, laminated copy of our wedding certificate. This is because often there is no charge for a spouse to drive a hire car, but you generally need to share the same surname. We don't, so we carry the wedding certificate. Some countries also have 'blue' laws on unmarried couples sharing accommodation.

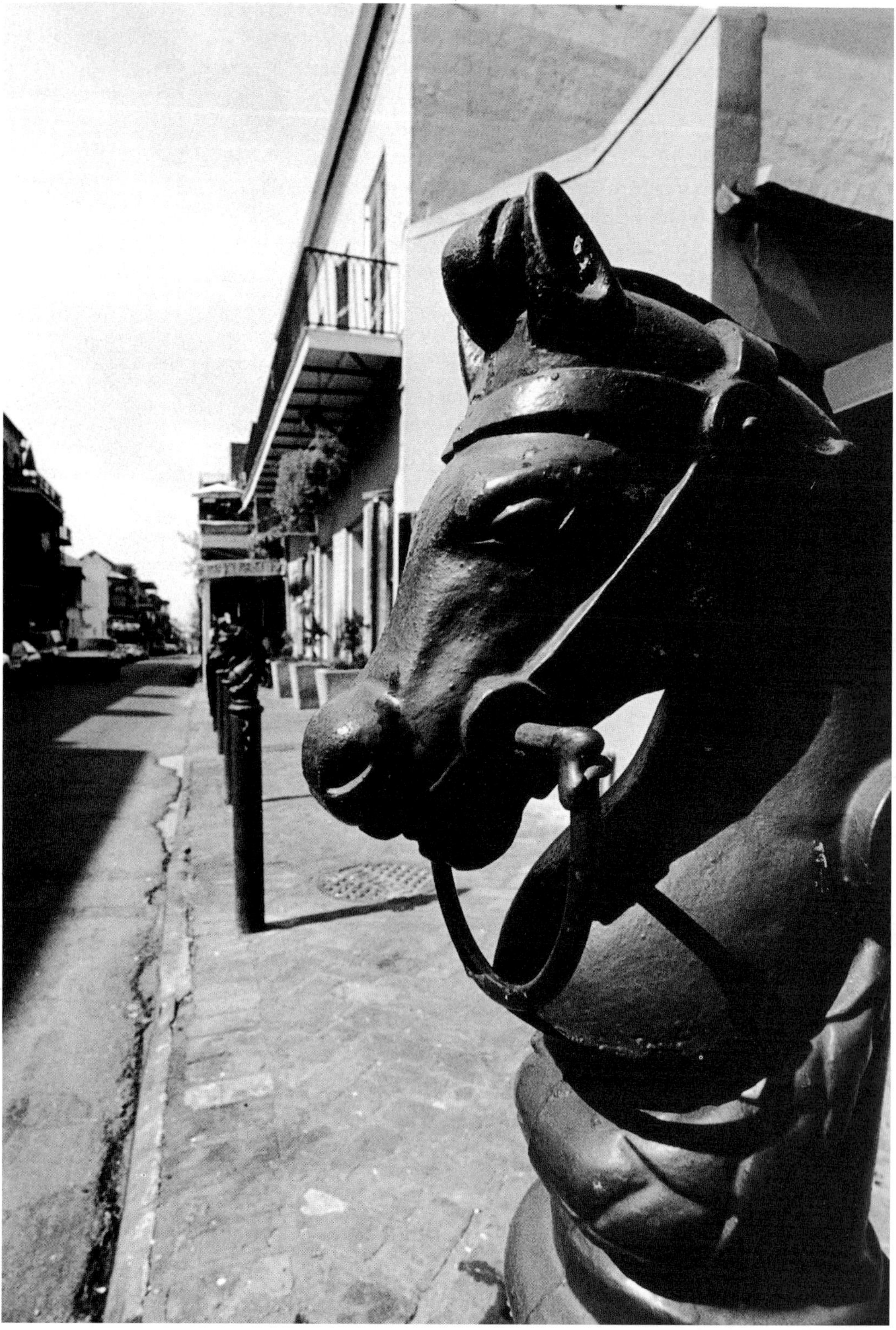

# 8 When you arrive

Culture shock is not limited to Third World countries. Indeed, it can be worse in countries which are superficially similar to your own – and even where the two countries are more similar than you imagined, the mere act of travelling can reveal aspects you had not previously encountered.

What is more, culture shock can continue throughout your trip, as you discover more and more differences. You break your glasses in California, a simple half-dioptre negative prescription? You'd better have your prescription with you, because otherwise you'll need an (expensive) eye test. Even then, some will refuse to accept prescriptions from out-of-state opticians (so it's an expensive eye test again) while others will refuse to re-glaze an existing pair of glasses. Even something as simple as getting a test sheet of E6 processed, something which takes at most a couple of hours in London, takes at least three hours at top Los Angeles custom labs. Why? It just does...

It is important, though, not to write off too much to culture shock, assuming that things are different (and maybe hard to deal with) just because you are abroad. For example, in many countries there is a choice of Western-style WCs and the squat or Turkish style. Many people struggle for days with the squat style before discovering that they have the choice, though in truth, the squat style can be more hygienic and you may even find, after a while, that you prefer them. We do.

Also, it is as well to examine what is actually happening, rather than what you think you are going to see. We met one young woman who was planning a trip to India, 'And I'm going to stop washing for three months before I go, so I can get used to going dirty.' We disabused her, pointing out that most Indians wash more often than many Westerners. Her world picture, based on her American upbringing and French domicile, was 'poor = dirty', which could hardly be further from the truth in most of India.

One of the best ways to exorcize the demons of culture shock is to talk to someone sympathetic to both your culture and the one you are visiting. Be careful whom you believe, though. There are always those who go to one extreme or the other, damning (for example) all that is American while praising all that is British or of course vice versa, and their own nationality is no guide: an American anglophile, or a Briton convinced of the superiority of America, can be as poor a mentor as the worst native chauvinist, so you have always to judge things with caution. The difficulty lies in framing your own questions and observations in a tone of inquiry, rather than of attack. Remember, too, that age can affect outlook: elderly French, who remember *la Libération*, and young French, who eat at American

***Figure 8.1*** *One of the most prominent features of the Vieux Carré of New Orleans is this distinctive pattern of hitching-post. Like many subjects, though, they may be obvious to the naked eye but they can be ridiculously difficult to photograph. Eventually, Frances decided to use an ultra-wide-angle lens and to fill the foreground with one of them. The result may be a little overly dramatic, but this is generally a better option than being too dull. (FES)*

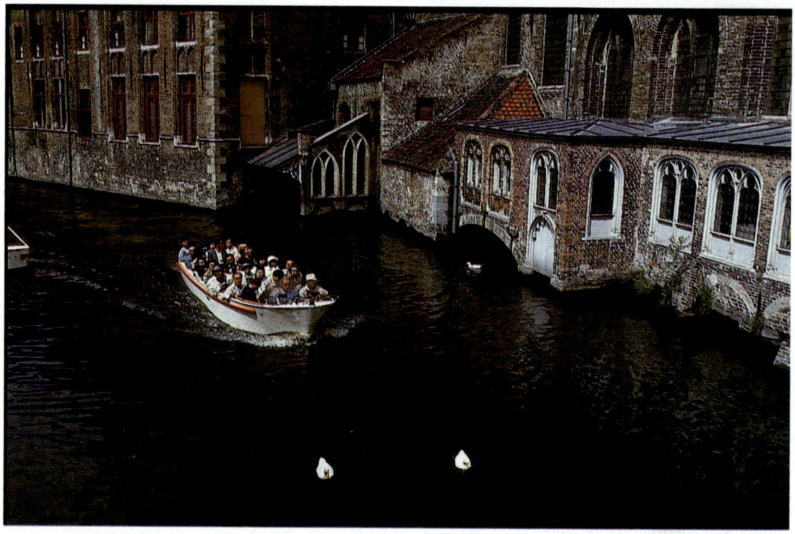

*Figure 8.2* *Bruges or Brugge is famed for its waterways, and boat trips are an essential part of most visitors' experience of the place. It is however surprisingly difficult to get just the right mixture of boat, water and background, because the waters are so crowded: all too often, the best shot of one boat includes parts of two others. This was our best effort, and it is a commercially competent shot, but we are not particularly proud of it. (RWH)*

hamburger bars, will have a different view of Americans from the middle-aged, who bemoan the disappearance of French cuisine and the spread of Anglo-Saxon cultural imperialism.

## THE IMPORTANCE OF SLEEP AND FOOD

Before you start talking to too many people, it is an excellent idea to get as good a night's sleep as you can – and to keep up your sleep levels whenever possible. When you first arrive, there is an obvious temptation to plunge *in medias res*, but the problem is, this is just when you are least adaptable and most likely to find fault. What we try to do is to take an easy stroll, staying awake until a decent bedtime and then going to sleep, but everyone has his or her own ways of trying to deal with jet-lag.

For the rest of the trip, we accept that we cannot always shoot both early in the morning and late in the evening, despite the fact that these are normally the best times of day: we must either go to bed early, or get up late. There are those who can go to bed late and get up early, relying on an afternoon siesta (when the light is normally at its worst) to mop up the sleep debt, but we are not among them; we have never mastered the siesta.

It is also worth adding that there are many archaeological sites and the like where you are more or less obliged, by opening hours, to shoot after the best of the morning light and before the best of the evening light.

Closely related to sleep is diet. To a modest extent, food and sleep are interchangeable: you can function better when you are either tired or hungry than you can when you are both tired and hungry. It is also worth checking out what the local snacks consist of. Most countries have their own types of fast food, and whether it is samosas in India, or a few mezedes with a glass of ouzo in Greece, or some pastizzi and a cup of coffee in Malta, a snack can be a valuable pick-me-up.

## Dealing with contacts

Whether or not you have had enough sleep and enough to eat, you are sooner or later going to have to deal with people. The importance of looking presentable has already been mentioned, and it is worth reinforcing the point here. You have to dress to meet the expectations of those with whom you will be dealing, and this can mean dressing down as well as dressing up. There is, for example, some interesting anthropological photography to be done among the Lost Tribes of hippies who still survive in India; but in order to gain their confidence, you would need to wear light cotton pyjama suits and an embroidered hat from the bazaars of Kathmandu. After all, people judge you first of all by appearance, so you want that first judgement to be favourable enough that they will continue to talk to you.

Some of those you meet, you may already know. Others, you may have planned to meet. Yet others, you will get to know quite well, though you have never seen them or heard of them before in your life. Then there are those whom you will meet once, and never see again. Recognizing the last category can be important: you can waste a good deal of time worrying about the impression you make on someone who really does not matter, such as the maître d'hôtel of a restaurant you walk out of, or the receptionist of a hotel where you reject the room.

We have found that clean, casual clothes, without too much concession to fashion (which can look ridiculous when divorced from its milieu) are all that is needed. Most of the people we meet know that we are passing through; that there is a limit to how much we can carry; and that we are working. We may apologize for our somewhat casual attire, but we have rarely found it a problem, even when dealing with headmasters, golf club secretaries, and others whom one might expect to set unusual store by appearances.

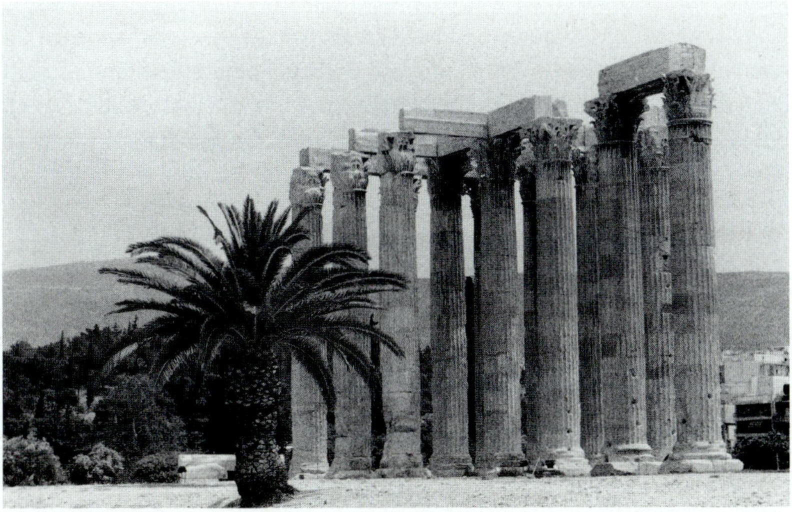

***Figure 8.3*** *The Parthenon dominates both Athens and the average visitor's perception of Athens; which means that 'lesser' sites (which would still be of major importance anywhere else) can often be explored at leisure, without crowds. We noticed the Temple of Olympian Zeus on our way in, and mentally noted it as a place to visit when the opportunity presented itself. The temple, the largest ever dedicated to Zeus, was begun in about 515 BC but not finished until 132 AD. (FES)*

## CLASS AND STATUS

By and large, we try to treat people as equals, except when this is totally inappropriate. In most cultures, a sweeper or a waiter does not expect to be treated wholly as your equal, though equally, there are cultures where to treat anyone as your social inferior can soon end in disaster: the United States, for example, or Australia. In general, though, politeness was devised as a means of getting around such problems, and words such as 'please' and 'thank you', or just a smile, are as appropriate to a beggar as to a king.

Going in the opposite direction, there are often plenty of people who see themselves as your social superior, even if you do not take quite the same view. Most of the time, it is easier to pander to them, especially if they have something you want; or again, politeness – slightly distant politeness, if need be – is the perfect social lubricant.

Regardless of your chosen or assumed status, you need to be fairly realistic about matters. On the one hand, you don't want to be the arrogant outsider, coming in and imposing your views on everyone, but on the other, you don't want to be Uriah Heep, ever so 'umble. In many societies, you will be expected to behave in certain ways in certain situations, so make an attempt to do so. Two good examples come from our own experience in India.

One was when the airline took us to Delhi, but dropped off Frances's backpack in Dubai. It took 48 hours to get it back – there was a general strike the day after we arrived, with the threat of riots in the wake of Indira Gandhi's murder – but there were no real problems. We asked the luggage attendant what had happened; he checked, and found out; and everyone was civilized about it. But another woman had had the same problem, and she was shouting and ranting, and demanding that they make telephone calls, and that they deliver the suitcase to her hotel first thing next morning. We doubt she ever saw her luggage again.

The other was when we were leaving Darjeeling. We reconfirmed the flight at both Bagdogra and Calcutta (the route was Bagdogra–Calcutta–Madras–UK), but when we arrived at Calcutta in the morning, there was no flight at all: all the Airbuses had been grounded. As this had happened 24 hours previously, after being announced 24 hours before that, and as both confirmations had been in the last 48 hours, we simply said that we understood, but we had an international flight out of Madras the next day and that we expected them to honour the flight; we could, after all, have taken the train down if we had had enough warning when our reconfirmation was accepted.

The ticket clerk made no attempt even to appear conciliatory or apologetic, so things rapidly grew quite heated. Things came to a head when he said, 'We will do our best', and Roger roared, 'You will do a great deal better than that, you will get us to Madras in time for our international flight tomorrow.' As he was speaking, the clerk crossed out the hotel he had written in – the Sheraton, from memory – and replaced it with the Grand, the most expensive hotel in Calcutta. We stayed there that night at Indian Airways' expense. Next morning, our tickets were ready and we made our connection.

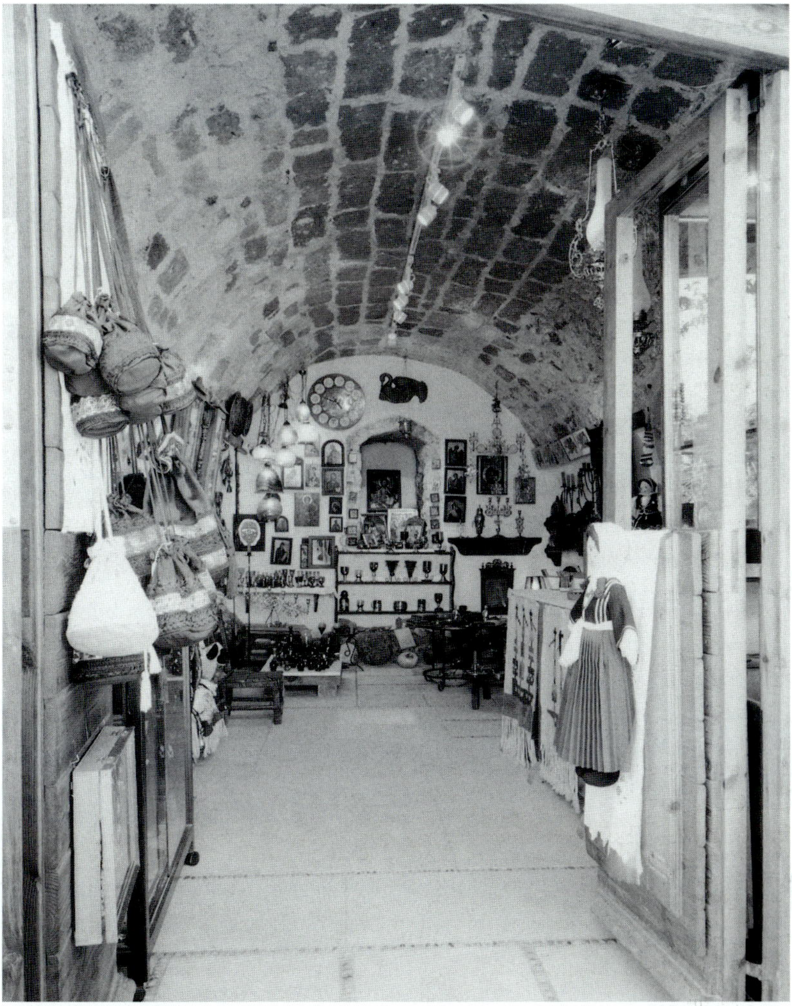

***Figure 8.4***
*Monemvassia suffered from being over-hyped in the guide books. To be sure, it is interesting, but there are plenty of places on the Greek islands which are at least as photogenic. The cave-like shops are very characteristic, and the owner of this one was more than happy when we asked her if we could photograph it. (RWH)*

The two situations may at first seem indistinguishable, but the difference is crucial. In both situations, we started out civilly. In the latter, when civility failed, we behaved as any well-to-do Indian would do. If we had not shouted, we might never have got our tickets. But the woman who lost her suitcase started out by shouting, which a well-bred Indian would rarely if ever do. What is more, we made no unrealistic demands. There were flights; we demanded to be on one. She, by contrast, seemingly did not know (or care) that telephone calls at that time could take hours to arrange in India, and in any case, in the middle of a general strike, her luggage could not have been delivered next day with the best will in the world.

As an aside here, in the event of overnight delays, most airlines will normally make every effort to book you either into the same hotel as you stayed at the previous night, or into a comparable hotel. As it happened, we had stayed in the Grand, and we should have mentioned this – though we did not know it at the time.

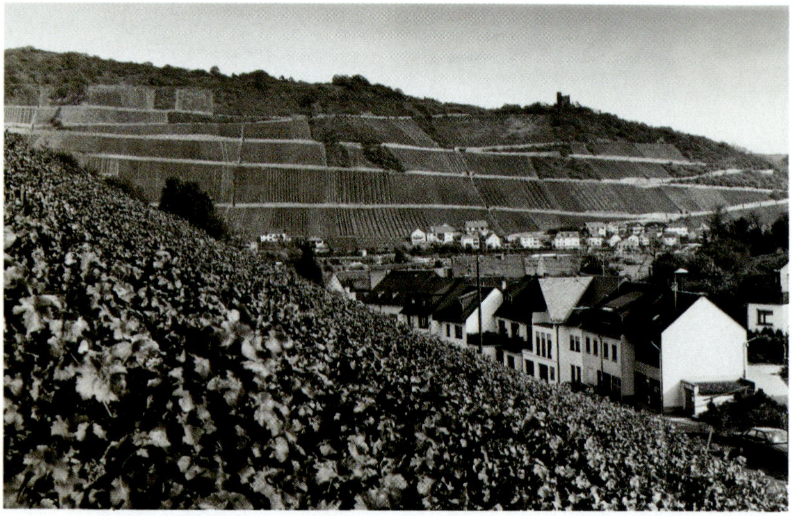

*Figure 8.5 The grape-covered slopes of the Rhine Valley are even more characteristic of the area than the castles and mediaeval towns which follow its length. The only way to show clearly that they are vines, however, is to fill the foreground like this. Otherwise, they could be fields of almost anything. (FES)*

## Bribery and corruption

In the example of the airline booking, there was no real scope for bribery; but we have more than once used a handful of rupees to expedite a train booking, again just as a well-to-do Indian might. Bribes must be offered during civil discussions, and they need not be very big: the equivalent of less than £5 or $10 (or for that matter, a £5 note or a $10 bill in many countries) will often smooth the path considerably.

As for whom you bribe, you need to be cautious. In some countries, police and customs officials are notoriously corrupt. In others, an attempt to bribe such a person will only land you in deeper trouble. In yet others, a bribe that is too small is one thing, but a reasonable sized bribe is another. In general, you should only attempt to bribe people in countries where you can reasonably easily afford it. Reputedly, some American police are very easy to bribe, but you won't do it with a $20 bill. You need specific local information on the going rate.

Curiously enough, when we were in Russia in the early stages of the break-up of the Soviet Union, you could buy things that were 'unobtainable' by judicious use of hard currency, but no-one had really cottoned on to the idea of bribery. A hundred grammes of caviar might cost a dollar, but to get a train ticket, the only thing to do was to queue, in person: hiring someone to do it for you, as you might in India, was not possible. On the other hand, a present such as a bottle of perfume for a booking clerk, passed on via an intermediary as a friend-of-a-friend, eased some paths considerably.

The bottle of perfume for a booking clerk is also an example of the value of connections. When we wanted to go to St Petersburg, for example, we did not pay the tourist rate. Rather, we paid the Party rate because we had connections (albeit tenuous and as a friend-of-a-friend) with the Supreme Soviet. A return first-class sleeper on the fast train was about a third of the tourist rate, and we didn't have to queue at all.

An entirely separate field is official theft. When we first went to Turkey, the immigration official simply stole the £10 which Roger had put in his passport to pay for his visa, and then demanded another £10 for the visa. He then tried to demand $20 for Frances's visa. If you can't handle this sort of thing, don't go to corrupt countries.

How do you learn this sort of thing, and how do you get a feeling for it? By a combination of reading beforehand; observation; and (once again) discussion with your contacts. Most people are genuinely concerned that you should like their country, so if you praise one aspect, be it the Moscow underground or the food in Turkey, you can then with decency raise a query on another: why is so-and-so like this, how do I make it easier to do that, is it possible to do this? Wade in with criticisms, and you are onto a loser from square one. Likewise, being a radical feminist in Saudi Arabia, or espousing even the most modest of left-wing views in most of the United States, will as already noted mean that you are cutting yourself off from precisely the subjects that you want to photograph.

## Networking

A genuine inquiry – 'I much admire so-and-so, how can I get to see it?' – will often result in useful networking. The person you are talking to may not know the answer; but they will probably know someone who does, and if you share an interest with this second person, you may well make a real friend. This was how

**Figure 8.6** *Another rendition of the Palace at Mysore appears in Figure 3.2, but this version, with the extraordinary sky, dates from our first night in Mysore when we did not really know what to expect. Although there is something to be said for exploring a place without a camera before you start shooting in earnest, there is also something to be said for carrying your camera even on your preliminary forays, in case you come across something you may not be able to shoot again later. (FES)*

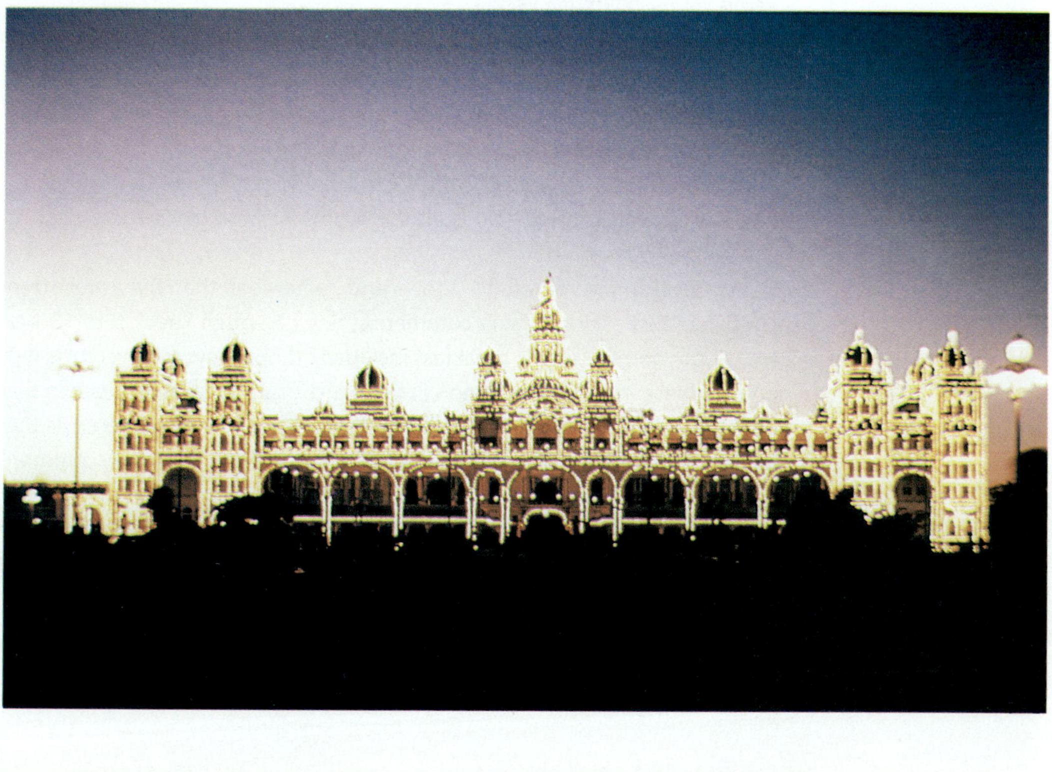

we got to know Jamyang Norbu, then Director of the Tibetan Institute for Performing Arts, through Frances's interest in theatre, and it was how Roger got to handle Voltaire's own books in St Petersburg (Catherine the Great bought his library).

Rules for dealing with contacts differ all over the world, but a visit to a café or bar, or even taking your new-found friend out for a meal, is normally well received. If you go out again, a small present can cement the relationship, preferably something not readily obtainable in their country. Straight malt whiskies are appreciated by just about anyone who drinks; after that, there are things like specialist chocolates, up-market pens, inscribed books or (something we have recently cottoned on to) subscriptions to magazines for which we write. Few things keep your name in front of a contact better!

## Checking out accommodation

As already mentioned, we almost never pre-book, but instead rely on finding somewhere when we arrive. We have even had considerable success from doing exactly what most guide books recommend that you should never do, namely asking a taxi-driver to take us to a good but modestly priced hotel. In some countries, to be sure, he'll be on a commission, but does this matter? The trick lies in agreeing a fare to an acceptable hotel, and making it clear that if the first place isn't acceptable, you will expect him to drive you to another (and another, and another, if need be) until you find somewhere that is.

You should never take a room, though, without looking at it first. The catalogue of possible failings could occupy a chapter in itself, but here are a few points to check.

How noisy is it likely to be? Look out for traffic, but also for discos and bars which may go on late into the night. Is the room reasonably secure, if you want to leave things in it? If it says 'with shower' or 'with bath', is there a WC as well? Is the bed comfortable? Look out for beds that are too soft, or where the mattress is so old that you fall into a pit in the middle. Are the mosquito nets and insect screens whole? Is the room air conditioned, or fitted with fans, or equipped with heating? Does all this work? Is there somewhere near at hand where you can eat?

Check prices carefully, too – and remember that they are often negotiable. Just asking for the commercial rate can often knock 5 to 15 per cent off the normal rate. Is breakfast included? If not, how much is it? Is it a non-optional extra cost (a common Parisian trick)? Are all taxes included in the quoted rate (Americans are good at hitting you for extra money here)? Is the rate per room (in most of the civilized world) or per person (still horribly common in Britain)?

Even if you check carefully, there are always things you cannot anticipate. We took a room in Mexico once which looked fine, but there were no curtains, only wooden shutters, so if you wanted privacy and darkness, you stifled. The bathroom door didn't latch, but swung gently open as you sat on the toilet, and after the first couple of hours the ceiling fan developed an infuriating intermittent squeak. This was bad enough, but in another couple of hours, it

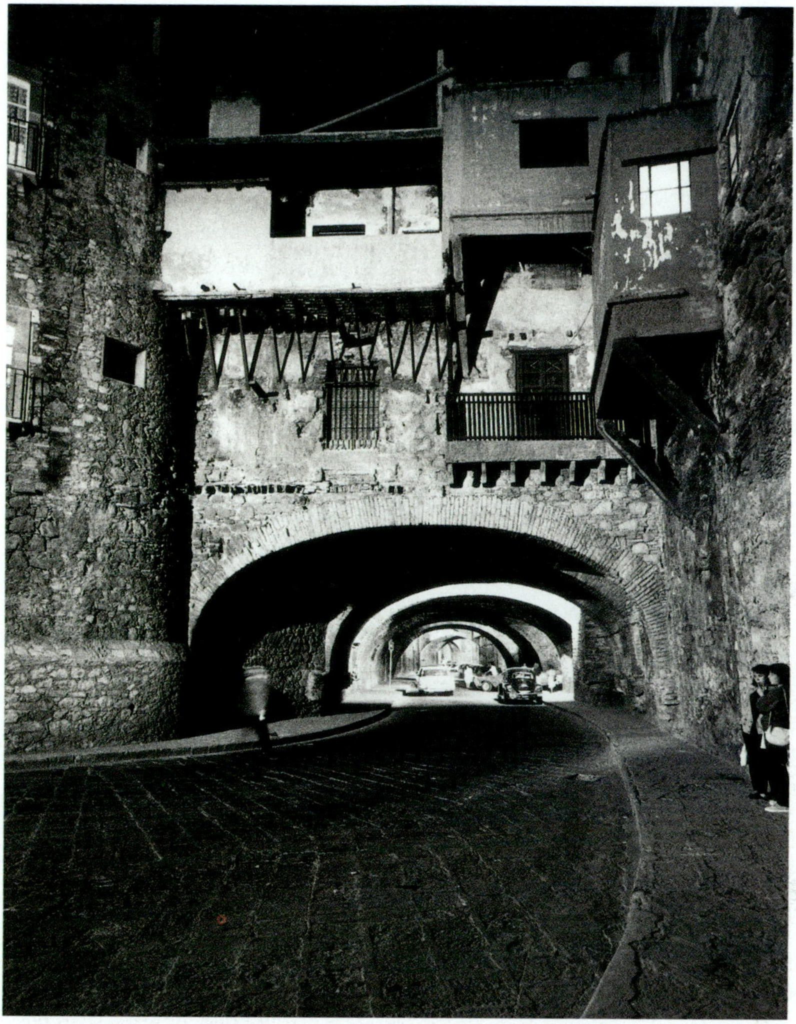

*Figure 8.7* Guanajuato is one of the most unusual places we have ever been. For centuries, it was the biggest silver-producing city in the world, and the wealth that the silver generated paid for extraordinary mediaeval architecture: Mexico was a century or two behind Spain, and Spain was a century or two behind most of Europe, so Guanajuato (founded in the mid-sixteenth century) has in many areas the mood of a place far older. (RWH)

developed quite a loud chirp as well. Trying to sleep under an intermittent squeak ... squeak ... squeaksqueak ...(longer pause) ... squeak ... CHIRP! squeak ... became so wearing that we left at five in the morning.

## LOCAL GUIDES AND TRANSLATORS

A guide or translator (or both) can under ideal conditions save you a great deal of time and money. He or she can also get in the way, slow you down, and be a general nuisance. If we are working on a commissioned shoot, we will work with whoever is appointed (this generally works pretty well), but if we are shooting speculatively, we see no advantage to guides. A hired guide, after all, tends to have a set patter and to want to whisk you around at his own pace, and this is rarely satisfactory for photography.

We may however engage for a day or half-day a taxi or auto-rickshaw with a driver who speaks English, so that he can act as a translator and expediter when appropriate, without trailing round behind us while we are shooting. Surprisingly often, too, we have met people who have acted as unofficial and temporary guides out of the kindness of their hearts, or out of a desire to have someone to talk to, or in order to practise their English. There have even been some whose principal interest has been in photography, though the danger here is that you will get stuck with a real 'anorak' who keeps trying to help and asks the most ridiculous questions at the most inopportune time.

A good guide book, something like a Blue Guide, should tell you pretty much all that the average guide would tell you anyway, and it is only if you have to work with people (which for us pretty much implies commissioned work) that you need on-the-spot, real-time translations.

For general translations, the sort of thing you need at hotels and restaurants and the like, we find that often there is someone who speaks English, and that even if no-one speaks English, we can get by with the merest smattering of French, German and Spanish, singly or in combination. Some countries are however much more flexible than others: Spaniards, for example, will often look blankly at you if your accent is not flawless Castilian, while in neighbouring Portugal you can successfully mix in chunks of French and English and German and even Spanish (provided you make it absolutely and abundantly clear that you have no time for Spain), in any old accent, and they will still understand most of what you say.

Wherever you go, learning a few words such as 'please' and 'thank you' and 'very good' will make friends, though it will not necessarily do much for your understanding: on the basis of a few words, people tend to assume that you speak far more of their language than you do. The real advantage of trying out halting Russian or Greek or whatever is that it makes people less shy of trying out their halting English. With goodwill, it is amazing what you can communicate across apparently insuperable language barriers.

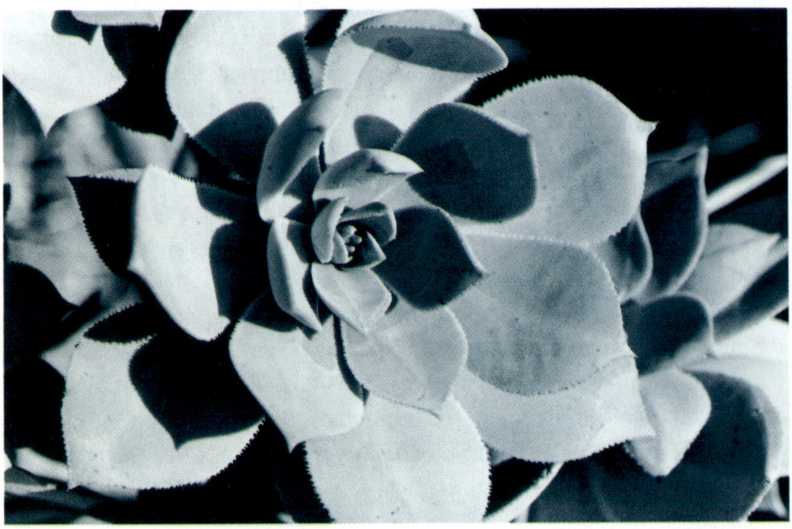

***Figure 8.8*** *Xerophyte plants – that is, those adapted to dry climates – are characteristic of many holiday destinations, and although they are not exactly a tourist attraction, they are something that most people with half an eye will notice and remember. They are therefore something worth photographing. This one was on Gran Canaria. (FES)*

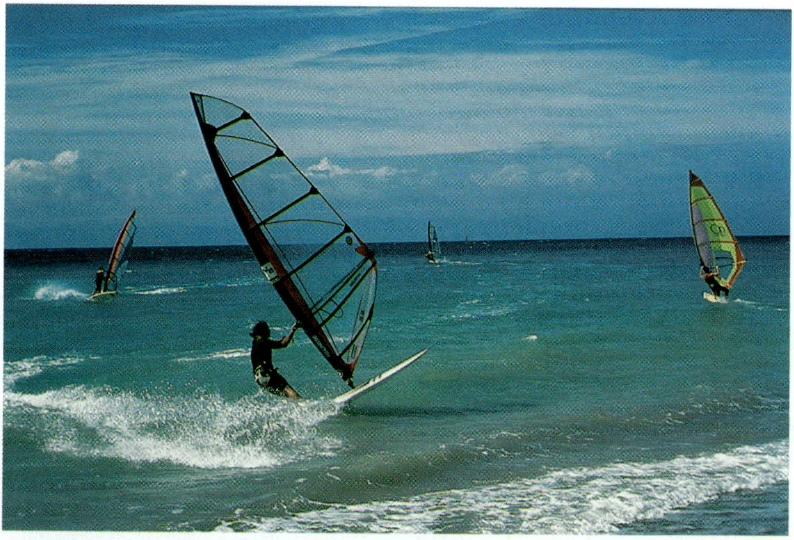

*Figure 8.9 The coast of Rhodes is awash with windsurfers – and yet, we did not get a good windsurfing shot until after we had checked in at the airport on the way out. The flight was delayed, and so we returned to the coast a few miles away and spent an hour and a half at a windsurfing school. We never return the keys to a hire car until we are sure that we are not going to need it any more. (RWH)*

## Friends and acquaintances

Friends and acquaintances in places you are visiting can be a mixed blessing. At their best, they can explain a great deal about how the place works, about local customs, about the going rate for taxis, tips and bribes, and so forth. At worst, they can be a ball and chain, hobbling your every move and trying to stop you doing anything without their assistance. They may also be a complete disaster while you are shooting, hanging around and making you feel guilty that you are concentrating on photography. You have to strike a balance between taking what you want, and taking what they want to give you, which may often be considerably more.

Broadly, the people you meet while travelling will fall into four categories. There are those who invite you to stay; there are those whom you know well enough to invite yourself to stay; there are members of clubs and organizations; and there are friends of friends. Which category they fall into will not necessarily affect how well you get on with them: until you try visiting them, you will never know how helpful (or how unhelpful) they can be.

The only category worth enlarging upon is clubs and organizations. Despite the many and obvious drawbacks of Mensa, it has over the years done a great deal for us. The only other clubs which might provide useful introductions for us are motorcycling clubs (we belong to the BMW Club), but others may have other interests: photographic societies (especially postal portfolios) and so forth. It is also worth mentioning that we met a good friend, with whom we have stayed in Moscow and Athens, through a letter he wrote after reading one of our books when he was stationed in Addis Ababa.

Obviously, if you impose on anyone in this way, you should be prepared to reciprocate, so always do as you would be done by, both in giving and in receiving.

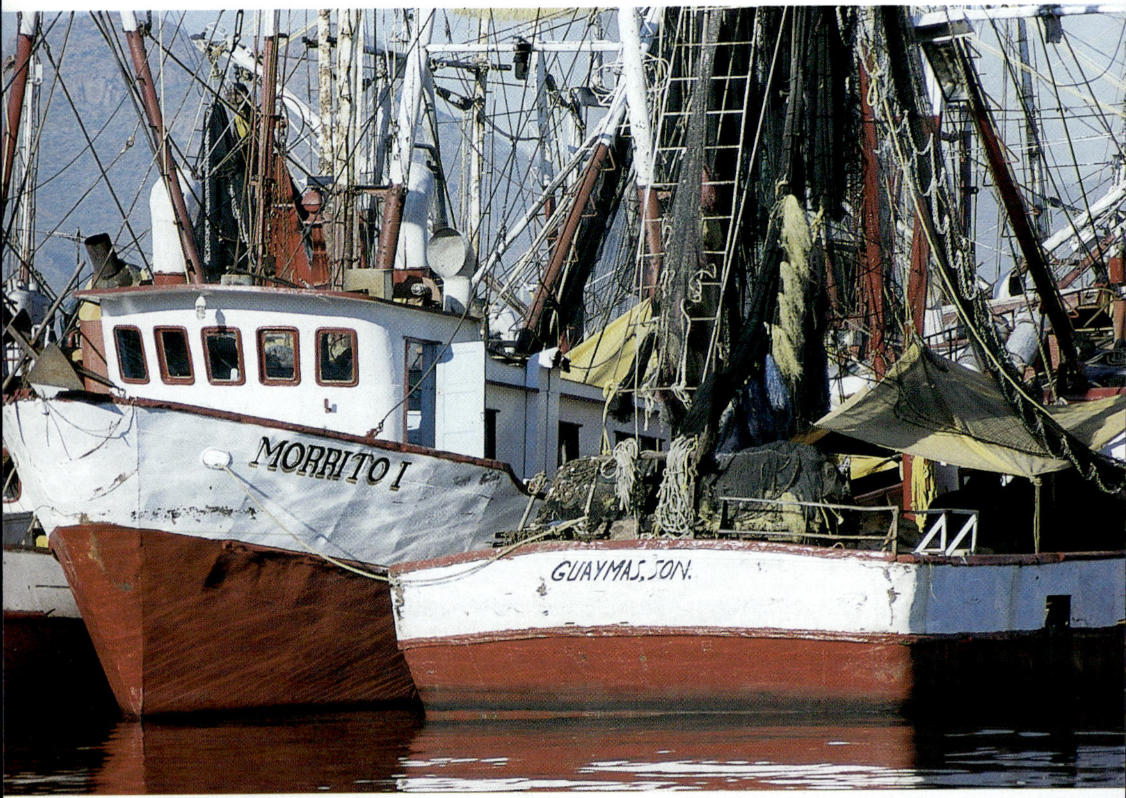
MORRITO I
GUAYMAS, SON.

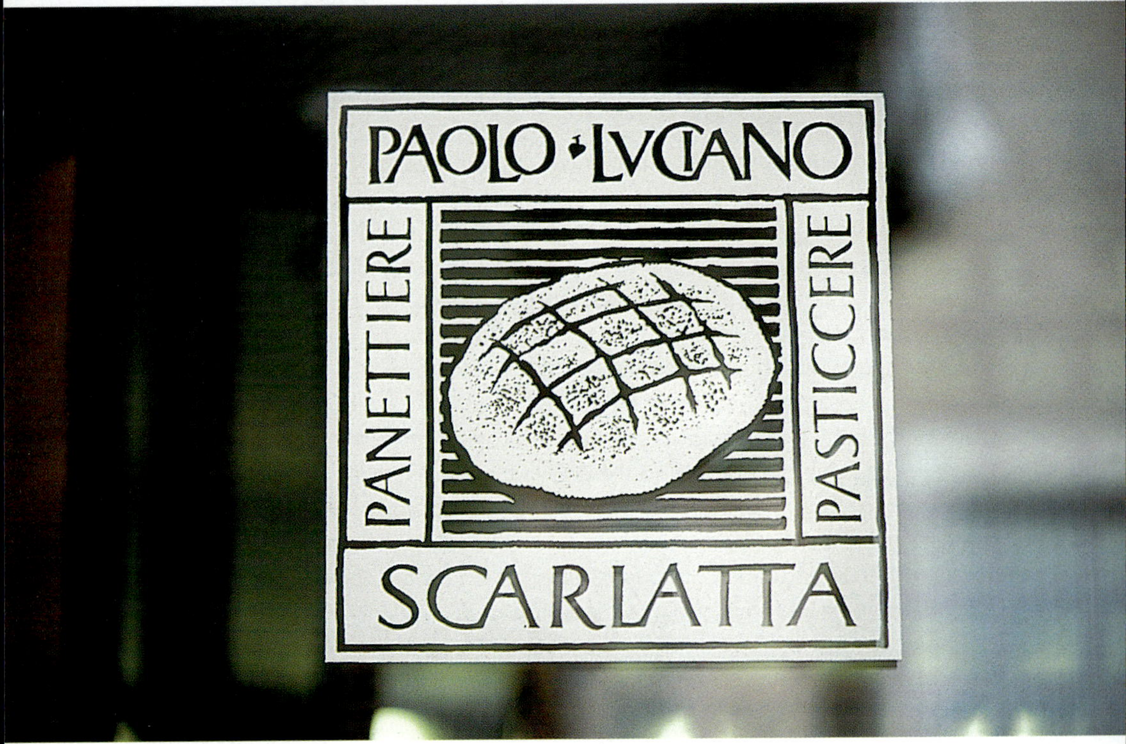
PAOLO LUCIANO
PANETTIERE
PASTICCERE
SCARLATTA

# 9 Stock photography

In the 1990s, the market for stock photography was in a state of flux. The libraries themselves were polarizing between big players such as The Image Bank and Microsoft on the one hand, and smaller, specialist libraries on the other – and the waters were being considerably muddied by the increasing availability of royalty-free 'clip art' photography on CD-ROM.

For some decades, the trend towards using library pictures (stock shots) instead of commissioned work had been growing, and it made sense. Often, the budget would not stand sending someone to New York to photograph the skyline, or to Bombay to photograph the India Gate; and even when it would, the photographer could never present the same range of pictures, under different weather conditions and at different times of day and so forth, that the picture libraries could.

The advent of royalty-free pictures affected principally the bottom end of the market, especially where small photos were needed and the often indifferent quality of royalty-free images would be less evident. Higher quality pictures, both technically and aesthetically, tended to go through conventional (and better-paying) picture library channels.

From the user's point of view, the advantage of the big libraries is one-stop shopping, usually together with superb technical quality. The advantages of the smaller libraries, on the other hand, are that they often have a wider choice in a specialized field; that they are often better able to help you, because they understand the subject; and that while some of their images may lack the slickness and gloss of the ones that are held by the big players, they may actually be more suitable for a particular application because they are judged on content as well as on glitz.

From the photographer's point of view, all three approaches – big libraries, small libraries, and royalty-free – have their advantages, and because the market is in a state of flux, it is necessary to look at all three quite carefully.

It is also important to remember that most stock photography is purely speculative on the photographer's part, so you normally have to fund the entire trip yourself and it may be some time before the money starts to roll in. A few photographers make a comfortable living from stock photography alone, but many more treat stock as a profitable second use for pictures which appear in magazines or elsewhere, or as an add-on to other work: if you have to be somewhere to shoot something anyway, then why not tack on a stock shoot where the marginal cost is limited to film, processing, and a few days' extra food and accommodation?

## WHAT THE LIBRARY DOES

All libraries take a hefty chunk of the reproduction fee for themselves, typically 50 per cent, though it may

**Figure 9.1** Fishing boats, Guaymas. *This is a classic stock shot: a simple, clearly identifiable picture of a place which can be used as an 'establishing shot' for that place, or as a general endorsement of seafood, especially as an illustration in a cook-book. It is generally captioned something like, 'Fresh seafood is central to Mexico's coastal cuisine...' (RWH)*

**Figure 9.2** *A saleable stock shot is not necessarily the same as a successful pictorial image. This picture of Paolo Luciano bread would win few prizes in a photographic competition; and yet it says a great deal about Italy, via both the elegant understated design of the sign and the subject matter. In its synthesis of good, simple food and superb design, it epitomizes much of what attracts so many people to Italy. (RWH)*

be higher or lower. Although some photographers bemoan this, the truth is that the libraries have good access to a wide range of clients, and are well placed to get the best possible fees. Also, they do all the work apart from the shooting and captioning: sales, invoicing, filing, chasing... It really isn't too unrealistic a deal.

The energy and skill with which libraries promote themselves is very variable, but it does not seem to have that much to do with their reputation or success. Some send out glossy catalogues on a regular basis, with frequent 'fliers' or newsletters to remind clients of their existence. Increasing numbers put their best-selling pictures onto CD, or allow on-line searches. Others seemingly put very little into promotion, and still do well.

What they sell is of course reproduction rights, not the image itself: copyright remains with the photographer, and the image is returned after origination. The size of the fee depends very much on the use: what the picture is used for, in how many markets, and whether or not it is exclusive. Bulk buys of ordinary images can be for as little as £20 or £30 each – $30 to $50, say – of which the individual photographer sees half. Exclusive year-long use for a world-wide advertising campaign by a major company may however net many tens of thousands for a single image.

## The library contract

Libraries often request, and sometimes demand, exclusive contracts with photographers. This means that you cannot put your pictures with any other library, and (in extreme cases) that you cannot use them yourself, though most libraries have some sort of clause which allows this.

The logic behind this is easy to see. They do not want to make an exclusive deal for $10,000, only to find that another library can then sell the identical image to someone else and blow 'exclusivity' out of the water. It is therefore entirely reasonable that you should agree to supplying a particular image or set of images to one library, but it is not reasonable that you should agree never to work for anyone else. The bigger libraries tend to be the most insistent about exclusive deals, and it is a matter of personal conscience and calculation whether you accept this limitation in return for promises of higher earnings per picture; or decline it; or lie.

Lying cannot be recommended, but we know several photographers who have cheerfully signed 'exclusive' contracts with a number of agencies in different countries in the reasonable expectation that because the images do not overlap, and because photographers are almost never credited, they will not find out about one another.

Even if you have non-exclusive contracts, it makes considerable sense not to put substantially identical pictures with different libraries, for the reasons outlined above.

### Library submissions

Libraries normally require quite a substantial flow of new work every year. They like to receive submissions of several hundred pictures at a time, and some may even impose minimum limits for the initial submission – rarely fewer than 100, and possibly as many as 1000. Of these, they are likely to accept anything from 10 per cent to 75 per cent.

The form in which they request the submissions will vary, but the minimum requirement is that the pictures should be well captioned: a caption on the mount is generally the easiest way around this, using the kind of software that was described in Chapter 3.

## ROYALTY-FREE IMAGES

The right to reproduce royalty-free images on CD-ROM is typically sold outright, by definition on a non-exclusive basis, to the publisher of the CD-ROM. Historically, most photographers tended to sell their rejects, leftovers, and second-bests for use on CD-ROMs, though this requires some discretion if the pictures in question are too close to pictures which have been used or accepted elsewhere, whether commissioned or in picture libraries. Fees are typically sufficiently low that you make your money on volume, not quality. Advertisements soliciting submissions for CD-ROM collections appear in both the amateur and professional press.

### What is required

The classic definition of a successful library shot is twofold: 'straightforward pictures of unusual subjects, or unusual pictures of straightforward subjects'. Of course, there is likely to be little objection to unusual pictures of unusual subjects, but they are rarely demanded as a *sine qua non*.

Perhaps the easiest way to get an idea of what a picture library requires is to go to one and take a look at the sort of category which you are interested in shooting. You may be surprised. There is an inevitable demand for what might be called 'touristy' shots – beautiful sunsets, the banks of the Ganges, the New York skyline, and so forth – but there is also a considerable demand for subjects which few tourists would shoot, or which would only appeal to specialists: steam trains leaving stations, aircraft taking off from airports, people sitting at an outdoor bar by a river...

What you need to do is to put yourself in the position of the library. Who are their clients? What do they want? Some specialize in record covers or book covers; others in textbooks or business magazines; yet others in the specialist press, be it yachting or motoring or child-raising. The library will probably be more than happy to tell you what kind of clients they service, though they may be less willing to show you examples or to tell you the clients' names, for fear that you will try to steal their customers away from them.

The point is, there is no such thing as a stock shot in isolation: it must normally be shot with a use in mind. It may well be that in due course it is used for something completely different, but if it is shot without some aim in mind, merely because it is a pretty picture, you may well find that it attracts little interest. It is almost worth setting yourself imaginary briefs, as if you were shooting a commissioned series on (say) Thai restaurants, from the fishermen to the markets to the kitchens to the restaurant itself.

## Set-up shots

An important point with some shots is that they are not the sort of thing which can be taken as a snapshot. Many countries are paranoid about photography at airports, for example, and anyone who has ever tried to photograph a bar or restaurant will know that people are typically distributed in all the wrong places, in the wrong positions, with their backs to you. Setting up a good bar or restaurant shot can take a while, and will require the cooperation of the management – and you have to explain that while it will be captioned 'Marco's Bar, Strada Somethingorother, Milano', you cannot guarantee that it will always be credited.

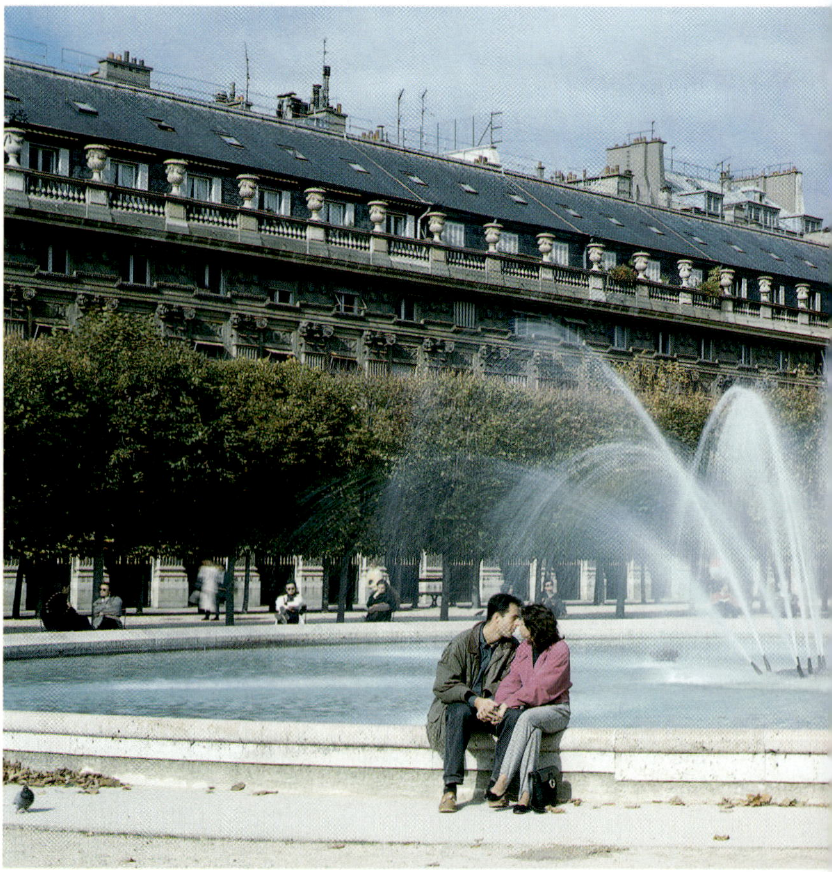

Some photographers, including those who make a full-time living from stock photography, go to considerable lengths to set up stock shots with models. Such things as 'stock' weddings have been set up, with good-looking models, hired or borrowed clothes, and so forth. Reportedly, for those with the resources (both financial and personal) to set up such shoots, the rewards can be considerable. You may care to discuss this with your library.

## Model releases

These are a very vexed question. Some libraries insist that you should be able to produce signed model releases from every identifiable person in a shot, but this is impractical more often than not. Just imagine trying to explain the concept of a model release to a room full of diners, in a language you don't understand!

In general (though far from invariably, and not in all countries) there is no need for model releases if the picture is used editorially and if the caption is factual. For an advertising shot, or if the caption tells untruths about the subject, the photographer can be in trouble. This is why model releases often contain the phrase that a model may be deemed to be an imaginary person. The leading

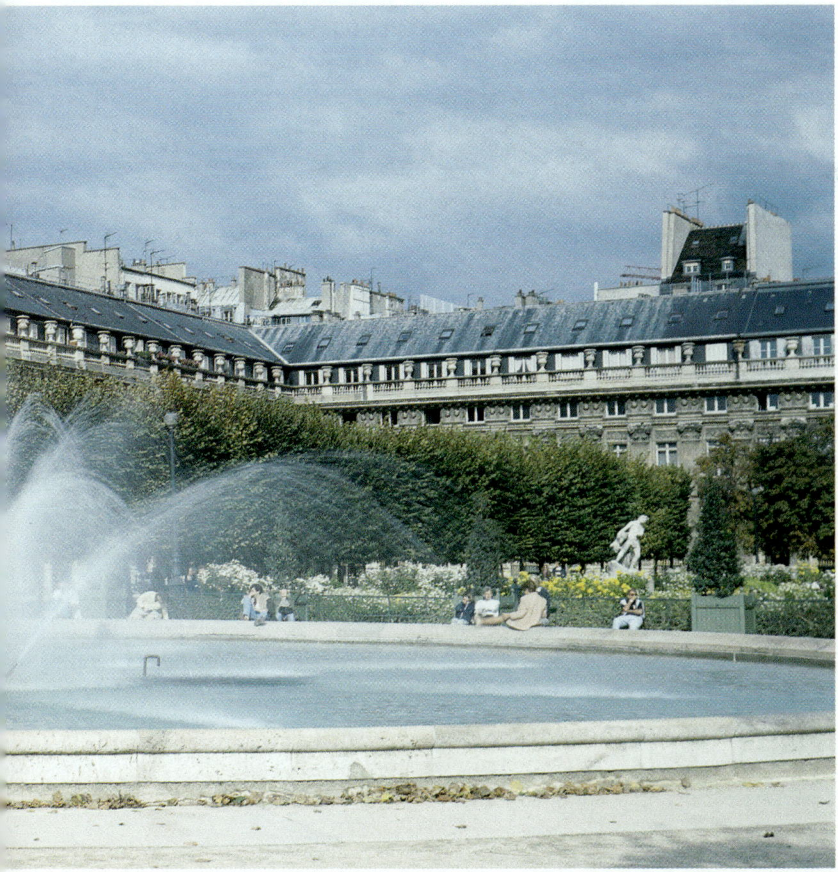

***Figure 9.3*** *If you do not have a model release, say so. There are countless purposes for which a picture like this could be used, especially if there is no caption or if the caption reads something like, 'The gardens of the Palais Royale are popular with everyone in Paris, young and old'. The risk comes when the caption says, 'Paris is for lovers' and the young couple in the shot turn out to be brother and sister, or married to other people, or whatever. (RWH)*

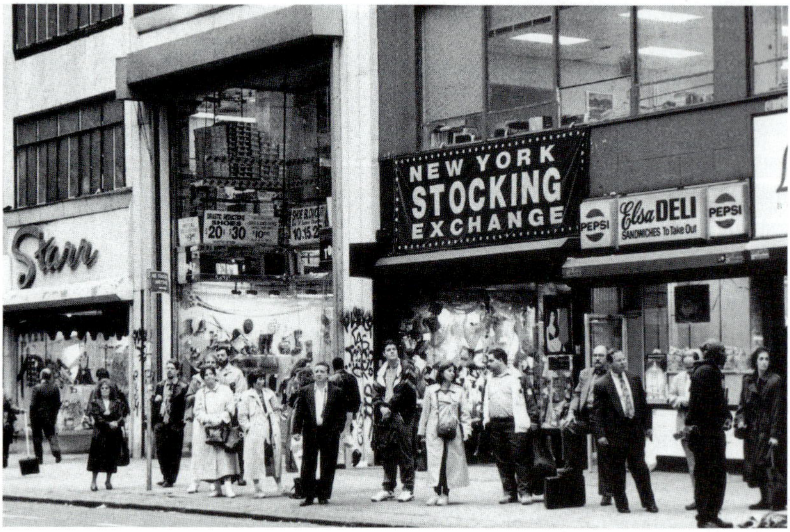


*Figure 9.4 Sometimes, a single image is all that is practicable, and all that is needed. The real appeal here is the way in which the queue of waiting people stands against a perfect New York backdrop of deli, graffiti, discount shops, offices... The people are related by waiting together, but otherwise totally separate, all looking in different directions, dressed differently, standing differently. It is like a set-up shot: every detail is spot-on, even down to the unswept gutter and the NO STANDING ANYTIME sign. (FES)*

case on the subject was a picture of a water-skier which was used in a men's magazine, with a caption advocating a hedonistic lifestyle. Unfortunately the water-skier was a prominent church dignitary with no great sense of humour, and he had not signed a model release.

Again as a general rule, a model release must be for valuable consideration, though this does not have to be financial, and if it is financial, it does not have to be of high value: 'valuable' in this context means 'having any value whatsoever'. We used to use kopeks as a novelty payment (a kopek is a hundredth of a rouble), but they are no longer available. Very low value coins such as 5 drachma, or 5 paise, or 1 penny (UK or US) are useful novelties when they are used outside their own country.

We normally include in the caption the words NO MODEL RELEASE or MODEL RELEASE AVAILABLE. This avoids any misunderstandings, and means there can be no come-back to us.

## *Formats*

Electronic media are making a difference to picture library requirements. Historically, bigger images always sold better. Give a picture researcher a hundred pictures and he or she would almost invariably look at the large-format images first. Any picture which was remotely suitable would be put to one side. Next came the medium-format images, but these had to be significantly better than the large-format transparencies in order to knock them off their perch. Only if there was nothing exciting among the medium and large-format images, or if there was something truly stunning in 35mm, would 35mm stand a chance at all.

Today, libraries which present their catalogues on CD-ROM or which allow on-line searching may actually discriminate in favour of 35mm slides, which are easier and cheaper to scan, and the quality difference on the average monitor is likely to be imperceptible. There is no question that if the image is to come up to more than about half page, a larger format than 35mm will usually reproduce far better; but the majority of picture researchers are more interested in the immediate impact of the image than in technical quality, even when the technical quality is sufficiently poor that it detracts from the impact of the image.

There is also the inevitable point that roll-film and cut-film images are several times as expensive to produce as 35mm: an entire 36-exposure roll of Kodachrome, processed, costs about the same as two or three sheets of 4 × 5 inch film. Although there is still a good deal to be said for exquisite large-format images of certain subjects – an image of Schloss Neuschwanstein on 13 × 18 cm Agfachrome rises unbidden in the memory – it is fair to say that today, commercial reality is probably on the side of 35mm. The only other format which we would seriously consider for stock photography is 6 × 12 cm or (possibly) 6 × 17 cm panoramic: 6-on-120 and 4-on-120. These have 'gimmick' appeal and stand out even when reproduced electronically, because of the format.

## Materials

In the past, only Kodachrome was acceptable in 35mm. Today, although no-one will ever object to a Kodachrome, and although Kodachrome 25 is still the sharpest general-application colour film in the world, it really doesn't matter much what film you use. In large format, it is even less important.

Most libraries handle only colour, but a few are also interested in monochrome and in hand-colouring. The only way to find out is to call an individual library or to contact an overarching organization such as BAPLA, the British Association of Picture Libraries and Agencies; at the time of writing, there were plans to set up an international coordinating body for other comparable organizations in other countries.

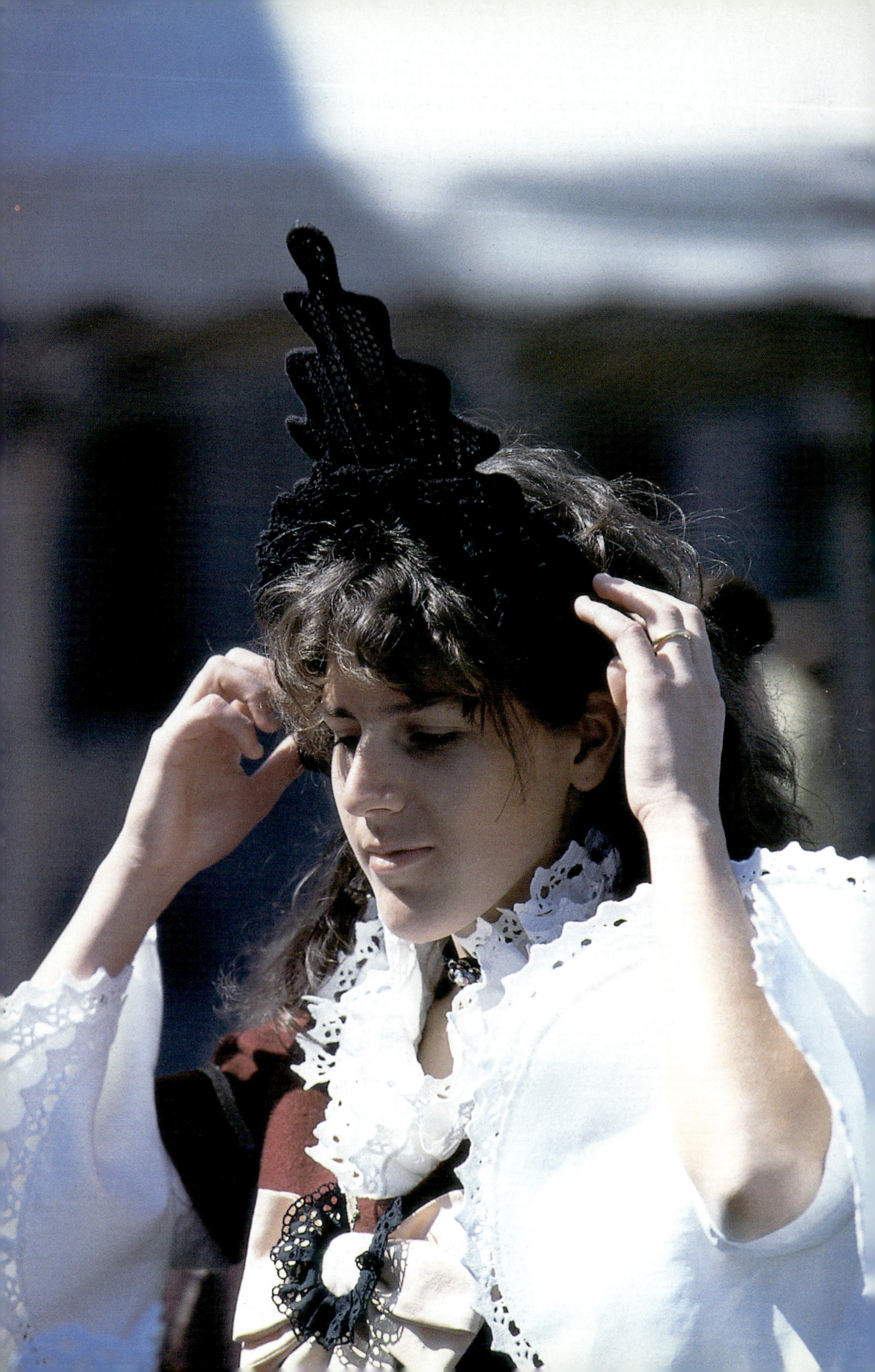

# 10 Brochure and 'walkie' photography

Researching the market for travel brochure photography is hardly demanding, though 'walkie' photography is another matter, and is described towards the end of the chapter. Most travel agents have stacks of brochures for the asking, or they can even be mail-ordered. Get a good handful, and go through them. Try for a good variety: family travel, 'golden age' (retired) travel, youth travel, special-interest travel (such as railway journeys, archaeology, etc.) and anything else you can find. Also, especially in Britain, visit two or three different travel agents: most of the major chains are owned by tour operators, who are understandably prejudiced in favour of their own offerings.

The first thing you will notice is that there are several levels of sophistication, as indeed there are among holidaymakers and their suppliers. Also, there are considerable national differences.

In Britain, and in much of the rest of Europe, most people get a minimum of 20 days' holiday every year, and 30 days is by no means unusual. A couple of weeks every summer in a Mediterranean resort (or increasingly, in Florida or even in the Dominican Republic) are practically taken as a condition of employment by most workers. Numerous travel operators in countless resorts fight for a share of an enormous and still rapidly expanding market. Spain, Portugal, Malta, Greece, Turkey, North Africa, Israel... the list goes on and on. Domestic and northern European resorts fight an increasingly desperate rearguard action to attract both local and overseas visitors, though there are inexplicable local successes such as Belgium's North Sea coast, which seems to exercise a disproportionate fascination over the hardy Belgians.

Seemingly in reaction to this, the more affluent traveller goes further and further afield, often with themed or highly structured holidays: studying art in Florence, travelling by train in India, trekking in Nepal. Even where the aim is a traditional '4S' (sea, sand, sun and sex) holiday, destinations as far away as Thailand and Sri Lanka are not regarded as particularly unusual.

In the United States, conditions are very different. By European standards, vacations are unbelievably short, and the choice of destinations is very limited. A surprisingly small number of mainland domestic destinations accounts for a surprisingly large proportion of travel: southern California, San Francisco, Florida, Las Vegas, New Orleans. An even smaller number of nearby destinations, some a part of the country, some not, soaks up another substantial portion of the market: Hawaii, Baja California, Bermuda, parts of the Caribbean. Cruises, too, are far more popular than in Europe, though this is changing: as so

***Figure 10.1*** *Distinctive folk costumes grow rarer every year, wilting before the onslaught of jeans and T-shirts. In affluent European countries such as northern Italy, such costumes are likely to be seen only on people who are consciously keeping traditions alive; people like this folklore troupe in Aoste. Even so, brochures are suckers for such pictures, especially at the lower end of the market. (RWH)*

often, where the United States leads, Europe follows, and cruises are increasing in popularity in Europe too.

For long-haul international travel, London and Paris remain favourite destinations among Americans, with China as a popular exotic choice. Yet many still see travel to destinations which Europeans might regard as passé to be somewhat adventurous, the preserve of the affluent or intrepid. Of course there are high-end, exotic destinations, and well-to-do Americans are apparently even more willing to pay large sums of money in return for travelling in some discomfort (such as Everest climbing expeditions or trips on Antarctic icebreakers) than Europeans; but proportionately, the American travel market is much less developed, much less adventurous, and much more expensive than the European market.

It is also worth knowing that to an American, a 'holiday' is a public holiday, and that if the words are used without further qualification, 'holidays' or 'the holiday season' generally means 'Christmas'. The American for 'holiday' is 'vacation' and a 'holidaymaker' is a 'vacationer'. This can lead to confusion if one or both parties are not aware of the different meanings of the words.

## What the client needs

Broadly, three kinds of pictures are used. There are the absolutely straight record shots, of hotels and hotel rooms and so forth. There are the 'lifestyle' shots, beside the pool and in the bar and the like. And there are the 'scene-setting' shots, which are very similar to general stock pictures, showing the attractions of the resort in general, the nearby countryside, and places you might like to visit.

For the most part, brochure shots are fairly literal: this is not the place for flights of artistic fancy. If there are any particularly evocative shots, they are likely to be fairly formulaic: sunsets, sun on water, self-consciously soft-focus images. Composition (where it is an issue at all) tends to be simple: especially at the lower end of the market, brochures tend to go for quantity in pictures, rather than quality, and pictures which are printed small must be simple and uncluttered enough to read easily.

A horrible tendency is over-use of effects filters, with the gruesome 'tobacco grad' being used without mercy. Although the market demands this, you may do better if you use the more sophisticated systems, such as Lee's 'stripe' filters, rather than the usual tobacco grad. You can get some impressive 'sunsets' with a stripe filter on its own or (more usually) with a stripe filter plus a grad.

## The importance of people

In all but the most sophisticated brochures, holidaymakers appear in almost every shot – often in quite large numbers. While the prospect of a 'tanning yard' beside a pool or on a beach, with two or three square metres per person for a sunbed, may repel many, there are apparently plenty more whom it attracts. The same is true of group activities in general, such as dances, games and keep-fit classes, and even of those activities where a bit of peace and quiet

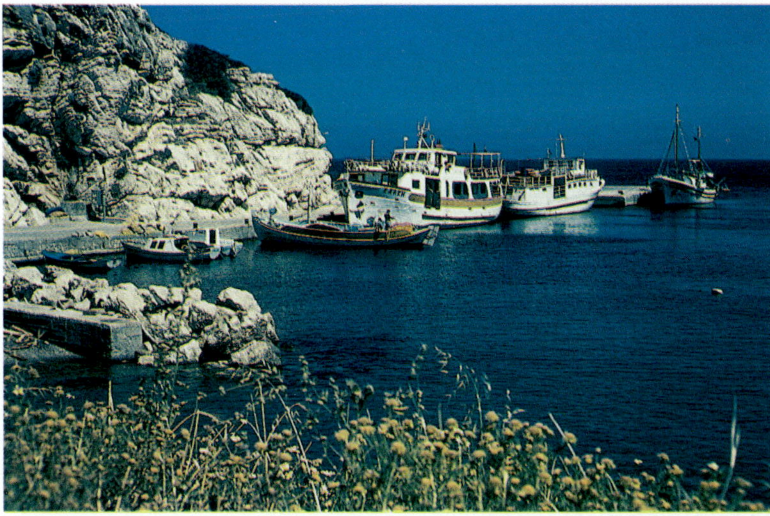

*Figure 10.2 'Colourful' scenes are a staple of brochures, and this sort of shot (taken in Rhodes) could be used at any level, from the most basic mass-market family-style brochure upwards. (RWH)*

might seem to be a selling point, such as a restaurant or a scenic walk.

What is more, the people in the pictures must be carefully matched to the market at which the brochure is aimed. Today, there are specialist companies aiming at families, at older travellers, and at the young. Most people seem to want to be with their own age group when they go on holiday, but it is curious that a family-oriented brochure will show only young couples with children: there will rarely be older people in shot, even in the background. The same is true, *mutatis mutandis*, of the other groups described below. The aim is to make the reader of the brochure identify with the people in the pictures: the 'it could be you' syndrome.

## Family brochures

These must have pictures of families, preferably with young children. Pictures will normally focus on a single family, often with a child in the foreground using a bucket and spade or suspended in a rubber ring, though there will be other families in the background.

The adults will normally be comatose, recovering from the pressures of their workaday jobs, though there will also be a few shots of children being lifted in the air by adoring parents, and a sprinkling of young couples together to convey the message that they can rediscover their romance or enjoy a drink in the bar without having to worry about children.

## 'Senior' brochures

Brochures appealing to the over-50s will inevitably feature older people, especially couples and groups: the slightest suggestion of being on your own, let alone lonely, is understandably frowned upon. Fitness and a generally healthy demeanour are particularly important in this market.

There will also be a good number of dance-floor pictures, with ballroom dancing, if the brochure is intended to appeal to the genuinely aged.

## Youth market brochures

These generally feature a judicious mix of couples and clearly available singles, plus group shots with as much action as possible. The couples stare into one another's eyes, entwine lovingly, or exchange banter. The singles are normally close-ups, to emphasize their physical charms as much as possible, and 'joke' poses (tongues out, hats on backwards, and so forth) are commonplace, especially among the young men. The groups jostle close together: as much skin contact as possible seems to be the norm.

Interestingly – perhaps it is a reflection of the fact that most photographers are male – there are quite often pictures of groups of girls together, or of young men with two or three girls, but pictures of several young men together or several men and one girl are much rarer. The marketing is overtly, and indeed aggressively, sexual, with explicit references to 'safe sex' and more.

## Models and releases

It goes without saying that all the people in all these pictures are attractive, or at least presentable: there is no call for the fish-belly white new arrival or the lobster-red sunburn victim.

Only rarely will budget, time-scale or organizational exigencies permit the use of models, so it is normal to inveigle holidaymakers into posing for pictures. It requires a certain amount of brass nerve to approach them, but most are quite flattered. Although model releases are desirable, they are rarely essential if the pictures are used honestly: they are, after all, straightforward representations of people at the hotel in question. As there are rarely extensive captions to such pictures, no-one is likely to be misrepresented in them.

The one exception to the use of models (and model releases) is that a day or two (or three) may be set aside for 'lifestyle' pictures such as a middle-aged, healthy couple walking hand in hand through the surf, or a younger couple staring into shop windows. The obvious problem with these, though, is that their subjects should not be too distinctive or their repeated presence will become rather too obvious.

## Low-end brochures

These are without question the dullest brochures, consisting of endless pictures of hotels, hotel rooms, swimming pools and tanning yards, leavened only slightly with attractive pictures of the destinations themselves. Also, quantity triumphs over quality: a typical spread may have as many as a dozen pictures on it, sometimes more, and at least half of them will be hotel exteriors or swimming pool shots.

There are however distinct differences between the different brochures for different age-groups, with people featuring more strongly in the youth and retirement-age brochures, and hotels featuring even more strongly in the family-oriented brochures.

Many of these pictures are taken by staff photographers, and being a staff photographer for a large tour company can (according to one, who wishes to remain anonymous) be somewhat wearing: 'You get the worst room in the hotel, over the disco, next to the lift-shaft, but fortunately you're so exhausted you can sleep through almost anything. You also tend to be there at the beginning of the season, when the weather is iffy: a whole week of white skies can go by, when you need blue skies or white puffy clouds. You end up doing a lot of interior shots! The schedule tends to be pretty punishing and uninspiring: they want a lot of pictures, and they don't allow you much time for shooting them.' This also helps to explain the popularity of the tobacco grad.

Tour companies also use freelances, usually under very similar conditions, but they tend to go back to the same photographers again and again. As in so

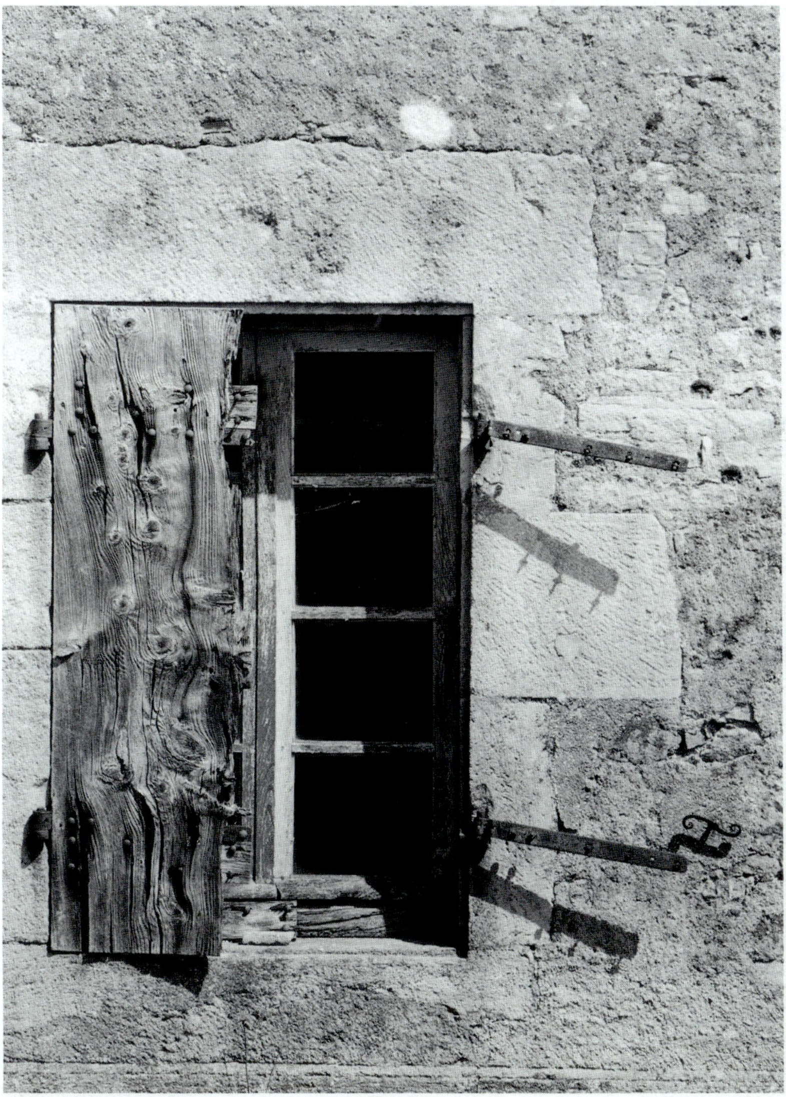

***Figure 10.3***
*Monochrome pictures such as this window in Burgundy are likely to appeal only to the more sophisticated brochures, where there is almost a 'fine art' element to some of the pictures (see Chapter 17). Even then, the preferred style is likely to involve bright, sunny weather: dramatic, bruised-looking skies are more likely to frighten people off than to attract them. (FES)*

much professional photography, reliability is more important than quality, and as in so much low-end professional photography, quality also ranks behind low prices.

Converging verticals are pretty much the norm on external shots, and on-camera flash is by no means unusual for night shots. For interiors, the general rule is to use the widest lens you can without excessive distortion, to make small rooms look larger; people, obviously, are stationed at the far side of the room to add to the impression of size, and in the middle so that they are not horribly distorted. Fill flash, often slightly over-generous, is standard for sunlit shots. Where off-camera flash is used, it is normally a simple one- or two-light monobloc set-up, typically with an umbrella. After a while, it becomes quite an amusing pastime to work out the (painfully simple) lighting in most low-end brochure shots, by looking at the shadows and reflections, especially at the catchlights in the eyes.

There is little or no need to use anything other than 35mm cameras, and while the vast majority of brochure shots have historically been on transparency film, it is not unreasonable to expect that direct scans from colour negatives will play an ever greater part. Although digital photography might seem to be a natural for this market, which deals mostly in small pictures of extremely modest resolution, 'real' film remains popular as it gives the brochure designer the option of the occasional large shot if the brochure demands it and if the picture warrants it.

The thing is, these companies are geared to doing everything on the cheap, shaving a few drachmae here, a few pesetas there, to keep costs to a minimum in this fiercely competitive market. Also, they know that their

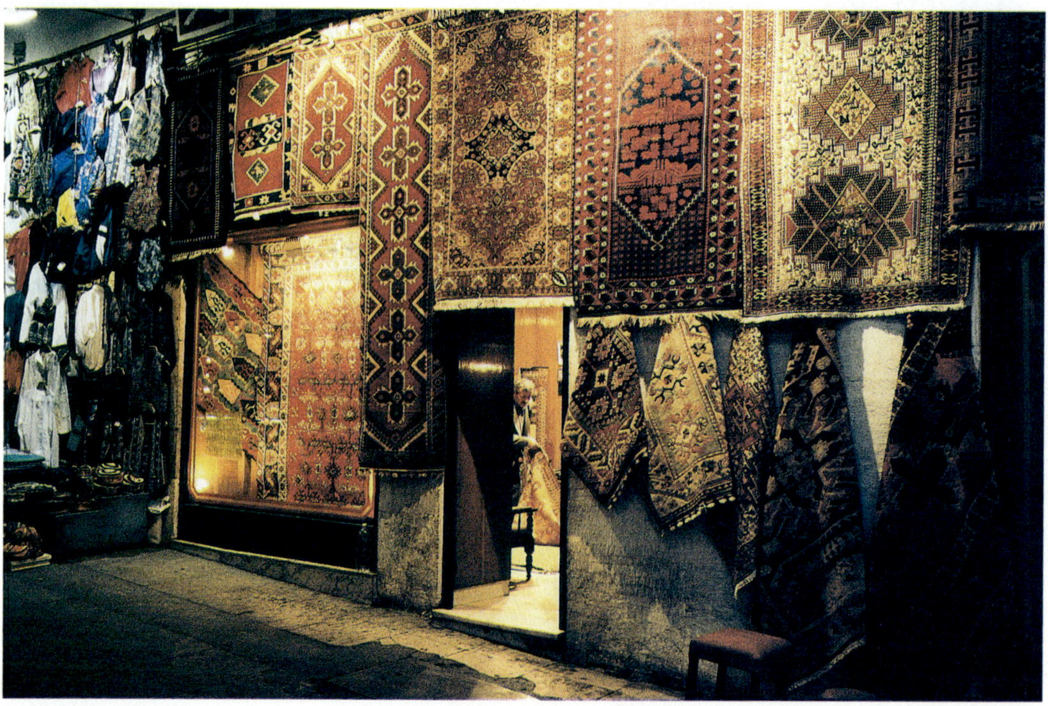

***Figure 10.4*** *Wherever possible, include people in your brochure pictures. The figure glimpsed through the doorway of this carpet shop in Istanbul is essential: without him, this is a very sterile snapshot. (RWH)*

customers are not particularly visually sophisticated: there is little point in appealing to anything other than the lowest common denominator. A direct approach, with your 'book', bearing all this in mind, may result in commissions – but it will never make you rich.

## Up-market brochures

As soon as you lift off from the rock-bottom mass market, where price is paramount, the quality of the brochures tends to rise quite rapidly. In particular, the number of hotel pictures often plummets (though there are a few exceptions) and the number of stock-type pictures of countryside, buildings and locals increases dramatically.

This is an inevitable consequence of the fact that they are dealing with a smaller, less demographically defined market. In the first place, they are less likely to take over whole hotels, and in the second, anyone with the money to spare might want to go to (say) Paris: young lovers, old lovers, art lovers, and indeed photographers looking for stock shots.

The pictures are therefore typically sourced in a number of ways. Some are straight, commercial library pictures: continuing with the Paris example, things like the Tour Eiffel, Notre Dame, the Champs Elysées at dusk. Others come from local tourist boards, from attractions, and from hotels: they are often out-takes or duplicates (or second use) of existing publicity material.

Yet others are locally sourced: a local photographer might well be hired to shoot a particular hotel or hotels, with the cost of the shoot quite possibly being split between the hotel and the travel company. This is less likely to be feasible in Third World destinations where some local photographers may be unable to work to the standards required, or where local styles may be rather old-fashioned for modern tastes, but it is likely to be entirely feasible in European 'package holiday' countries such as Spain, Portugal and Greece.

If hiring a photographer locally is not a realistic option, then there may be some chance that the tour operator will send a freelance out to a particular destination, but for specialist tours such as railway journeys, historical tours, and the like, a surprising number may come from the tour leaders or even from guests who volunteer their shots for nothing or who receive a discount off a subsequent trip in return for use of their images.

Rarely – only very rarely – will an operator 'comp' a photographer. As noted elsewhere, 'comps' are normally reserved for writers, often for fairly indifferent writers, who can be relied upon to sing for their supper, and to sing the right tune fairly loudly. On any comp deal, it is essential that both parties have a clear idea of what is expected in terms of numbers of pictures, quality of pictures, and exclusivity: the operator does not want to be fobbed off with all the spares which are unsaleable through a picture library, and the photographer does not want to relinquish all rights in all his or her pictures to the operator.

Because the situation with up-market brochures is so much more confused than with the mass-market offerings, it is fairly clear that the usual rules of professional photography obtain: catch as catch can, with a good slug of luck added in.

## Cruises

The situation with respect to cruise photography is still unclear in Britain, so what follows comes principally from an American contact.

First, remember that the cost of travel in the United States is normally considerably higher than in Europe, and that cruises tend to be a high-profit undertaking. Operators can therefore afford to hire photographers and to send them on a cruise – and indeed, this is normally the only way to get the pictures they need.

Inevitably, as a 'non-revenue' passenger, the cruise photographer rarely gets the best cabin, but with a little smooth talking it may be possible to upgrade if the best cabins are unsold: after all, the walk-in trade on a cruise can safely be neglected.

Remuneration is not high, but it is a realistic, living wage and the conditions of work are indeed very agreeable. Personal appearance can however be important: if you are the sort of person who does not care to dress in anything other than jeans and a T-shirt, you would do well to check with the operator what their expectations are.

It may yet be that as cruising broadens its appeal and (inevitably) loses its per-capita profit margins, conditions will deteriorate at the lower end of the market, even to the point where the 'walkie' photographer is expected to double as the cruise photographer.

## 'Walkie' photographers

If you see an advertisement for a cruise photographer, it is a safe bet that they are not looking for someone to shoot brochures. Rather, they are looking for something like the old beach photographer or holiday camp photographer, whose job it is to take pictures of people enjoying themselves, and then to sell their victims those pictures. Indeed, although cruise photographers are most often advertised for, other group entertainments may also have very similar demands.

The general level of technical and artistic skill which is required is roughly the same as that which is required for a news photographer on a free sheet, or on a very small newspaper. There is normally a mini-lab on board, which the photographer is expected to operate, so you need to be able to shoot, process and sell. You may also have to put the punters' films through the mini-lab, though this is not (yet) the norm. On a big ship, there may be a photographer and a mini-lab operator, though it is not likely.

Those who have tried 'walkie' photography generally report that they tried it for a lark when young and foolish. All the reports that we have ever heard, however, indicate that it is incredibly hard work, and that as you are usually working on a commission basis, there is little or no opportunity to take things easy. One of the major advertisers, even in Britain, is an American-based company; this gives you some idea of where the market is.

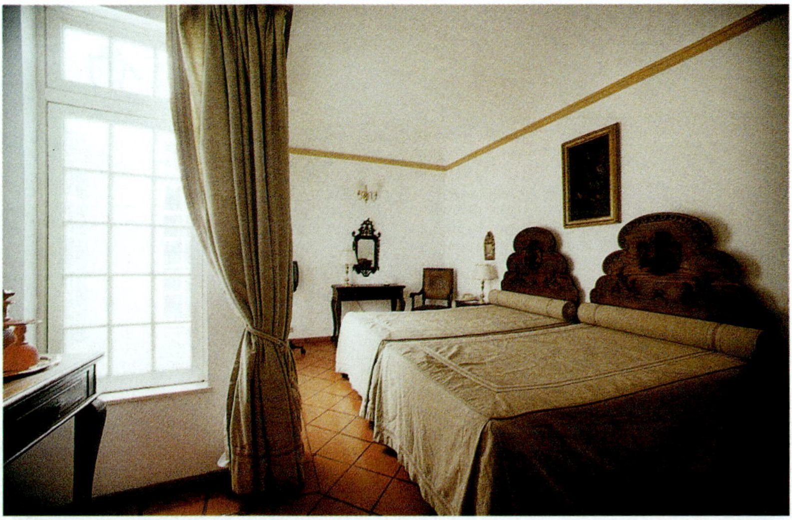

***Figure 10.5*** *Even the more up-market brochures may use room shots, especially if the rooms are particularly attractive; and even if the rooms are particularly attractive, you may still need to use extreme wide-angles to give a fair idea of the interior. This was shot with a 14mm lens. Also – an interesting point – it was shot on the (now discontinued) Agfachrome 1000, which had a delightful tonality and could handle a long subject brightness range with ease. (RWH)*

## Trend spotting

Each year's brochures are subtly (or sometimes very noticeably) different, with the possible exception of the low-end family brochures. While the hotel shots (including pool-side shots, bar shots, etc.) mostly change very little, the shots with people in them change rather more and the 'mood' shots – the couple walking hand in hand, or in front of a noteworthy attraction – change quite rapidly.

Sometimes, the fashion may be something which anyone with an ounce of aesthetic sensibility would utterly deplore. A good example, already mentioned, is the fashion for the 'tobacco grad', where all skies are rendered as a pinkish-brown. Another would be over-use of starbursts. Of course, any trick is legitimate if it gives an attractive effect, but over-use of any technical trick (and especially of any filter) soon becomes very wearing.

At the time of writing, however, monochrome photography was becoming more popular in the better brochures, and was even percolating down into the mid-market. Well-executed toned pictures might well be expected to follow this. Another trend – barely perceptible – seemed to be for an increased use of panoramic shots. At the reproduction sizes normally used, these could perfectly well be cut down from 35mm, but panoramic shots in the portfolio (Chapter 20) might pique a picture buyer's interest.

As with so many other areas of photography, too, you might do well to look at what is fashionable elsewhere, and to consider the possibility that new fashions might move into the rather conservative and unimaginative holiday market. Again at the time of writing, hand colouring was a distinct possibility. Another was pictures which were manipulated in Photoshop or some similar program, to create the impression of brush strokes or whatever. Actual comping together of pictures would be risky, as there is a strong likelihood of ever stronger pressures for 'truth in advertising' (something of an oxymoron, a cynic might think) and cleaning up beaches, removing roads, improving sunsets, and other such tricks might well attract the wrath of consumer groups if not of regulatory bodies.

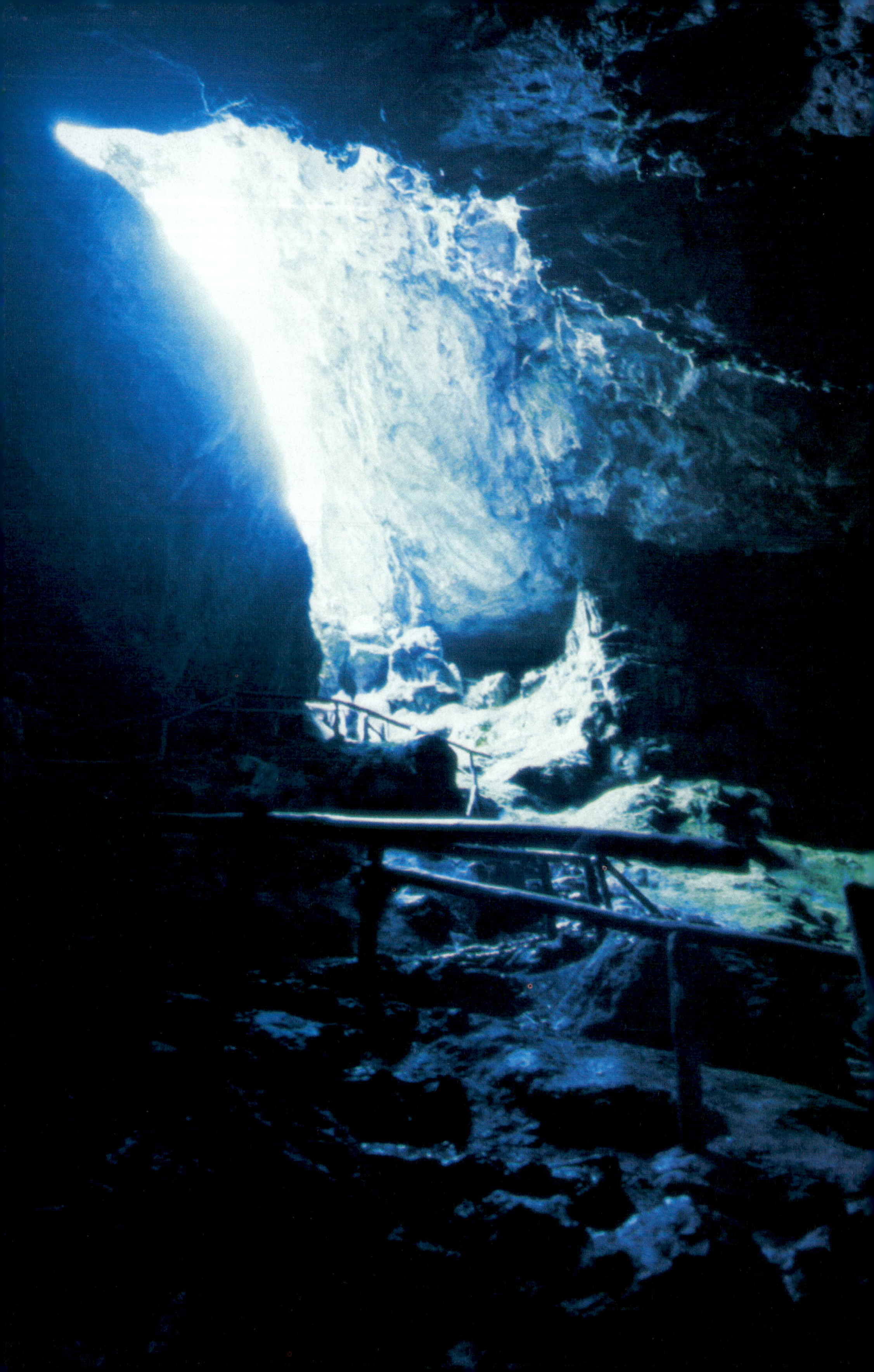

# 11 General travel articles

Figure 11.1 Dikteion cave. *The birthplace of Zeus, in Crete, is a memorable place – but hard to photograph. We were not particularly proud of this picture, but photographers are not always the best judges of their own work: it was used full page as the lead picture in a magazine article. (RWH)*

At first sight, the market for general travel articles is immense, and the standard is fairly undemanding. Just about every print medium, from the local free sheet to the glossiest of glossies, seems to run at least some travel material, so the market is clearly enormous. From a literary point of view, the vast majority of travel articles are little better than a ten-year-old's school composition about What I Did On My Holidays, and most of the rest are wont to indulge in prose so purple as to veer into the ultra-violet. What is more, many of these frankly awful articles are illustrated with mere snapshots, and when a photograph is any good, it is as often as not a well-executed cliché. How difficult can it be to produce something which is vastly better than the average?

The answer is that while it is quite easy to produce both words and pictures which are quite considerably better than average, it does not necessarily make financial sense to do so, either for the photographer or for the editor who commissions the work. This may seem an exceptionally jaundiced viewpoint, but it is (alas) all too defensible. If what follows is too much of a jeremiad, console yourself with three thoughts. The first is that there are a few shining exceptions, such as the *Los Angeles Times,* to which we shall return at the end of the chapter. The second is that there are other ways to make money from travel photography. And the third is that as long as you do not expect to make very much money from general travel articles, you can comfortably offset the cost of some of your travel by this means.

## Why travel sections exist

To return to the less palatable side of things, you need to begin by asking yourself the reason why most magazines and newspapers have travel sections, or run travel features. The answer is that they want to sell advertisements. Next, ask yourself who advertises, and why. The answer is that those with the highest profits can afford the biggest ads. How are profits generated? By volume – in which case, most people shop from the brochures (Chapter 10) or on price alone – or by very high margins. Where are the highest margins to be found? Suddenly it becomes clear why the articles are the way they are. The people at whom they are aimed are generally well-to-do, but they lack the skills, the experience and indeed the time to organize very much independently, or to cope with the inevitable mishaps and delays which characterize genuinely independent travel.

The destinations themselves need not be everyday, and the journeys need not be luxurious; but you may depend upon it that when a travel supplement talks about going up the Amazon, or climbing Mount Everest, or journeying into the Antarctic on an ice-breaker, they are rarely retailing the experiences of an intrepid traveller who sets everything up for himself (or herself). Rather, they are far more likely to be describing the latest ultra-expensive package holiday.

In any case, when you read the magazines and the supplements, you can see that the majority of destinations are pretty conventional. There may be a gloss on the whole thing, emphasizing the cultural aspects of visiting the Hermitage in St Petersburg or the historical significance of travelling by private train in India, but ultimately, all these reflect is a slightly greater sophistication than is exhibited by the customer who buys a Club 18–30 trip to Greece: instead of sun, sand, sea and sex, the middle-class, middle-aged travel article promises a brand of self-improvement which is as irresistible to its readers as sun, sand, sea and sex are to Club 18–30 buyers.

It is clear, then, that the market has its requirements. A little more research will also make it very obvious indeed that almost all general travel articles are word-driven. Sometimes, there may be a good lead picture to act as a 'hook' and to get the readers' attention, and even more rarely, there may be a set of very good pictures, often accompanying a well-written article; but while it is not uncommon to find a competent article either without illustrations or illustrated with little more than snapshots, it is very unusual to find a set of brilliant illustrations supported with minimal or incompetent text. First-class pictures with minimal text are normally presented either as a single image – normally just one page – or as a spread or (at most) as three pages of pictures.

## Why words prevail

It is not immediately clear why this should be, though several possibilities suggest themselves. One is that words sell. People who buy newspapers and magazines are in many cases reasonably well educated, and therefore place a premium on the written word.

Another argument is that big, beautiful editorial pictures are hardest to integrate with advertisements. You can run a couple of thousand words of text across two or three or even four pages, mixed in with middling-sized editorial photographs and with ads which rely on words or pictures or both, and no-one blinks; but a spread without text makes it much harder to fit the ads in.

Yet a third possibility is that it is often easier for a skilled writer to paint the right picture with words than it is for a skilled photographer to paint the right picture with light. Bad weather, mechanical mishap, or simply unphotogenic conditions are no problem to a writer, who can re-create the entire sequence of events in his or her head, without worrying about what actually happened. The writer can describe feelings, and transient events which passed almost unnoticed, and an enormous gamut of things which are difficult or impossible to represent in a photograph. Think of the smell of rain or of sea, the taste of sea-urchin roe, the feel of a sea breeze or of a flower touched to the lips, the first flake of the coming winter's snow on your cheek after you have walked past a row of snow-ploughs on Kalinin Prospekt.

Think, too, of things which are not as they seem: of someone covered

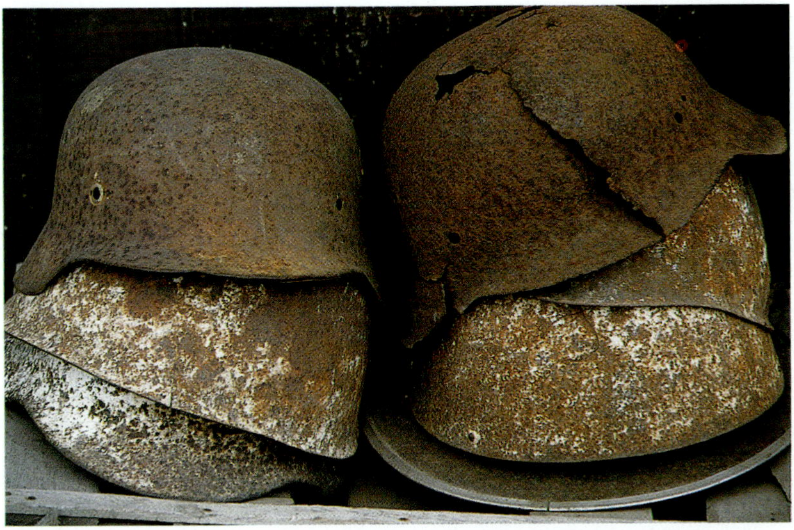

*Figure 11.2* *Although Crete is sometimes held up as the textbook example of what airborne troops can do, it is also the textbook example of what they cannot do. Fliegerkorps XI was effectively wiped out during the invasion of 20–27 May 1941, and massed parachute and glider landings were not attempted again by the Germans during the war. What is more, Cretan resistance was considerable and German reprisals were ferocious. Knowing this kind of background suddenly makes it clear why these rusting steel helmets are so important. (RWH)*

head to toe in mud, after they have slipped and fallen full length while trying to un-bog a four-wheel-drive. There is (or can be) a moment between the rueful disbelief that it has happened at all, and suddenly seeing the funny side of it. This would be very difficult indeed to represent in a single picture, and it would look contrived if you tried to shoot the whole sequence; but a writer can dispose of it fully, drawing us all into the event, in a sentence or two. A picture may be worth a thousand words, but in a travel article above all, a few words may often convey something which could never be described convincingly with a thousand pictures.

A fourth consideration is that in order to sell a picture set, you have to sell the idea verbally. It is possible (though rare) for an editor to see a picture set and to be knocked out by it; but one of the reasons it is so rare is that the editor will not even deign to look at the pictures unless he or she has been presented with good (verbal) reasons for doing so. Editors tend, in their very nature, to be word-oriented, so the whole market in word-driven articles is self-perpetuating.

## People who give their work away

If all this seems bleak, be not of good cheer; it gets worse, at least for the would-be professional. In essence, freelance professional travel photographers are competing against five separate groups of people, many of whom are prepared to work for next to nothing, or whose work is heavily subsidized, and some of whom are already highly skilled photographers and writers.

The first category consists of those amateurs who want nothing more than to offset the expenses of their photography and their travel against tax. Their 'day job' may be accountancy or medicine or almost anything – many of them are far from short of money – and by a combination of the law of averages and sheer weight of numbers, some of them can and do turn in very good sets of travel pictures. What is more, they are often the ones who go to the latest and most exciting destinations, simply because they can afford to do so. The financial return on their photography may be a mere fraction of what they spent, but they don't care. Nor should their desire for fame, rather than fortune, be underestimated; many non-professionals are so delighted to appear in print that any financial rewards are secondary.

The second category consists of 'celebrities', often defined as those who are famous for being famous, but also including newspaper columnists, writers, models, pop stars and the like. It matters not that they may have the photographic equivalent of a tin ear (a glass eye, perhaps). No: the editors' assumption, all too often correct, is that people will swallow any old drivel as long as they have heard of its originator, and so they assign these people travel articles, often with budgets which are considerably more handsome than a full-time professional travel writer could ever hope to see. In all fairness, some of these people are very good indeed, but it can be galling when you see the work of those who are not.

The third category comprises members of staff of the various newspapers and magazines, again substantially regardless of talent. The PR value of being written up in a major publication is not lost on travel companies, airlines and tour operators, so 'comps' are fairly readily available to any magazine with a reasonably large circulation. Sometimes, indeed, they are proffered even when they are not requested: 'Have you anyone who'd like to do an article on...?' Comps of this type are often distributed as rewards, or simply as a perk of the job. The editorial view, which is not entirely unjustified, is that travel is not all that difficult to write about: people will read the article if it is about a place which interests them, almost regardless of the quality of the information.

The fourth category consists of tourist boards and other promotional bodies whose job it is to give away pictures. Some of these pictures are very good, and even the ones that are not in the first rank are usually well selected to fit in with everyone's preconceptions of a given destination. Given the average editor's priorities, if there is a choice between a good free picture, and a superb picture at a substantial price, the free picture will win more often than not; the

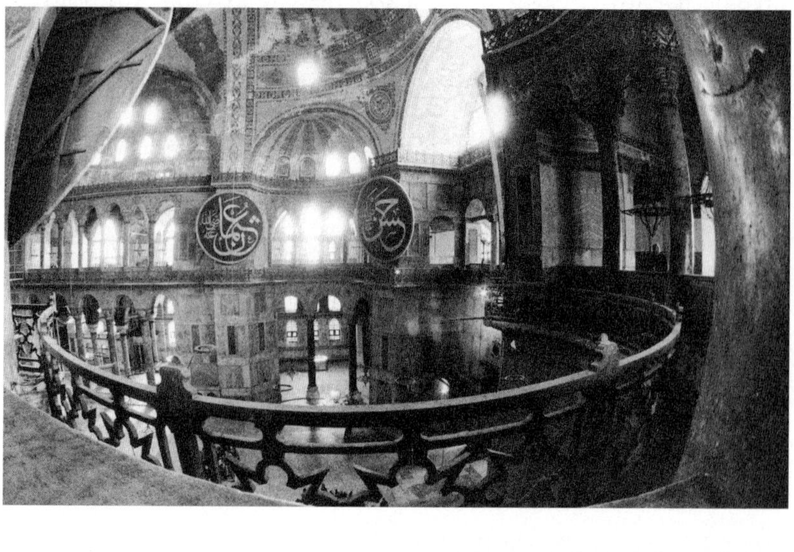

***Figure 11.3*** *Some photographers have a greater natural sympathy with fish-eyes than others, and are better at spotting pictures which will benefit from their use. Frances has considerably greater sympathy with fish-eyes than Roger does, and we both agree that this is one of her best fish-eye shots ever; the curvilinear forms of Ayia Sofia seem to be emphasized, rather than distorted, by its use. (FES)*

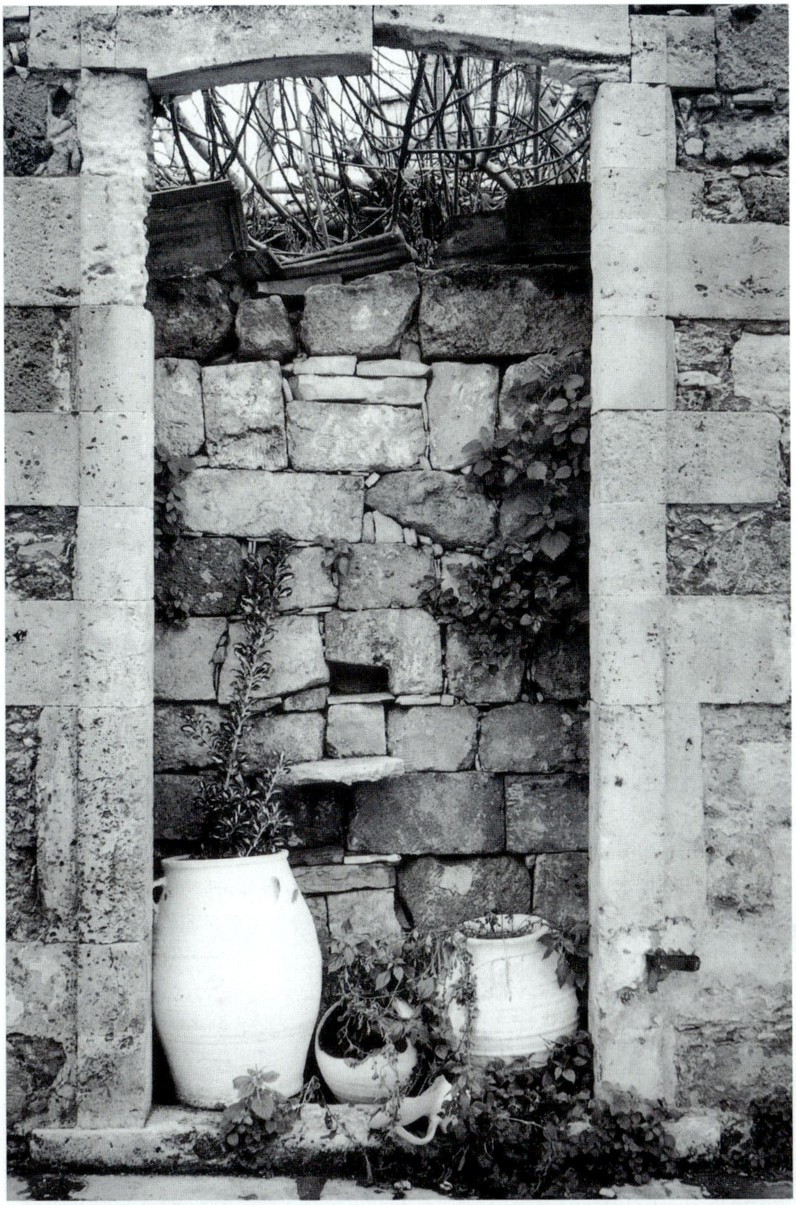

***Figure 11.4*** *Mood is as important as fact in a travel article, so you need to shoot a good mixture of what might be called 'record' shots, and shots like this which give more of a feeling for a place. On its own, this could be almost anywhere in the Mediterranean; as part of a set of pictures on Crete in general, and Chania in particular, it reinforces the overall tone of decaying splendour which characterizes so many Greek destinations. (FES)*

more so, given what we have already said about travel articles being word-driven.

The fifth category takes us back, in effect, to the first; except that this time the amateur travel photographers are professional photographers in another field, such as advertising or portraiture or celebrity photography, who turn their hand to travel photography for the fun of it. After all, a professional photographer can already offset film and processing and equipment against expenses; and if enough pictures appear in print to pay for the trip, then by definition, the trip is tax allowable. The tax authorities do not say that you must not enjoy what you do, or even that you have to make a large profit on every project, so travel photography may well be cross-subsidized by some other branch of photography, with the missing 'profit' being taken in pleasure.

*Figure 11.5* *This photograph of Chania at dawn was taken from the balcony of our hotel room. It may cost a little more to stay near the centre of things, and it may cost a little more again to get a room with a view; but early in the morning, or late at night, it can be well worth the extra money to shorten as far as possible the distance from where you are shooting to the comfort of your bed. Of course, not all views from hotel balconies are as successful as this one. (RWH)*

In other words, the main reason why so many travel articles are so bad is that the majority of editors are unwilling to pay for anything better; and indeed, they have no great incentive to pay for anything better. In general-interest magazines and newspapers, many readers will be entirely satisfied with mediocre articles which are little more than a puff for an uninteresting destination, written by someone who is clearly singing for his or her supper and illustrated with tourist office hand-outs; and even those who are not satisfied with these articles are unlikely to cancel their subscriptions merely because of the very low standard of travel writing and photography.

Go to the magazines which are devoted to travel alone, and although the standards are usually (though far from invariably) higher, there is an even greater likelihood that someone reasonably skilled at writing or photography or both will be prepared to work for knock-down rates, just in return for subsidizing their travel. Also, because these magazines depend almost exclusively on travel advertising for their profits, they have a higher incentive than most to dwell on exotic and expensive package tours; their advertisers would be less than enchanted if they said, in effect, 'Don't waste your money buying tours from the expensive operators who advertise in our pages, because you can have more fun and save a lot of money by doing things yourself.'

## Shining exceptions

At the beginning of the chapter, though, we said that there are shining exceptions; and one with whom we have some experience is the *Los Angeles Times*. Although it is sometimes a little too clear that some of their travel articles are aimed at a largely comfortable and not always worldly readership,

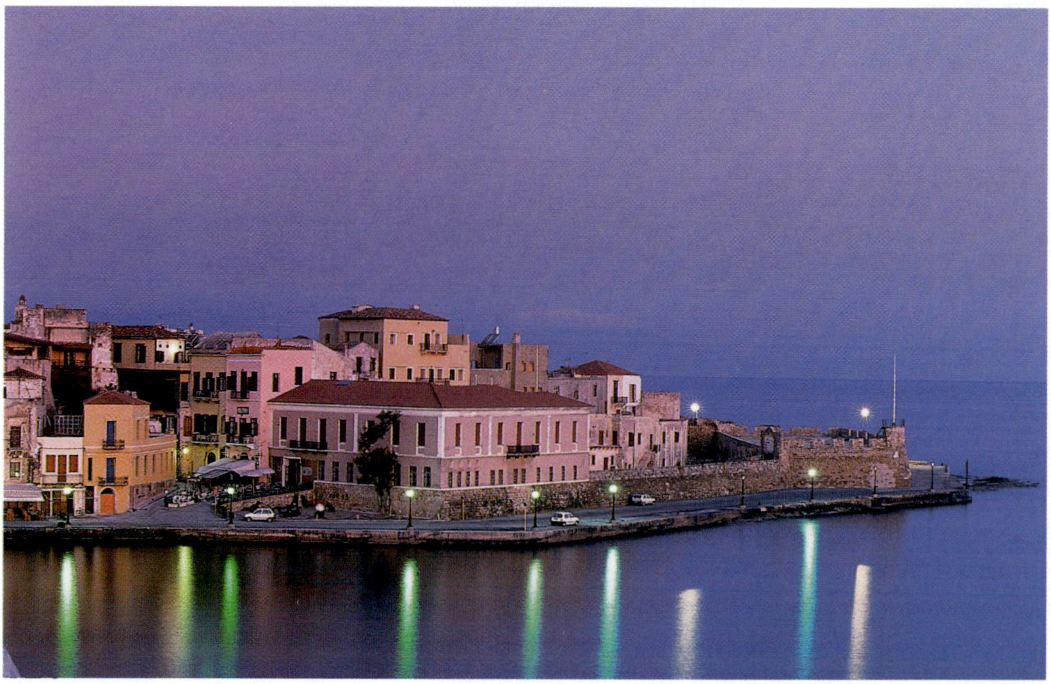

they do publish many superb articles. Some are clearly intended to inform the Great American Vacationer about the practicalities of travel in Foreign Parts, while others are about places where few if any would go just for fun: Gail Fisher in particular has covered wars and revolutions, as well as feature news stories about the resurgence of the church in Russia, problems engendered by pollution, and more.

The great strength of the *Los Angeles Times* is that their travel articles are for the most part held to the same journalistic standards as the rest of the newspaper. That is, facts must be accurate; captions must be useful; and there must be no suggestion that the writer has been 'bought'. If any part of a trip has been 'comped', they will not run the article; and if they run an article and find that they have been deceived on that point, they will never use that person's work again.

This does not mean that the articles are dry, and indeed their guidelines go to particular lengths to stress the importance of creating mood by describing smells, regional dishes, and all the things that you cannot capture in photographs. In common with all newspapers, the likelihood of selling a package of pictures without words is slender, so you need either to be a writer yourself or to work with a writer.

Reading the guidelines is, if anything, even more important with this sort of market than with any other. Familiarity with the publication is taken for granted, but other requirements, such as length, number of pictures, the amount of information required for 'boxes' or sidebars, and so forth, will far more easily be gleaned from the guidelines. Most major publications will send a copy of these on request, or on receipt of a stamped, self-addressed envelope: they typically consist of a few sheets of photocopied instructions, and while they are rarely absolutely binding, you depart from them at your peril.

The reason for this is not hard to see. Major newspapers are regularly deluged with articles, many of them first class. They simply have no need to take on articles which require heavy work or criticism or re-working; they can afford to throw them aside, and reach for the next article, in the hope that it will be better. If it is not, well, there are always dozens, scores and hundreds more.

From the photographer's viewpoint, the most important thing is the number of pictures required. Even if the magazine or newspaper is only going to use two or three, they will frequently request far more from which to make a selection: typically twenty to forty. Why this should be is not entirely clear, but it may again relate to the point which has repeatedly been made above, that travel articles are for the most part word-driven, and photographs are regarded as a sort of optional extra. What is worse, many magazines (including the *Los Angeles Times*) will insist on seeing originals, not dupes, and they may hold on to them for an altogether unconscionable length of time. If you can get or make reproduction quality dupes at a reasonable price, you may do better simply to lie about whether or not they are originals.

Once you are established with a particular publication, you may be able to get away with sending fewer pictures, perhaps as few as ten or a dozen

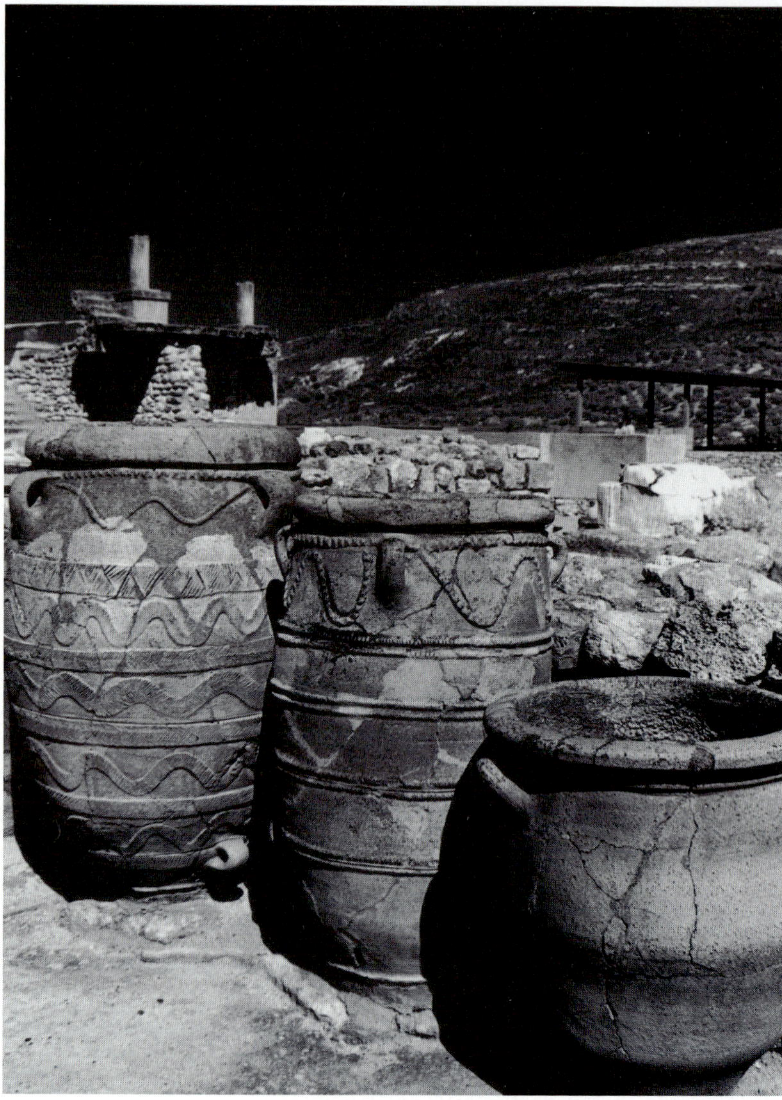

***Figure 11.6*** *Sometimes, you may decide to resort to unusual film stocks in order to create a particular effect. These storage pots at Knossos were shot with Konica 750 IR and a red filter: the 'green gap' (missing green sensitivity) of the film makes the sky go black, and adds still more dramatic contrast. It is always a good idea to experiment with such shots, for the right subject, but it is rarely a good idea to rely exclusively on off-beat techniques and materials. (FES)*

if you know they are only going to run two to five images, but if you are wise, you will wait a while before you ask your editor if this is acceptable. Also, you want a good mix of pictures, which is another reason why you are frequently asked for what may at first seem like an unreasonable number of photographs.

## Cinematic vision

As so often in travel photography, thinking in cinematic terms is a good idea. You want the establishing shot, the one which tells you immediately and unquestionably where you are. You want close-ups, mid shots and long shots. You want pictures of the actors – the locals, or the models if that is the sort of shoot you are doing. And you want cutaways, pictures of details or events which are not central to the main story, but which help set it in context and create a mood. Superimposed on this, and quite separately from cinematography, you want a good mixture of both portrait and landscape formats. Although many pictures in newspapers and magazines – perhaps most – are run landscape, there is a peculiar thrill in seeing one of your pictures run as an unexpected full-page, or at least very large; a thrill which once experienced is never forgotten, and which seems to bear very little relationship to the pictures you thought were best.

The normal standard for newspapers and magazines alike is 35mm, both because there is no need for anything better and because it would not be feasible from a financial viewpoint to shoot on roll-film or large format. The reason there is no need for anything better is that pictures in magazines are rarely run big enough for it to matter, while in a newspaper, newsprint masks the quality differences between the different formats. Although staff photographers on the *Los Angeles Times* typically work with colour negative, which is scanned straight in from the negative, freelances are still expected to provide colour transparencies. General travel articles are sometimes illustrated in black and white, but to a large extent, readers' expectations of colour are so strong (or at least, they are perceived that way) that colour is very much the norm.

If the weather is not good when you visit a particular destination, you will often have to exercise some ingenuity. Over the years, we have had to use almost every trick in the book. Night shots are always useful (and can even be improved if the streets are rain-slicked); interiors can start to feature very heavily; high-contrast, high-saturation film such as Fuji Velvia can conceal dull days, if there is no sky in shot; and an 81-series filter can add to the deception. You may even be reduced to using coloured grads to liven up the skies.

## Yes, but does it pay?

Finally, the subject of payment is vexing. For understandable reasons, few newspapers or magazines are willing to set out pay scales, and different contributors' rates can vary very widely. If you can make a name for yourself, and if your pictures are run across several pages in a major publication, you can look forward to four-figure fees (in pounds or dollars), though three-figure fees will be much more usual, even in respected newspapers and magazines, and by the time you come down to local free sheets, you can be looking at two-figure fees. At the lowest level, which is the one that is so often bruited in 'make money with your camera' articles and courses, you can at best regard it as a way of building your 'book': it won't cover the cost of any but a comped trip (and then only if it is fully comped), it will barely cover film and processing, and it certainly won't cover your time.

In the final analysis, we have never recovered the full cost of a trip and of materials from a single, general travel article, but we rarely travel comped; we always travel together; we are fond of good food; and because we are always shooting with an eye to two or three markets, our expenses are perhaps higher than those of most travel photographers, who might reckon to base an article on as little as three days' travel.

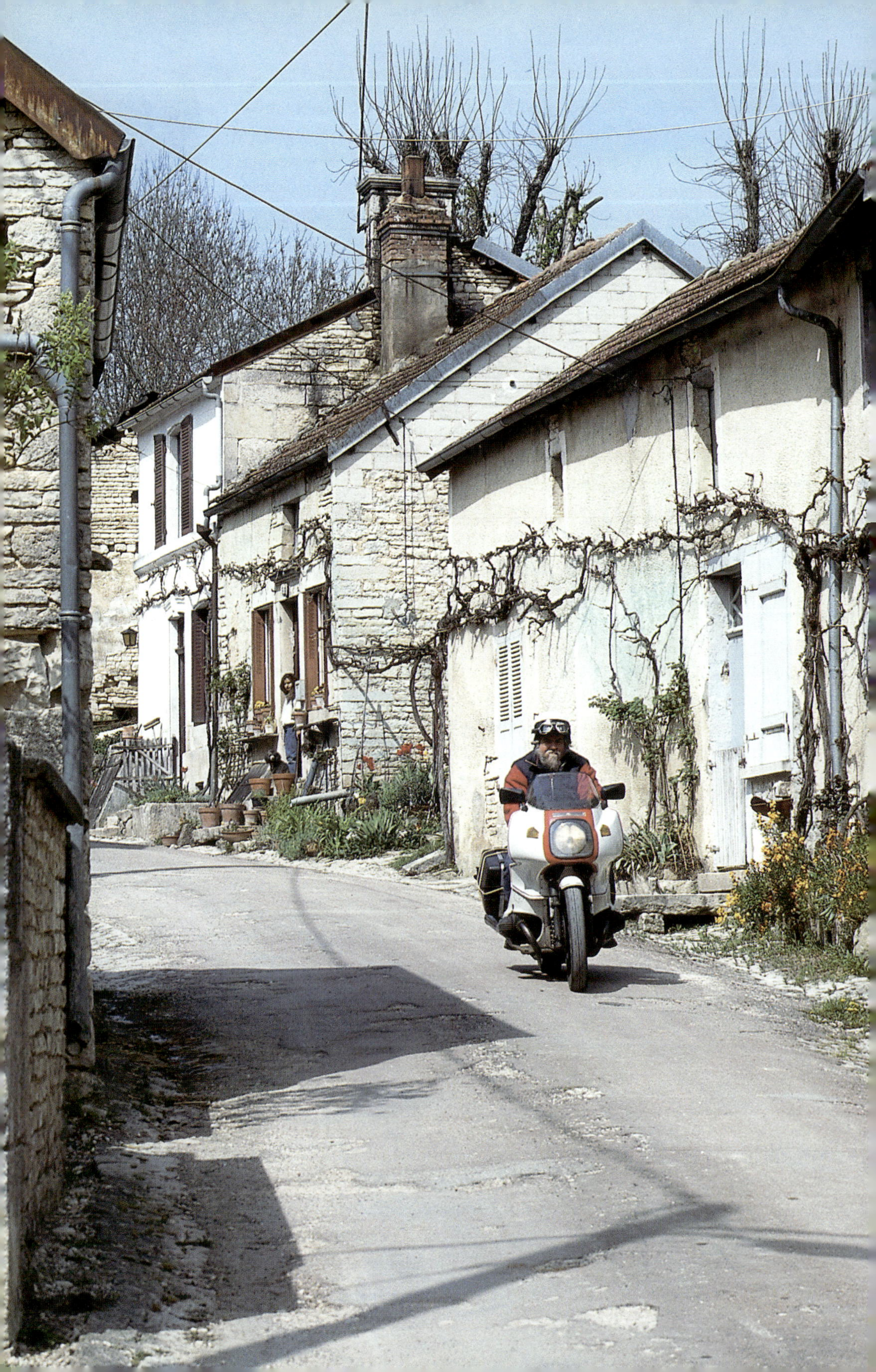

# 12 Specialist travel articles

The good news about specialist travel articles is that the market is very large, and that it generally (though not invariably) pays better than the lower end of the general travel market. Even the most relentlessly domestic of subjects lends itself to a travel article, just to see how things are done abroad: cookery is an obvious example, but it is hard to believe that (for example) a magazine about embroidery would not be interested in the work which was done in an area noted for its embroidery, or that a publication aimed at the home weaver would not be interested in the ancient looms used to make Malta weave. Magazines aimed at those with an interest in homes and decorating would almost certainly be interested in exotic carpets. Collectors' magazines are interested in foreign collections, museums and fairs; and so forth.

The bad news is that specialist travel articles still do not pay very well, except at the uppermost reaches of the glossies. A typical motorcycling article, for example, might (at 1998 rates) pay £100 to £200 a page, or $100 to $300, while photographic articles generally start lower (as low as £50 or $75 a page). This is about the minimum you should expect, but equally, you would be lucky to see much more than double the maximum rates quoted above.

The reason why rates are so low is because (once again) the majority of travel articles for the specialist press are written and illustrated by people who are not so much trying to make a living, as trying to offset some of their expenses in travelling. Others are written by magazine staff members, who may have access to company credit cards, company hotel rates, and so forth.

***Figure 12.1*** *Motorcycles parked in front of things are a staple of motorcycle touring magazines, but motorcycles on the move often make for better images. Unless you are travelling with a partner (as we normally do), you will have to enlist the help of people you meet while touring. Fortunately, motorcyclists are generally ready to extend a fraternal hand to their fellow riders – though they might draw the line at negotiating a road like this five times, as Roger did in order to allow a variety of pictures. (FES)*

## THE PACKAGE

Again as with general travel articles, you are in with a far greater chance if you can provide a package of both words and pictures. This is even more important than it is with general travel articles. After all, there are plenty of writers who go to (say) Crete or New Orleans, and there are plenty of photographers and sets of photographs to match to them. Even if a writer goes somewhere exotic, it is generally quite feasible to find a set of pictures which more or less fit, and which can be made to look even more as if they are a part of the same package by careful captioning. But if an editor is presented with a brilliant selection of pictures of (say) motorcycle touring in India, there are likely to be far fewer writers who can provide the words to accompany them. The general rule about travel articles being word-driven is thereby reinforced: it is far easier to get more-or-less right pictures to suit existing words, than it is to get words which suit existing pictures.

## Knowing the subject

With all of this in mind, the most important thing in shooting and writing specialist travel articles is that you really need to know your subject. References to tensioning the chain on a BMW Boxer in a motorcycling magazine would be akin to referring to Linhof compacts in a photography magazine; your credibility would be blown straight out of the water. Worse still, editors will not always spot such errors – but when the general readership does, and starts writing stiff letters, as it invariably will, your name will be mud.

You do not need to be a world authority, but you do need to have a genuine interest in the subject and you have to be able to practise what you preach. The advice so often given in 'how to' books and articles, to adapt the same story for different but seemingly related markets, is substantially worthless in the form in which it is given, for two reasons. The first is that as soon as you stray outside the realms you know, you are likely to make the kind of egregious error described above, and the second is that experience simply is not transferable.

To take an obvious example, consider European touring by motorcycle, and by motor caravan. With the former, you can stop more or less anywhere; narrow roads present no problems; and of necessity, you travel very light. What is more, unless you are camping, you are interested in hotels, gîtes, pensions and guest houses, not camp sites. With a motor caravan, not only are the opposites likely: you are also going to be concerned with water and power supplies and sewage dump tanks, and you may well be interested in remote areas where you can stop unimpeded and where you can see the sun rise in beautiful scenery.

On the other hand, most people can see several angles to a story which they might be able to sell in different and substantially unrelated markets. For example, we could slant an article on 'La France Profonde' ('deep' or rural France) for a general travel market; a motorcycling market; a photographic market; (possibly) a food and drink market; and a market for active retired people (we are not quite that old, though we sometimes feel like it).

The point is that these markets are all ones where we feel at home. We travel anyway; we have ridden motorcycles for many years; we write regularly for the photographic press, on both sides of the Atlantic; we are fond of food and drink, and have written several cook-books; and we are nearing the age where our interests are congruent with those of many retired people, such as reasonable comfort, modest expenditure (or at least, good value for money), and a lifestyle which eschews discothèques and the like. We could not however write for the youth (or 'yoof') market; for the laddish magazines apparently aimed at young professional men; for publications intended for parents travelling with children; or for the Sunday supplements, with their relentless emphasis on consumerism and their seeming determination to spend money as fast as possible.

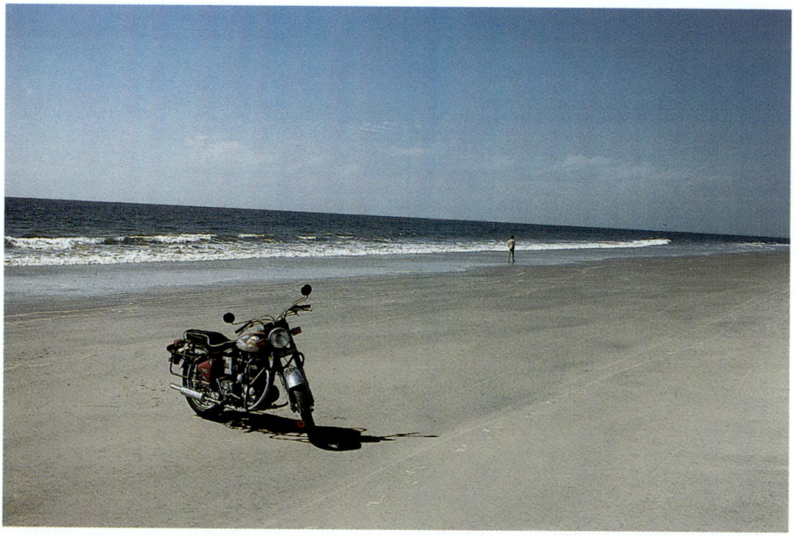

*Figure 12.2 Always ask yourself what a particular picture says, before you include it in a submission; try to divorce yourself from what you saw, heard and felt when you took it, and rely on the content of the picture alone. Here, the message is clear: almost deserted beaches, warm sun, freedom to ride where you want... (RWH)*

In practice, we would probably omit the active retirement market and the food and drink market, unless we were unusually lucky or persistent in our picture-taking: ideally, you want pictures of fit and happy retired people for the one, and food for the other, though there are ways around the latter. You can do a lot by photographing markets and locals (general 'lifestyle' pictures), and then shooting the food in the studio – though food photography is an entirely separate skill from travel photography, and one which you may or may not already possess or wish to cultivate.

## Seeking multiple sales

From the above, it is clear that a major advantage of the specialist market is the possibility for multiple sales, if (and it is a big if) you can work out the right angle and sales pitch for each market. There is however the inevitable question of how often you can bear to go over the same ground, and, for that matter, of how often you decently can go over the same ground without growing stale.

If you are aiming for multiple markets, you need to do your research (and to plan your shots) even more carefully than usual. To a considerable extent, you have to visualize each article in its finished form, and to make sure that you have the right pictures for each. In fact, sticking with the example given – La France Profonde – it is worth going through all the markets in question, sketching them mentally.

- *General*: Up to three magazine pages, or a page and a half in a newspaper. Maximum of about seven shots run, 20 to 40 submitted (see page 121). Colour for newspaper of first choice; black and white for newspaper of second choice. Subjects: rural accommodation, restaurants, things to buy, food, old villages and farmhouses, scenery.
- *Motorcycling*: Up to four pages, maximum of ten shots, 20 to 30 submitted (motorcycle magazines are generally pleasantly surprised to

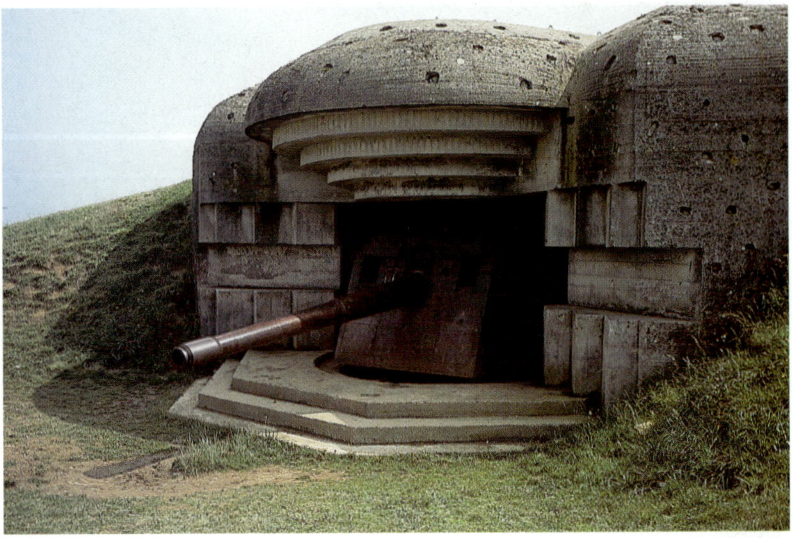

*Figure 12.3 Most photographers, and most editors, would prefer the version of this picture which has the children in it (opposite): the contrast between the rusting engines of war and the innocence and hope of the future is clearly poignant. But there is a certain type of military history magazine which would run the other picture (right) instead. (RWH)*

get good pictures, let alone a good number of them). Colour. Subjects: motorcycle parked in front of things, other motorcycles/motorcyclists, riding on good roads/riding off road (useful to have a partner here!), possibly camp sites/rally sites, scenery preferably featuring winding roads, wayside eating and drinking establishments.

- *Photographic*: Up to three pages, probably no more than half a dozen shots, ten to 20 pictures submitted (we could get away with less, because we would normally do an article like this for one of the magazines we write for regularly). Colour or mono – probably mono. Subjects: principally pictorial: attractive buildings, colourful locals, activities (fairs, boules), markets. There should be as many 'establishing' shots as possible – pictures which are unique to this part of the world, rather than ones which could have been taken anywhere.
- *Food and drink*: Up to four pages, eight to ten pictures, 20+ submitted. Colour, or colour and mono mixed – mono probably toned. Subjects: farmland, farms, markets, shops, restaurants, food if at all possible, but supplemented with a few (two to four) 4 × 5 inch food shots of re-creations of regional specialities prepared at home and shot in the studio.
- *Active retirement*: Up to three pages, six to ten pictures, 20 to 40 submitted. Colour, or colour and mono mixed – mono probably toned. Subjects: accommodation, shops, restaurants, museums, scenery, as many shots with retired people in them as possible, whether tourists or locals – boules players would be a natural, as would a grizzled farmer enjoying a glass of pastis at a café table.

In addition to the above specific ideas, you need to have a set of visual notes or departure points, all the things that you think of in rural France. These

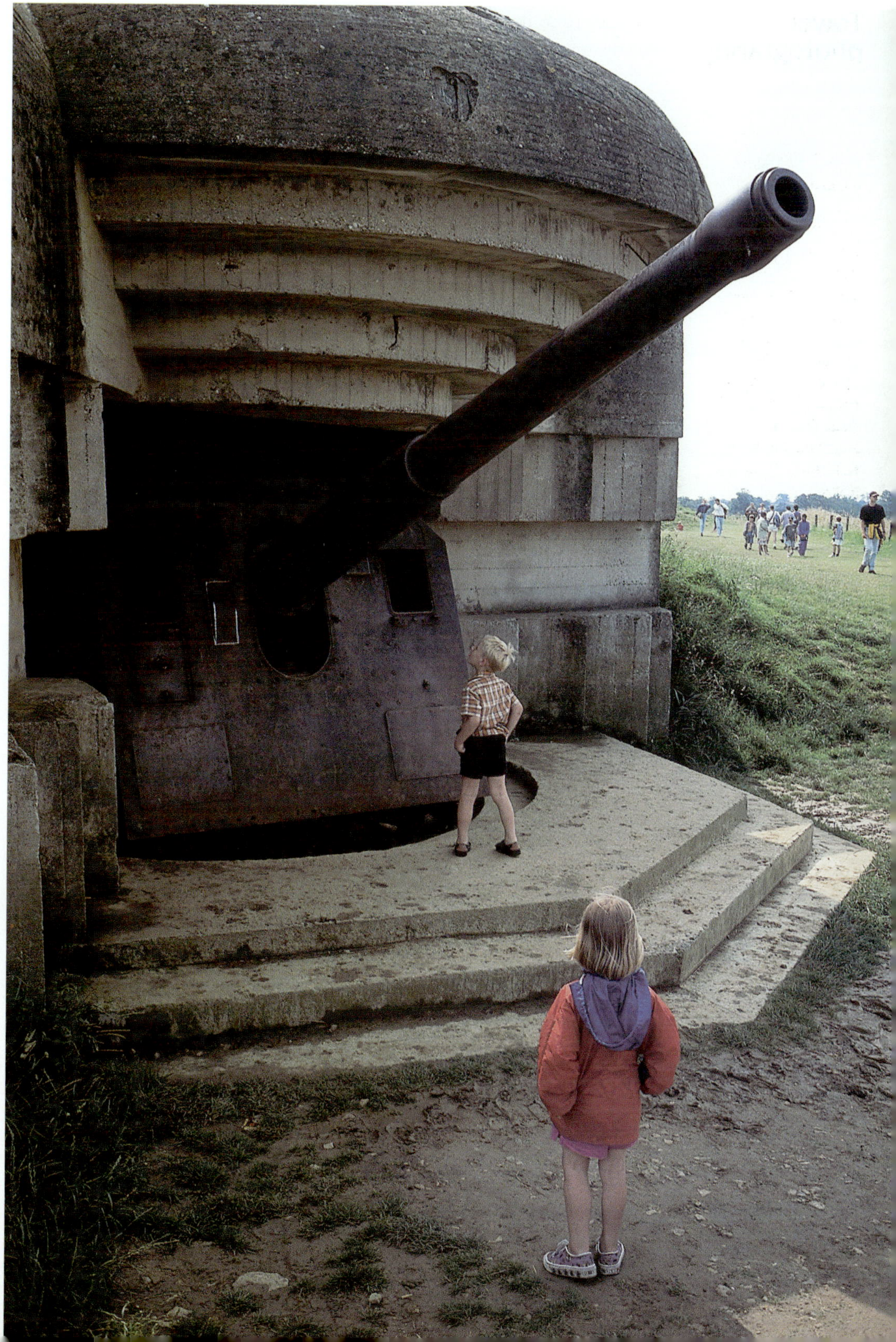

will vary to some extent with the area and the season – poppies, sunflowers, tall dry grass – but others are there at any time of year: faded and weathered paint, wooden shuttered windows, old tin advertising signs, decaying farm machinery, wayside crucifixes.

Of course, you have to remain sufficiently open-minded that you do not neglect shots merely because they are not on your mental shot list: 'hardening of the categories', in the wonderful phrase we first heard used by Lucille Barringer. We all do this, though: when we get back, we think, 'Why didn't I shoot that?' As usual, the general rule is to shoot first and ask questions afterwards.

Once you have mentally sketched out the articles, it is a very good idea to write your query letters before you go. Provided you are reasonably competent, and provided the idea is reasonably appropriate to the readership, the main reason for the rejection of articles in any magazine is duplication: a similar article has either been run recently, or is already commissioned for the near future. In general, if the topic was last covered more than three years ago, you should be safe; and if you are familiar with a more recent article, but can convince the editor that your idea is sufficiently different, you may be able to sell an article with a gap as small as three or four months.

Your query letter should always make it clear what you are offering, and how certain the trip is. It is perfectly acceptable to say that you are considering a trip to (say) Iceland in July, and that to some extent your decision to go will depend on what response you get from the person you are writing to, and from your picture libraries (even if you don't have one, this sounds good and provides an uncheckable excuse for either going or not going). Do not enquire too early, because editors mostly work on a fairly short time-base, and if something is more than three months away, it might as well be thirty years. Also, don't make a habit of enquiring, and not going (or going, and not delivering pictures). You can get away with it twice, or maybe even three times; but if you never deliver anything, you will sooner or later be seen as a time-waster.

The query letter should also make it clear why you are the person who is best equipped to illustrate this article: you have been riding motorcycles for thirty years, you have won cookery competitions, whatever it takes. Stick reasonably close to the truth, but equally, do not be afraid to put yourself in the best light. Make it clear that you are familiar with the publication, but equally, don't pretend to be a life-long subscriber if you have only read three issues (or just one!). Obviously, request guidelines.

Ask when they would like the article. Obviously, people want to read about a place before they go, at the beginning of the season; but equally obviously, you cannot send in the pictures until after you have gone. Timeliness rarely means delivering the article a few weeks after you get back: rather, it means delivering it several weeks (typically up to three months) before it is due to run.

## SIMULTANEOUS SUBMISSIONS – AND DUPES

If you want or need to make all of your submissions simultaneously – and if you do not, you may lose timeliness – then you will need a lot of pictures: at least 100 good ones, which means shooting at least 20 rolls of 36-exposure film, unless you have a hit-rate which is considerably higher than average. With certain subjects you want half a dozen identical or near-identical pictures, because they are common to all five markets, whereas others will often fit only into one category – unless of course you find retired motorcyclists or a motorcycle museum, which could provide good cross-overs.

If you can make (or have made) genuinely reproduction quality duplicates, you may find that some magazines do not actually require originals; or, of course, you may simply decide not to tell them that you are not giving them originals. Except for the photographic markets (and not always then), they are unlikely to be able to tell the difference, provided there are no tell-tale black lines around the edge from sloppy copying.

You will also need to exercise considerable care in how you divide the pictures up, for several reasons. You have to avoid the inevitable temptation to send all the best pictures to the magazine that most reflects your interests, regardless of the fact that they do not necessarily pay the best; but equally, you have to resist the temptation to send all the best pictures to the magazine which pays best, despite the fact that you are not as enthusiastic about that subject and may therefore have a smaller chance of selling. You need to try to put yourself in the shoes of the person who will actually be buying your pictures: don't send moody setting-sun shots if you can see that almost all their pictures are taken with the sun high in the sky. On the other hand, you want to place your stamp on the article, your own uniqueness of vision, or why should the editor buy it? You want passion, but not so much passion that it obscures the content.

Whatever you do, avoid sending too many makeweights to any one magazine. There will be makeweights, of course, but if you are short of genuinely good pictures, send the minimum that is requested in the guidelines, rather than the maximum; and by intelligent use of presentation, disguise the makeweights as far as possible. If you are sending 40 pictures, in two 20-sheet sleeves, try to avoid sending the 20 best in one sheet and the 20 also-rans in the second.

We have also found that it makes sense to lay the sleeves out on the basis of overall density and colour, wherever possible. In other words, if you can possibly avoid it, do not put a bright, light transparency next to a dark, moody one. Both may be perfect exposures for the subject in question, but they will suffer from juxtaposition. The ideal layout, which is not always feasible, is to lay the sheets out in diagonal stripes. Put the lightest transparencies in the upper left and lower right corners, the darkest transparencies in a diagonal line from lower left to upper right, and grade the others in between. Sometimes,

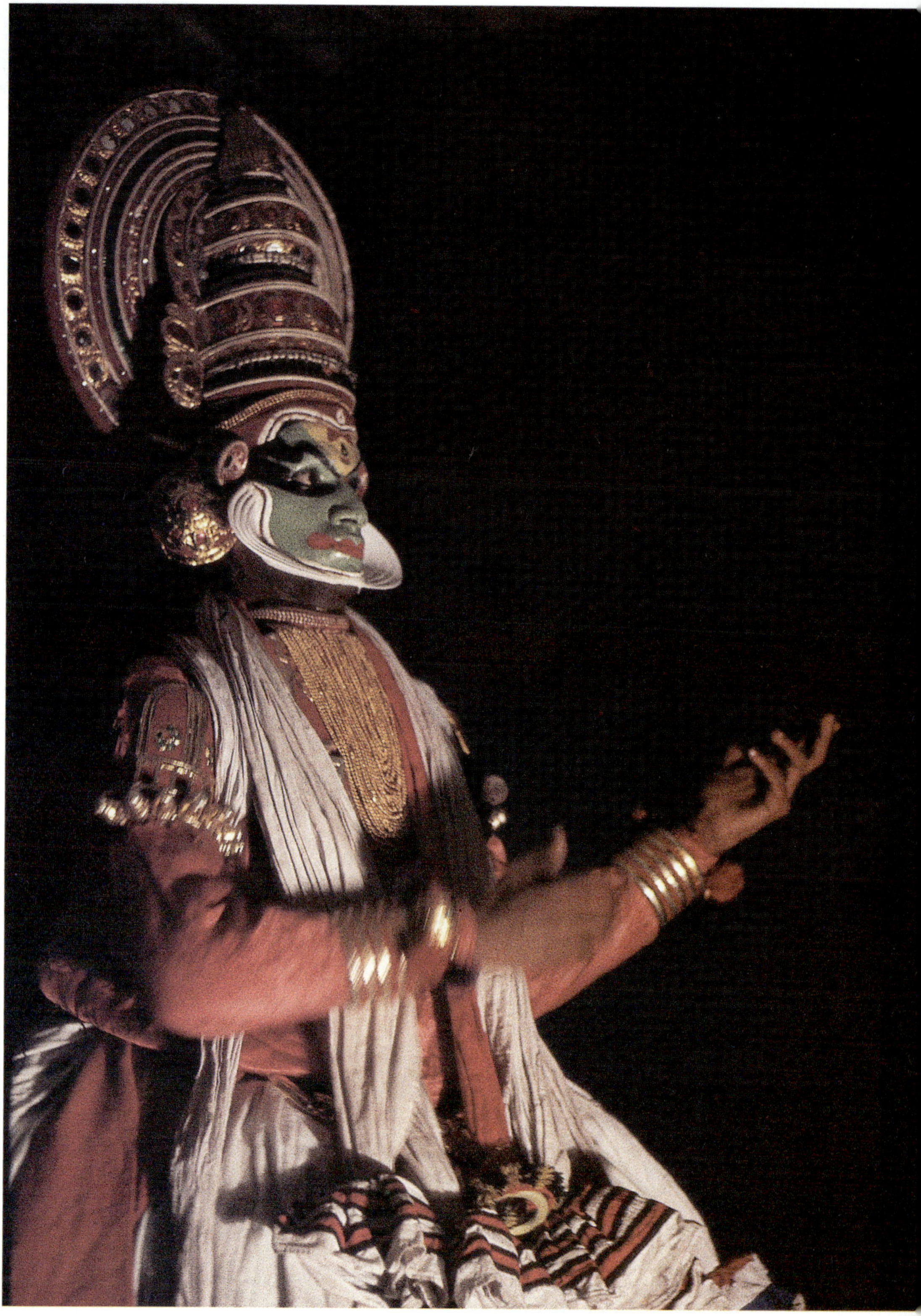

the logic of captioning makes this impossible; but when you can do it, the immediate impression on seeing the sheet is much better than a chequerboard.

The easiest way to divide the slides between the various journals is probably with a seriously large light table. We have a monster which we bought very cheaply at auction, 24 × 36 inches or 60 × 90 cm, and even this is not quite big enough: we repeatedly toy with the idea of making one 60 × 150 cm. A 20-pocket sleeve is approximately 25 × 30 cm, so you can conveniently fit five of them onto our table, with a small area for sorting the sleeved trannies as returned from the lab. A 60 × 150 cm table would allow nine sleeves, but what stops us making one is the sure and certain knowledge that, like every other horizontal surface in our offices and indeed in the entire house, it would soon grow a surface layer of papers, books, photographs, and equipment. It is hard enough to clear the light table we have!

All in all, we have found that specialist travel articles are an easier and better bet than the general market, but that (once again) we rarely make back the full cost of a whole trip, even if it is of modest cost, from a single article. We have quite often managed around $1000 (about £600 to £700 – these are late 1990s values), but equally, we are not particularly surprised to see as little as one third of this. This is for a package of words and pictures, remember. A highly respected specialist, or a columnist whose name is well known elsewhere, might double or conceivably triple our normal maximum, but to go beyond that sort of income is not something that the majority of photographers can hope to do.

***Figure 12.4*** *One of the big differences between illustrating a specialist travel article, and merely providing 'mood' pictures for a brochure, is that your captions (and your knowledge) need to be more extensive. This is one of a series of pictures of Kathkali dancers which begins with the application of the make-up. Make notes at the time, or use a tape recorder, or memories will fade. (RWH)*

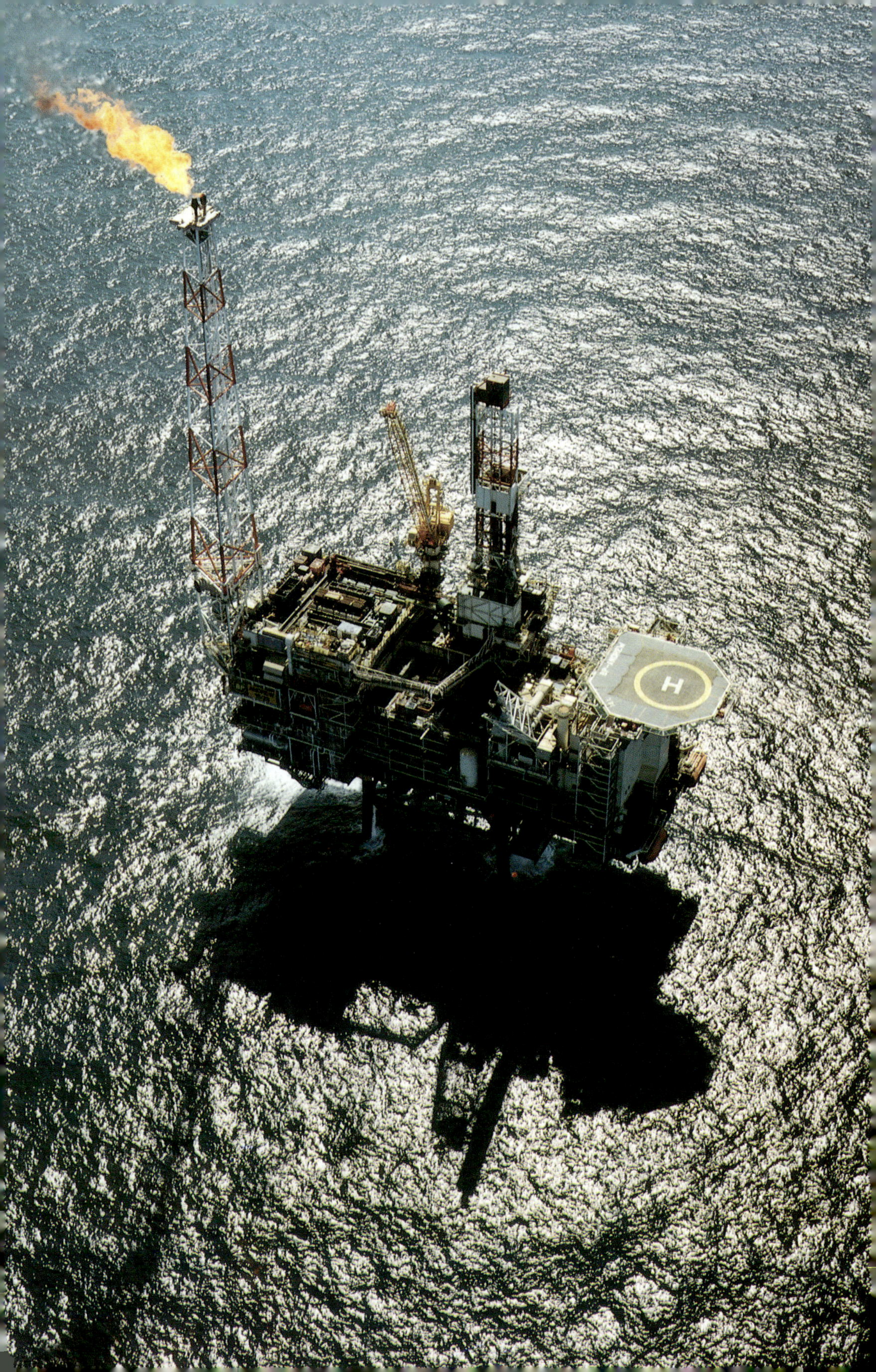

# 13 Corporate, industrial and advertising photography

Corporate, industrial and advertising photography may seem to be a somewhat disparate bunch, but considered in the context of travel they have a lot in common. By corporate and industrial photography, we mean the kind of thing which appears in annual reports and prospectuses, while in this context advertising clearly refers to location shots: studio pictures can almost invariably be shot anywhere in the world, so it usually makes more sense to bring the subject to the photographer rather than bringing the photographer to the subject.

Corporate photography tends to lean more towards people in office environments, while industrial photography is more a matter of factory floors, people making things, and product and plant, but the distinctions are very blurred if they exist at all. Advertising photography tends to be of two kinds, either highly product-oriented (though the 'product' may be an oil refinery or a racing car in the pits) or almost completely divorced from the product: those companies who are perceived as endangering the environment are particularly keen on landscapes in general and pastoral scenes in particular.

The first and most important thing to remember is that in all three cases corporate, industrial and advertising photography – you are still expected (by most clients) to shoot the same kind of pictures as they expect from their domestic photographers hired for the same purposes at home. BP, who kindly supplied pictures for this chapter, is particularly well known for the quality of its industrial and corporate photography, though a photographer who wants to break into this market might be well advised to set his or her sights lower to begin with.

The skills you need are those of any location photographer in these fields, overlaid with the skills which you need in order to work abroad, quite possibly in an unfamiliar language and within an unfamiliar business culture. On the bright side, you should have the countervailing advantage of assistance from your subjects, though this is far from invariably the case, and sometimes you may find your alleged helpers to be downright obstructionist.

In practice, most overseas corporate, industrial and location advertising work goes to photographers who are already known for the same sort of work at home; and often, it will go to photographers who already service the client in question in the domestic market. This is of course assuming that the work is not given to a local photographer in the place where the pictures are to be taken: unless your work has a particular look, a particular originality, there is little reason to hire you and fly you to (say) Paris or Rio de Janeiro, instead of hiring someone locally.

***Figure 13.1*** *Many of the best pictures of drilling platforms are taken from the air, typically from the supply helicopters which shuttle between the rigs and the shore. If you are unusually persuasive, and if you find the right person on the right day, and if you are prepared to sign the appropriate disclaimers and waivers, and if the weather is not too bad, you may be able to shoot this sort of thing for your portfolio; but for the most part, pictures like this one (courtesy of British Petroleum) are shot by specialists who enjoy a good relationship with the oil company.*

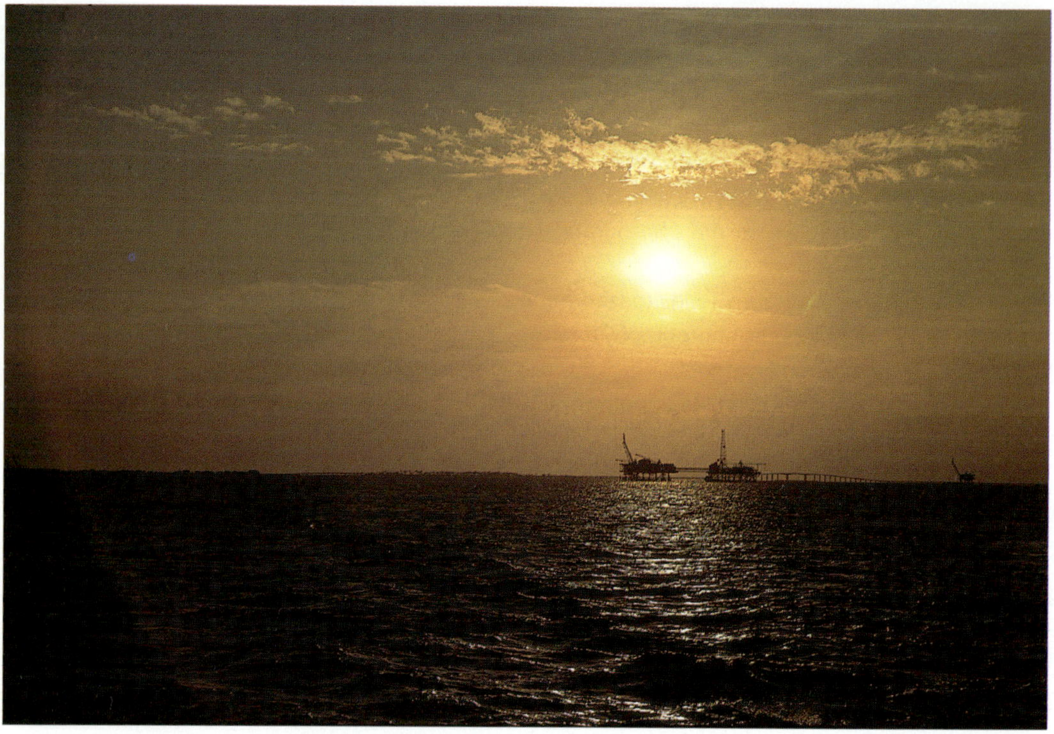

*Figure 13.2 Drilling rigs are inherently visually fascinating, and if your interests lie in the direction of industrial, corporate or advertising photography you will do well to try photographing them. Sometimes, attractive pictures can be obtained surprisingly easily; this was shot from the deck of a public ferry off the southern coast of the United States. (RWH)*

## SPECIALIZATION

By the same token, you are more likely to be assigned to a place where there is little or no chance of hiring a local photographer capable of working to the necessary standards, either because it is a Third World country – in which case, living conditions may be harsh and facilities may be primitive – or simply because the subject is highly specialized.

And specialization is most certainly the name of the game in many areas of corporate and industrial photography. We know one photographer who is an acknowledged ace at photographing petrol stations (gas stations, garage forecourts) and another whose speciality was trucks. Even if someone else was retained to shoot other parts of a corporate report or prospectus, these photographers would be jetted in to shoot their speciality.

On the other hand, there can also be room for the generalist if, as has already been suggested, he or she has a particular vision which can unify a whole report or campaign. Either way, the skills required are so different from the majority of travel photography as to warrant devoting a fair part of this chapter to technical matters.

## EQUIPMENT AND MATERIALS

To begin with, you are normally going to be shooting on medium format or even large format, instead of the 35mm which is all but universal in so many branches of travel photography. This is, quite simply, a matter of technical quality, combined with the expectations of the client; the latter have been summed up in the phrase, 'he's paying a big price, so he expects a big camera'.

Precisely what sort of equipment you use is obviously a matter of your personal choice and of what you already have, but several points are worth making.

Among roll-film SLRs, the Hasselblad is extremely popular with industrial photographers, not just for the superb quality and excellent reliability which endear it to photographers in so many fields, but also because it is so small and light. When you are shooting from a crane bucket, or when you have to climb a steel ladder which is surrounded with a safety cage, or when you have to shoot from a precarious platform; in all of those cases, the small size and weight of a Hasselblad are very welcome. To be sure, there is much to be said for the sheer versatility of a Mamiya RB67 or RZ67, or of a big Fuji, to say nothing of the larger image, and many industrial photographers use them; but with industrial photography, it is very much a case of 'horses for courses' and you need to look hard at your choice of SLR.

Equally, an SLR may not be the best camera. In particular, the Mamiya 7 rangefinder camera is light, fast-handling and easy to use, while delivering a usefully bigger image than a Hasselblad; and some of the best industrial pictures ever taken have been shot with the 'baby' Linhof, which can be used equally as a rangefinder camera (the 'anatomical grip' makes it particularly easy to carry and use) and as a technical camera with movements.

Although 4 × 5 inch is no longer regarded as the norm in industrial photography, as once it was, there can be a good deal to be said for this and for still larger formats. The apparent universality of the monorail can be challenged by the metal field camera or (still more) by the technical camera such as the 4 × 5 inch Linhof Technika or even the long-discontinued MPP. Extreme movements are rarely necessary in commercial, industrial and this sort of advertising photography, so the field or technical camera can provide all the

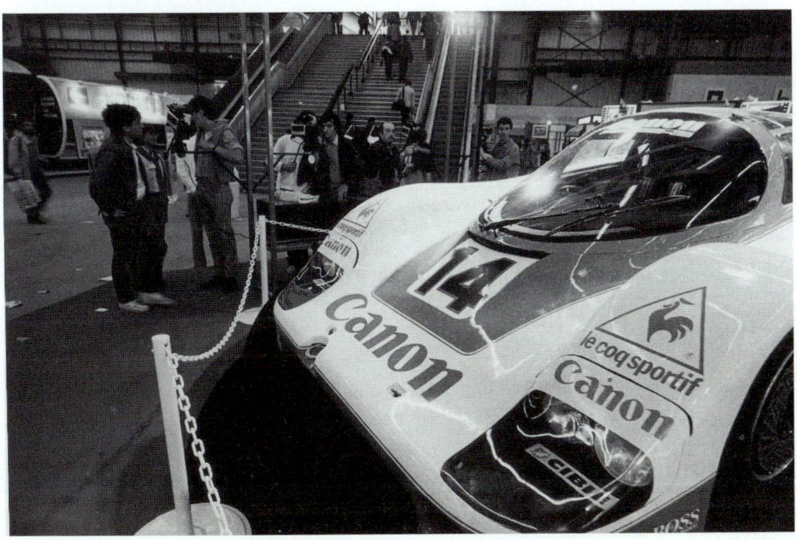


*Figure 13.3 Do not neglect pictures like this if you are building a portfolio to appeal to corporate markets. A reportage, almost snapshot, look might be just the thing to catch the eye of someone who is after something different for the annual report. (RWH)*

movements that are needed, while their big advantages are that they are quick to set up, that they fold away very compactly, and that they are enormously strong. It can even be surprisingly feasible to shoot hand-held 4 × 5, which gives a unique look – always a potential selling point – as well as impressing at least some clients. Really determined extroverts can even shoot 5 × 7 inch hand-held, if they can find a (now discontinued) Linhof Technika in this size.

A useful tip on 4 × 5 inch materials (and 5 × 7, if your tastes run that way) is to shoot colour negative film. To show the client, all you need is a reference print, and for origination, increasing numbers of origination houses can scan straight off a negative. Using negative instead of transparency means, of course, that fine filtration is no longer an issue (colour can be corrected at the printing or scanning stage) and that precise exposure is no longer very critical: as long as you err on the side of over-exposure, you will be all right.

No matter what equipment or materials you may use, dirt and dust are a perennial problem in some kinds of industrial photography in particular, and enclosing the whole camera in a heavy-duty plastic bag can make a lot of sense. Camera cases may also need to be particularly dust-tight, and to afford more than usual protection if you are working in difficult locations.

## LIGHTING

The real nub of a great deal of commercial, industrial and advertising photography is however lighting, and we are indebted to Garry Hume for some of the ideas that follow; he mis-spent a good deal of his youth in photographing large trucks.

Much of the time, you can work by daylight with little or no auxiliary lighting; and even if you do need fill flash, you may need little enough that it can be achieved with a reasonably powerful on-camera flash, something like a Metz 60. Very often, though, you can get a much better picture by shooting early in the morning or around sunset, because you get dramatic skies. Also, there are times when

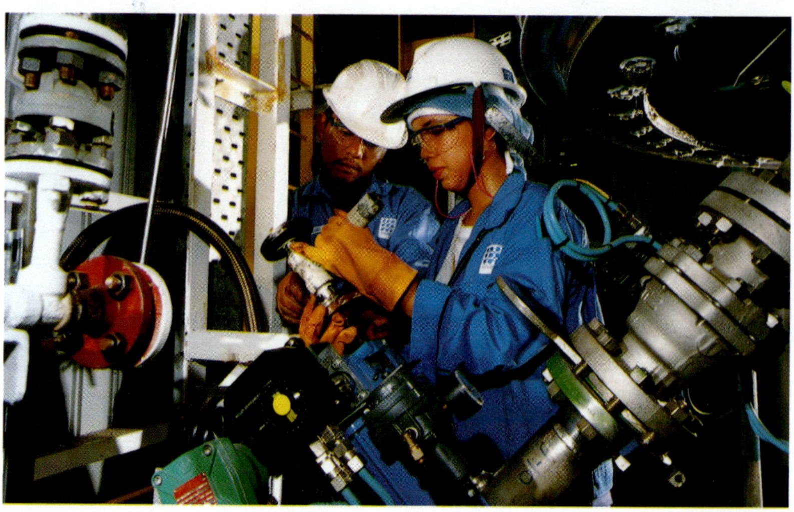

***Figure 13.4*** *An important point in industrial shots showing people is that they must be wearing any appropriate protective equipment. Note the hard hats, safety glasses and gloves in this picture – and remember that there is always someone who wants to leave them off! It is not always possible to convey to the non-expert exactly what is going on, but the valves, motors and pipes show very clearly that this is a sparkling, high-tech plant. It is in Kertih in Malaysia, and appears courtesy of British Petroleum.*

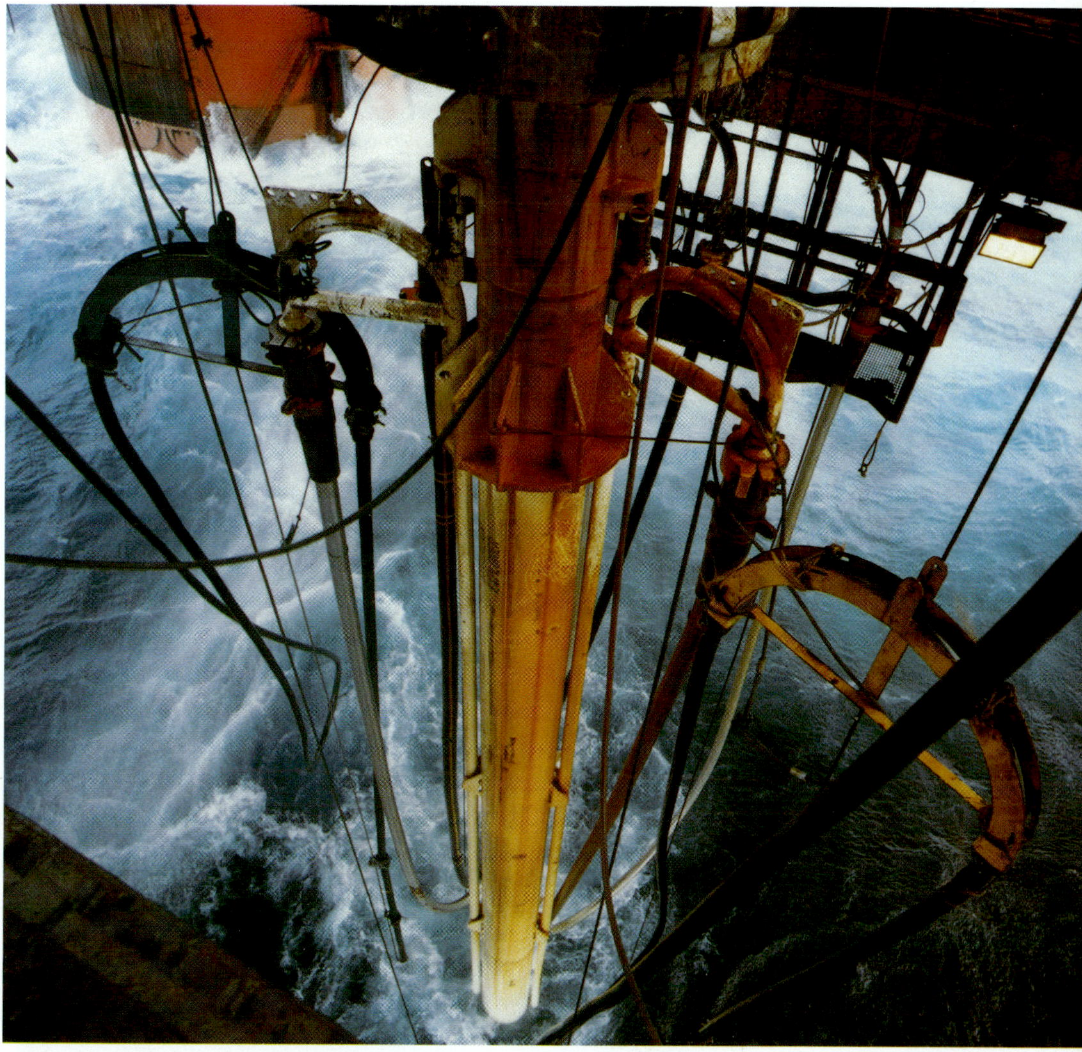

either practical or aesthetic considerations dictate that you must shoot at these times, or even at night. Then there are interiors, often ill-lit, and there are occasions when you need to add a lot of light to a particular area of a subject.

Sometimes you can get mains power, and work with conventional electronic flash units, though the difficulty often lies in getting enough light. Out of doors, or inside a large building, even 1000 Watt-seconds is soon swallowed up, and carting about large numbers of 1000 Watt-second monobloc heads or (worse still) 2000 Watt-second power packs with separate heads is difficult and expensive.

The next choice, therefore, is normally a generator plus continuous lighting. Provided movement is not a problem, you can do a surprising amount with a 5 kilowatt 'jenny' and a few tungsten lights – though we have met people who have used 10 kW and even 20 kW jennies on location. The noise tends to be deafening, though.

***Figure 13.5*** *Some pictures can be taken at a distance, without special facilities. This is not one of them. In order to get a shot like this – described in the caption as 'Onboard semi-submersible rig "Sovereign Explorer" drilling in the Foinaven Field, west of Shetland' – you need careful planning, consider-able cooperation, and a good awareness of safety procedures. (Photograph courtesy of British Petroleum.)*

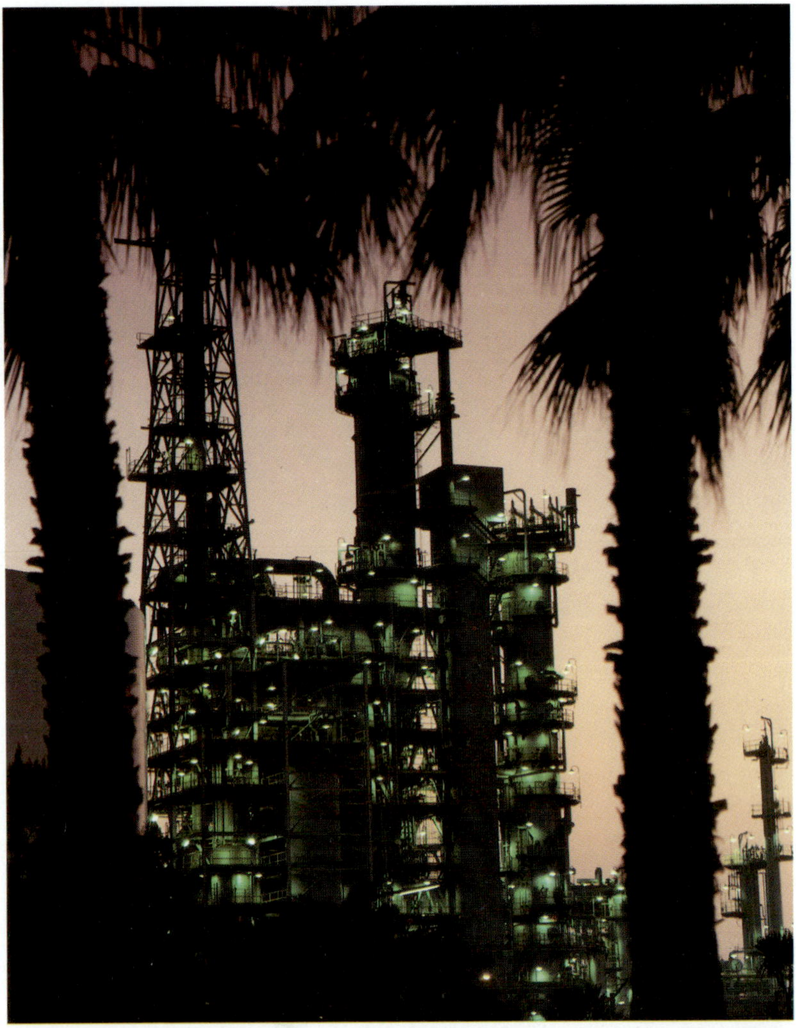

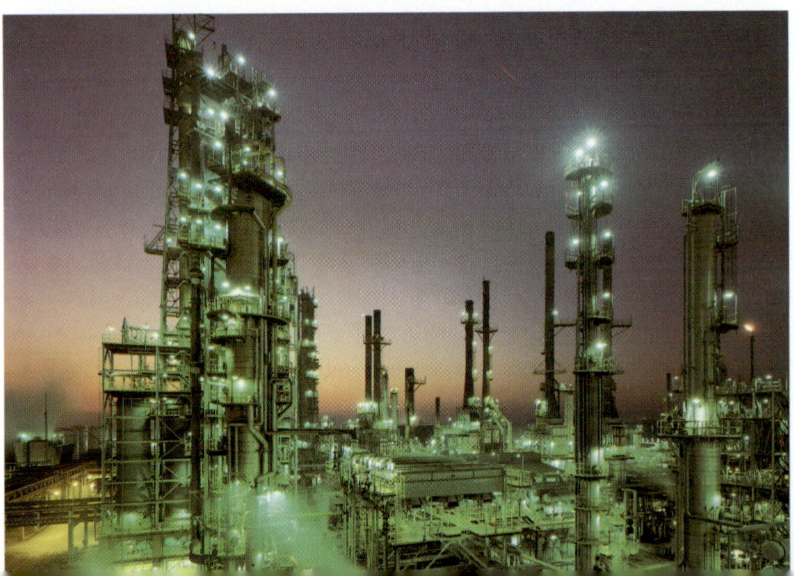

*Figure 13.6* Castellon Refinery, Spain. *Refineries at dawn or dusk are fascinating subjects, brightly lit, often wreathed in steam or condensation, sometimes punctuated with brilliant flares of burning-off gas. It is sometimes possible to get good night shots too (i.e. with a true dark sky), but daylight shots are much more difficult. The shot with the palm trees is an unusual variant, and might well attract attention simply because it is a less usual sort of shot. (Both photographs courtesy of British Petroleum.)*

Where serious power is required, there arguably remains no better choice than seriously powerful flashbulbs, which were still readily available at the time of writing. A single big bulb is roughly comparable with a 1250 W-s electronic flash, and it is quite feasible to use two or three clusters of three (or more) bulbs each, plus two or three others as effects lights. Ten bulbs is pretty much like having 10 000 to 15 000 W-s of electronic flash, and there is no particular reason (apart from the cost) why you should not double that; a single bulb costs about the same as a single sheet of 4 × 5 inch film.

Metering is however a major problem with single-use bulbs. For obvious reasons, you do not want to fire off (say) a dozen bulbs, just to take a meter reading, so considerable experience plus careful calculation can be required in order to get into the right ball-park; and even then, you will need to be uncommonly self-confident not to shoot a Polaroid first.

A traditional trick is to bracket exposures using two cameras, on open flash: even if there is some movement, it need not be obtrusive, and it is possible to adjust some double cable releases so that the shutter of the first camera opens a fraction before the shutter of the second, which is synchronized to the flash. With a little experience, this can be done reliably at speeds of ⅛ second or less, at which point ambient light should rarely be a problem.

Whenever possible, it is of course desirable to shoot brackets – normally, two on the button, one at one under, and one at one over – and together with the Polaroid this translates into five sets of bulbs unless you are using two cameras, in which case you can do it with three sets. Speed adjustment in processing is then used to get the exposure spot on; one of the middle exposures is processed normally, and with a realistic range of a one-stop pull to (in desperation) a two-stop push, you have an effective range of –2 to +3 stops around your metered or calculated exposure. Alternatively, of course, you can shoot colour negative and simply over-expose.

An unconsidered problem of big flash, though, is that it is literally blinding when used in this sort of quantity. Garry tells the story of shooting a truck by a motorway bridge under construction, using about a dozen bulbs. After the third shot, he was told politely but firmly that he had finished. When he protested, the point was made more forcefully. The men working on the site were losing their night vision for several minutes after each flash, and the after-images were persisting for a good deal longer than that. Where people can simply stop work if they are temporarily blinded, this is not necessarily a great problem; but it does not take a great deal of imagination to create a scenario where big flash could be very dangerous indeed.

In sum, although commercial, industrial and advertising are very specialized areas of travel photography, they are also the best-paying, and we have met photographers who sustain a very comfortable lifestyle indeed on the strength of their skills in these areas. All three are arguably more disciplined and more technically demanding than almost any other aspect of travel, but this is definitely reflected in the rewards available.

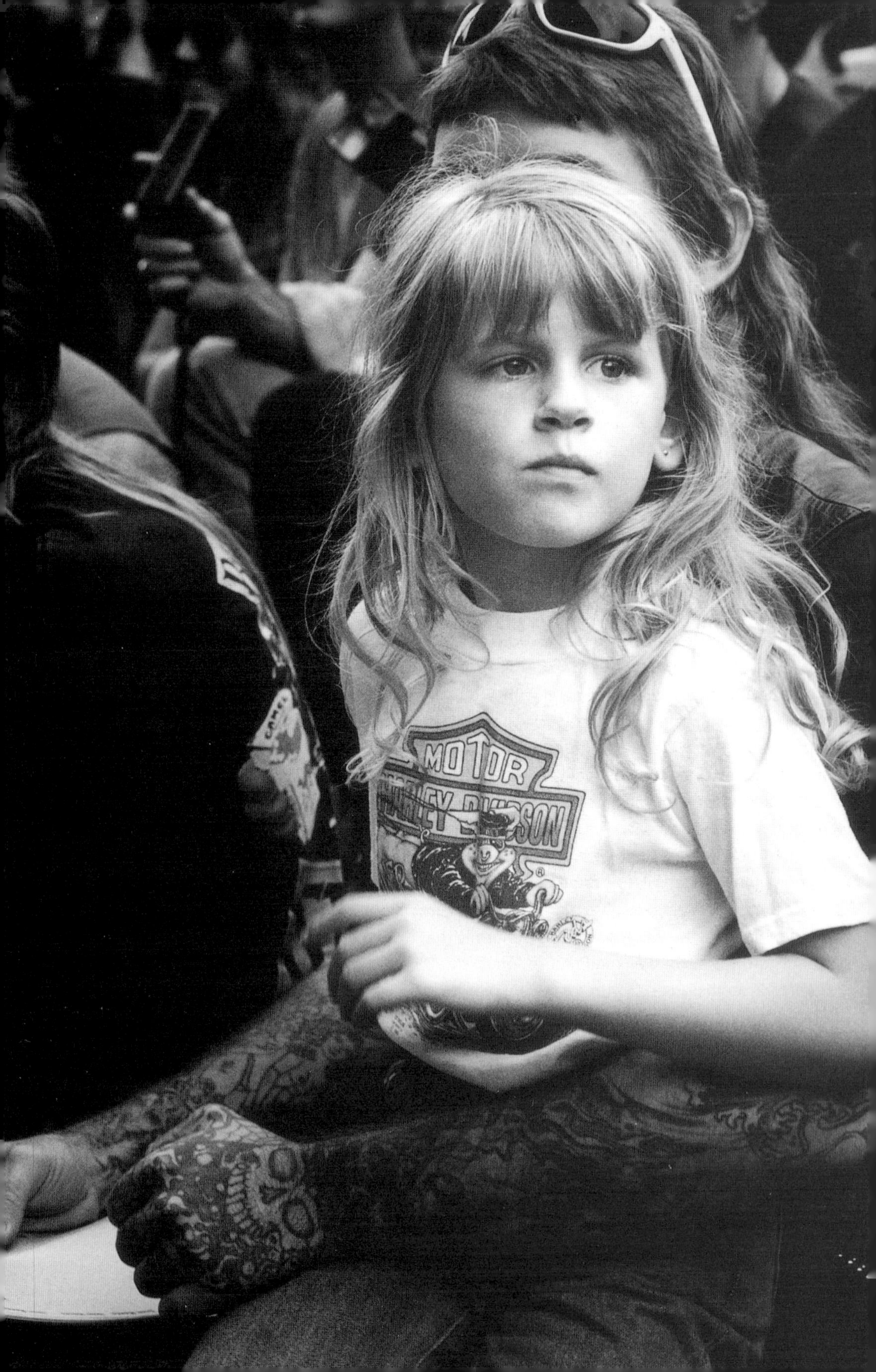
MOTOR

# 14 Reportage

It is possible to make distinctions between reportage, photojournalism and news photography, and some people exercise themselves greatly in trying to do so; but in general, the only practical differences are between 'hard' news and 'soft' news. Even then, there is plenty of crossover.

The majority of hard news pictures are extremely time-sensitive, and have little staying power. The archetypal hard news pictures are 'doorsteps' and 'grip and grins'. 'Doorsteps' are people in the news, entering and leaving buildings; getting them consists mainly of waiting for long periods, then hurriedly shooting someone who either does not want to be photographed, or will devote only as much time to the photographers as is expedient. 'Grip and grins', on the other hand, are made with the connivance of the subjects. Memorably described by Claire Leavey as 'pictures of grown men holding hands', they traditionally centre on the handshake which symbolizes the completion of a business deal, a treaty, a successful negotiation, an election, or anything else where both parties are feeling more or less pleased with themselves. To be harsh, many hard news pictures are there to hold the words apart, breaking up what would otherwise be large areas of grey text.

Soft news pictures, on the other hand, are considerably less time-sensitive, but they mostly have to be considerably more interesting pictures in their own right. Instead of being a bare representation of a person or (less often) a place, they try to tell the reader something about context and history and background.

The overlap arises principally because there is a continuous spectrum between hard news and pure froth. If war breaks out, or a president or a prime minister is assassinated, or a princess dies, this is real, hard news: it is something which most people want to know more about. At the other extreme, there are increasing numbers of solipsistic columnists who have little or nothing to say, but say it at great length. In between, there is news of minor international interest – remember the famous headline, guaranteed to deter readers in a British paper, of 'Small earthquake in Chile, not many killed' – and there is a curious brand of pseudo-news about 'celebrities', who, as mentioned elsewhere, are best defined as 'people who are famous for being famous'.

But even a celebrity, in whom there is constant low-level interest, can become hard news if he or she does something genuinely interesting or scandalous, or dies; so the whole gamut of reportage is well confused.

**Figure 14.1** Young girl, Iron Horse Saloon, Daytona. *Since this picture was taken, Ilford's XP2 chromogenic film has been challenged by Kodak's T400CN. Both offer an excellent speed/grain ratio, with lower grain in the critical light mid tones than in the shadows – but more importantly, both offer tremendous latitude, and if rated at EI 200 instead of EI 400 they can take two stops' over-exposure and two stops' under-exposure while still delivering superb quality. (FES)*

## News and public opinion

From the photographer's point of view, the important thing in all cases is that a really good picture (or set of pictures) can powerfully influence public opinion, creating the public mood as much as catching it. This is true whether you are talking about hard news – few will ever forget the memorable picture of the execution of a suspected Viet Cong sympathizer – or about matters which really are of somewhat limited interest. For example, rumours and even factual reports of illicit (or for that matter licit) romances are one thing; but a photograph of a couple together, or better still a kiss or some other expression of love or lust, somehow attracts people's attention more.

The power of pictures is an extremely interesting subject for speculation, as the more you think about it, the more puzzling it becomes. The importance of shock value is not hard to understand, and war pictures often have this quality; but when a picture is not shocking, it is curious that people who would not look twice at the written word will look at the picture and then read the article which accompanies it. This is however not the place for such ruminations. What is more important is what sort of pictures sell, and how they are obtained.

Even doorstepping can produce excellent pictures, if you can capture the right expression of elation or dejection (or arrogance or weariness or whatever), or the right little girl presenting a bouquet of flowers, or the right conspiratorial aside, but doorstepping (like shooting grip and grin pictures) is pretty much the same skill the world over. Traditionally, except for the most important subjects, such shots were assigned to the local stringer; when the people were important enough, a staff photographer might be flown out.

The freelance travel photographer who wishes to specialize in reportage will generally do better with a picture set than with an individual picture, though (as noted elsewhere) an individual picture may surprisingly often be abstracted from a set and run as a single image. The real key to success in freelance travel reportage, no matter what you are shooting, lies principally in understanding the subject.

## Life and Death

Understanding the subject can literally be a matter of life and death. If in a war zone you make the wrong greeting, or betray what appear to be the wrong sympathies, you may be inviting death or imprisonment. But even if you are doorstepping celebrities, you need to know the politics and cast: who is whose lover, who is whose friend, who is whose bodyguard. This means that you have to take a real interest in the subject, whether or not that interest would exist independently of your desire to take pictures of the subject and to sell those pictures.

War photography is perhaps the purest (or at least the most dramatic) form of reportage, and the simple truth is that most of the greatest war photographers of the twentieth century have succeeded principally by taking risks. Many have died, and their successors continue to die today. They generally begin young, when (like most young people) they have a fairly firm belief in their own immortality, and they discover a talent for photography. In some cases, they would never achieve any fame or notoriety if it were not for their chosen subject matter. In other cases, the pressure of war acts as a forcing-

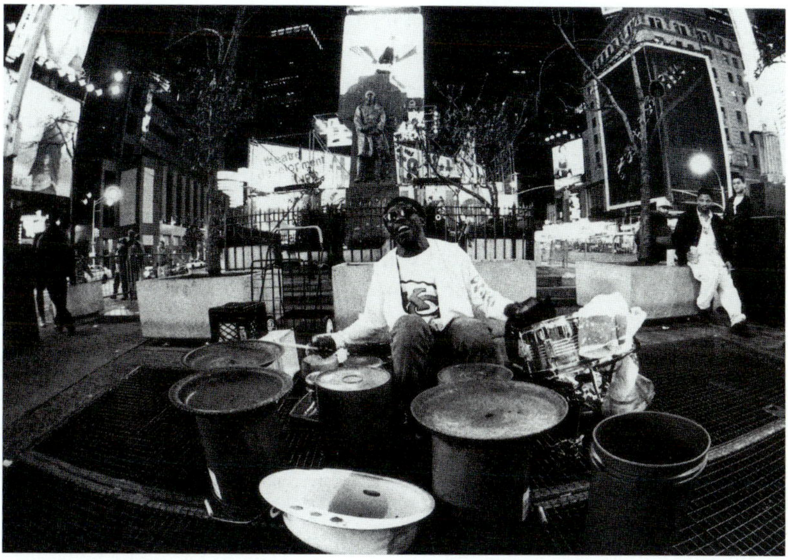

***Figure 14.2*** *We much prefer ultra-fast film to flash: this drummer in New York City was shot with Kodak TMZ P3200, rated at EI 12,500. With such speed, it is possible to hand-hold the camera even in very poor light and even with a relatively slow lens, in this case a Sigma 15mm f/2.8 fish-eye. As well as giving pictures which look more natural, fast film is much less disruptive than flash, and you do not have to wait for the flash to recycle. (FES)*

house for their talent: they become great photographers, far quicker than would otherwise have happened. And in yet other cases, they seem to come fully-fledged to war photography, as if it were a special talent which had only been waiting for the right circumstances – a war – to be revealed.

Like most photographers, too, war photographers tend to find their métier by accident. In some curious way, they may not even be tied to the subject of war. Although there are some who roam the globe, seeking out wars here, there, and everywhere, others seem almost by accident to have been somewhere where there was a war going on, and to have photographed that. Tim Page, one of the master chroniclers of the Vietnam War, was essentially a wandering hippie who found himself in the middle of a war. Since the end of the Vietnam War, South East Asia has continued to fascinate him, and he returns regularly to cover other stories in the area: the drug trade, reconstruction, economic rebirth.

Although much war photography is the hardest of hard news, there is also the undeniable fact that the logistical exigences of covering a war will mean that when the pictures are published, they are treated more in the nature of a feature. Gail Fisher of the *Los Angeles Times* has covered a number of war-related topics in Eastern Europe; she goes away for a while, shoots the pictures, then comes back and puts the story together.

Most war photographers are a fund of extraordinary stories. Gail Fisher tells of sheltering in wine cellars in a war zone, sharing the simplest of food but drinking rare vintages. It is all, without doubt, wonderfully romantic. But it is also extremely dangerous, and it can exert a literally fatal fascination over people who really can't hack it – and who, if they are lucky, simply blow a great deal of money on going somewhere exceptionally unpleasant, lose all their equipment, and come back without any pictures. If they are unlucky, they die.

*Figure 14.3* Cafe, Aosta. *Photos which pander to people's prejudices are often successful, and this one has it all: the handsome, well-dressed gentleman of a certain age in his dark glasses, the fascist-era architecture, the café tables, the perfect sense of Italian style pervading the whole thing. It could be used either 'straight', or slightly self-mockingly. (RWH)*

Even the ones who can hack it may also die. Tim Page was so badly wounded by 'friendly fire' that he was pronounced dead on arrival at hospital. Admittedly, being pronounced d-o-a was something he already had experience of (the first time was after a motorcycle accident), but it is only the fact that there is a certain indestructibility about the man which allowed him to survive: in the vast majority of cases, the diagnosis would have been accurate. His friend Sean Flynn, also a war photographer, did die in Vietnam.

If you want to shoot war, you already know why, and you already know that nothing that anyone can tell you will deter you. From a purely business viewpoint, you will be less well placed than people like Tim Page or Don McCullin. *Life* set the style for picture-oriented news magazines in the late 1930s, and although there was still plenty of serious still photography around at the time of the Vietnam War, it was by then television which provided most people with most of their news. Today, the markets are negligible, and the Sunday supplements which were arguably the last great outlets for serious reportage are now paeans to the consumer society, filled for the most part with gardening advice and fashion. Only the newspapers themselves are a real market, and competition is fierce.

Today, the actual technical side is not particularly demanding. With the arrival of ever-increasing automation; with the widespread acceptance of 35mm colour negative film as the standard medium for reportage; and with ever-cheaper mass travel, it has never been easier to turn in competent pictures of shocking subjects.

As a result, there are still plenty of young photographers who imagine that they can make their name in a war zone. At the time of writing, Bosnia was probably the favourite destination. But the sad truth was that there were so many young photographers trying to make their names in Bosnia that most newspapers and magazines refused to take them seriously. The only way to get someone's attention was to show them extraordinary photographs, and the best way to get extraordinary photographs for most people is to take extraordinary risks – which is also, of course, the best way to get killed.

Two other factors also influence the ease with which one can become a war photographer. One is that all the parties to wars are now a lot more skilled at news management than they were. Everyone wants to put the right spin on the news, so that they come out as the good guys and their opponents come out as the bad guys. Of course, this was always the case; but now, people are more aware of it, and try to do it more consciously.

A second factor is the ever-increasing improvement of battlefield communications. The 'fog of war' still exists, without question, but it refers principally to one's lack of knowledge about what the other side is doing. Centralized command and control are now very much more efficient than they used to be, and if the commander does not want a photographer in a particular place, then his or her chances of getting to that place are greatly reduced.

To be sure, there are still features on wars in many magazines and newspapers, but the chances of fame and fortune are slimmer than ever, while

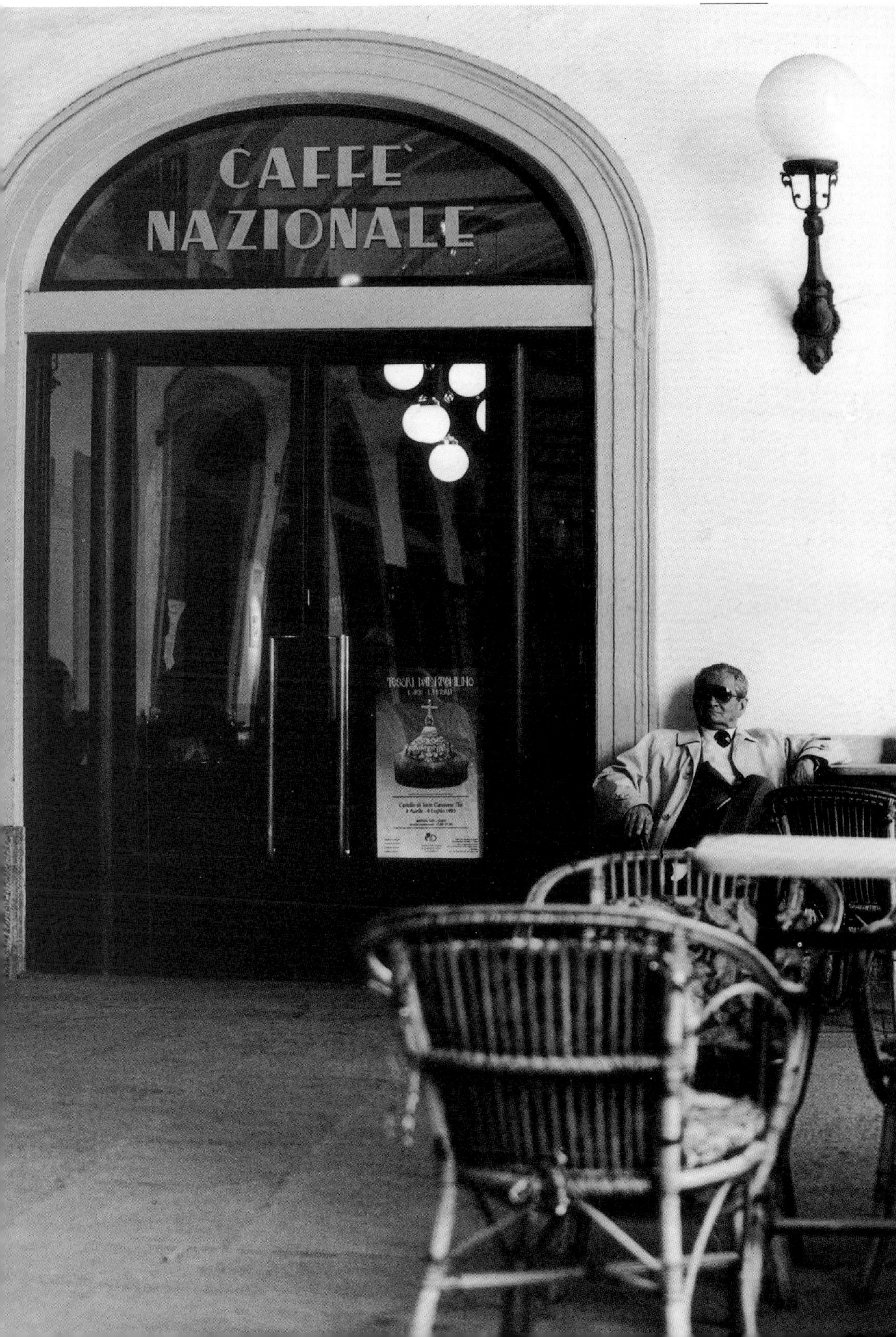
CAFFE`
NAZIONALE

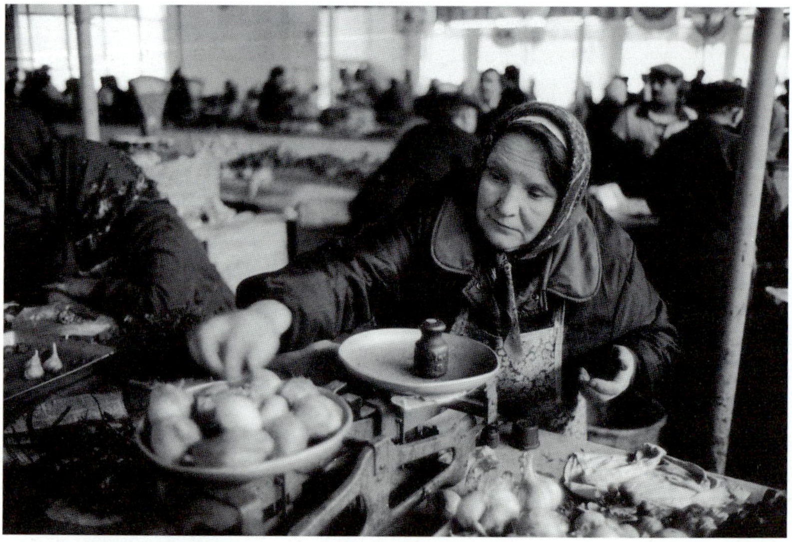

***Figure 14.4*** *It is always disputable whether it is better to use flash, which is easy and allows plenty of depth of field while 'freezing' movement, or available light, which may require longer shutter speeds and faster lenses at wider apertures but allows more of the surroundings to be seen. This picture of a garlic seller could probably be shot equally well either way, though we prefer to see the market hall behind the main subject, even if it is out of focus, instead of the murk which would have backed a flash picture. (RWH)*

the chances of sudden death are at least as great as ever they were, and quite possibly greater.

## Paparazzi

For fame and fortune (and obloquy and opprobrium), perhaps a better example of reportage would be the so-called paparazzi. We say 'so-called' because the term is neither clearly defined, nor particularly susceptible of clear definition. The paradigm case of the paparazzi must surely be their obsession with the Princess of Wales, culminating in her death. Of course, their obsession was no more than a distillation of the obsession of millions of readers, world-wide, who eagerly purchase the most intrusive pictures while tut-tutting over the way in which they were obtained.

Whether the activities of the paparazzi were a contributing factor to Diana's death or not – and many would argue that a thoroughly drunk driver was a rather more important consideration – they well illustrate a number of things. One is the enormous amounts of money to be made. The right picture of the right person can earn literally millions, as was reputedly the case with a picture of the Princess of Wales kissing Dodi al-Fayed a few weeks before their deaths.

Another important point is the blurring of the distinction between news of world events, and news of celebrities. Diana was the celebrity par excellence: a picture of an unknown person in a gymnasium, or on a jet-ski, would have had no news value whatsoever. Yet another point is that for this sort of picture, content repeatedly triumphs over technique and aesthetics. As long as a picture is recognizable, and shows something which titillates people's interest, that is all that is required. It is salutary to remember that a blurred, grainy but recognizable picture of the right person will earn far more money than a technically and aesthetically superb picture of almost anything else.

The relevance of the paparazzi to travel photography is fairly simple, in that there are a number of places where celebrities are likely to be fairly easy to capture, and they are mostly quite pleasant resorts. It may be an odd way to make a living, and it may not make you many friends (though without the paparazzi, many celebrities would sink without trace, so there is a pact between the two). Like war photography, it has its risks, and like war photography, the photographic skills required are not necessarily very great: once again, automation and colour negative films cover a multitude of shortcomings.

## THE BUSINESS SIDE

Viewed as a business undertaking, the principal disadvantages are that fast, long lenses are very expensive, and may in the nature of the job be lost, damaged or destroyed; that in some countries, fines and bribes are a way of life; that competition is fierce; and that income tends to be 'boom or bust', so you can be living in a flea-pit on the day you make the million-dollar shot. It is not realistic to say that paparazzi 'are not photographers', because the same criterion would reveal that many columnists are not journalists, that many chauffeurs are not drivers, and so forth. Even those paparazzi who are reviled as the lowest of the low will be treated with remarkable respect if they have a picture which someone wants.

Most other forms of travel photojournalism are less extreme than either war photography or joining the paparazzi, and the same general observations apply as are repeated throughout this book. It can be very hard to draw the distinction between a general travel article, a specialist travel article, and a news travel article. Again taking one of Gail Fisher's stories, on the renaissance of the church in Russia, one could view it as a general travel article (many people are interested in Russia, and this is an aspect of life in Russia); or as a specialist travel article (do not neglect the size of the religious market – though religious publications may pay very poorly); or as a news travel article (in that this describes a change which is taking place in an important part of the world).

One last category of travel photojournalism does however warrant mention, and this is typified by a single magazine with an enormous circulation: *National Geographic*. Sophisticated readers may look down upon the middlebrow ethnography, and not all photographers may be particularly impressed with the pictures. The fact is, however, that the circulation is enormous and the pay can be very good indeed. Normally, the photographers (and journalists) spend a great deal of time with their subjects, so expenses are high too, and there is little point in trying to shoot for *National Geographic* 'on spec': commissioned work is the route. The publishers are remarkably open-minded about ideas, and about photographers: they will use anyone whose work is good enough, and which fits their needs, so there is no need to worry about gaining admission to a secret clique or inner circle. Competition is however extremely fierce, and we cannot help feeling that if you are ready to work with *National Geographic*, you do not really need this book.

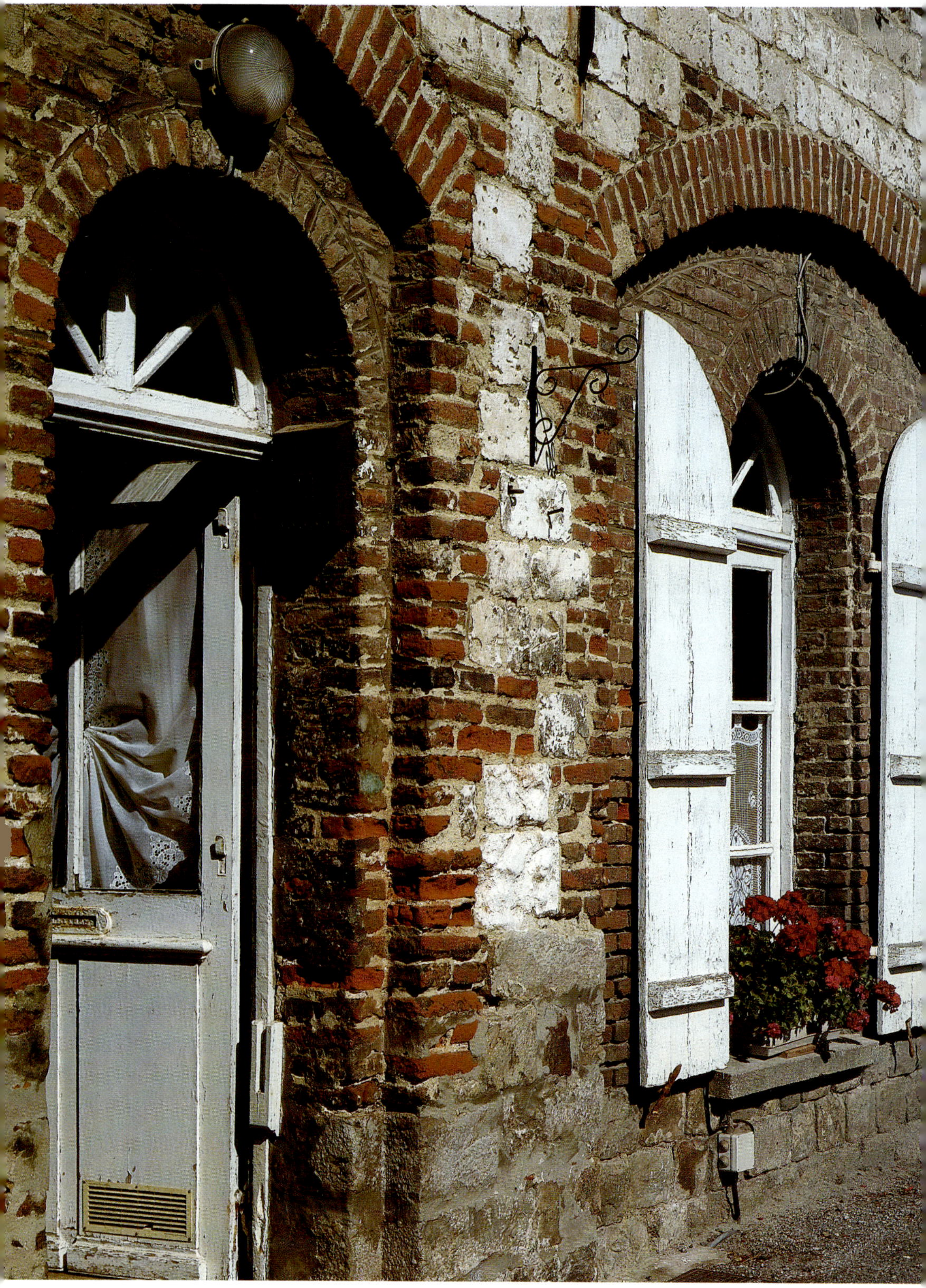

# 15 Photo tours

The popularity of photo tours is explained by a single question. It is this. How did you learn to take pictures?

For most people, the answer is that they began by blind experiment; then started to read books and magazines; and then began to refine their expertise and technique by a combination of practice and reading. Some, a rather smaller proportion, study the subject at college, either in its own right or as a part of a larger course. A few take evening classes, and then there are always the camera clubs. But a resource of ever-increasing importance is the photographic tour or short course.

These are extensively advertised in the photographic press, and seem to be growing steadily in popularity. Broadly, they fall into two categories: those where there are photographic opportunities, and those where there is photographic tuition. For our purposes, we need to consider both kinds, from both sides of the counter: as participant, and as leader.

A seeming paradox immediately arises. For the professional, the kind without tuition is likely to prove the most useful; leading a tour like this is much more a question of being a professional travel courier, and of sorting out the hassles and problems of often inexperienced travellers, than of being a professional photographer. But equally, participating in the kind with tuition is likely to be of limited interest to the would-be professional travel photographer, as the level of tuition is normally aimed at the (fairly well-to-do) amateur. Here, leading the tour is likely to be of considerably more interest.

***Figure 15.1*** House in wall of church, Montreuil. *Novices at architectural photography frequently need guidance on striking a balance between getting everything in, and choosing significant details. Many will try to show too much in a single image, and others will choose details which in isolation tell you very little about the overall subject. (RWH)*

## Photo opportunities

The first kind of tour, the one without tuition but with photo opportunities, does however have two or possibly even three significant advantages over other types of travel photography.

To begin with, it allows you to concentrate on taking pictures. The courier or tour leader takes care of all the accommodation and most of the other practical details. If you can afford the extra cost of a trip like this – and remember, you are paying for the tour leader's trip and remuneration, plus the operators' profit – then it can be an excellent introduction to some of the more demanding destinations, which you might later wish to re-visit under your own steam with fewer restrictions on your time. We owe a good deal of our insight into this side of the market to Roger Williams, who leads this sort of tour for a major American operator and has led tours to Tibet, Nepal, South East Asia, and many other places. Luxury may or may not be a part of the agenda, but if you are camping, you will generally be able to rely on porters, cooked meals, and all sorts of other things which look very like luxuries when you have been trekking all day at 3000 metres (10 000 feet).

The second great advantage

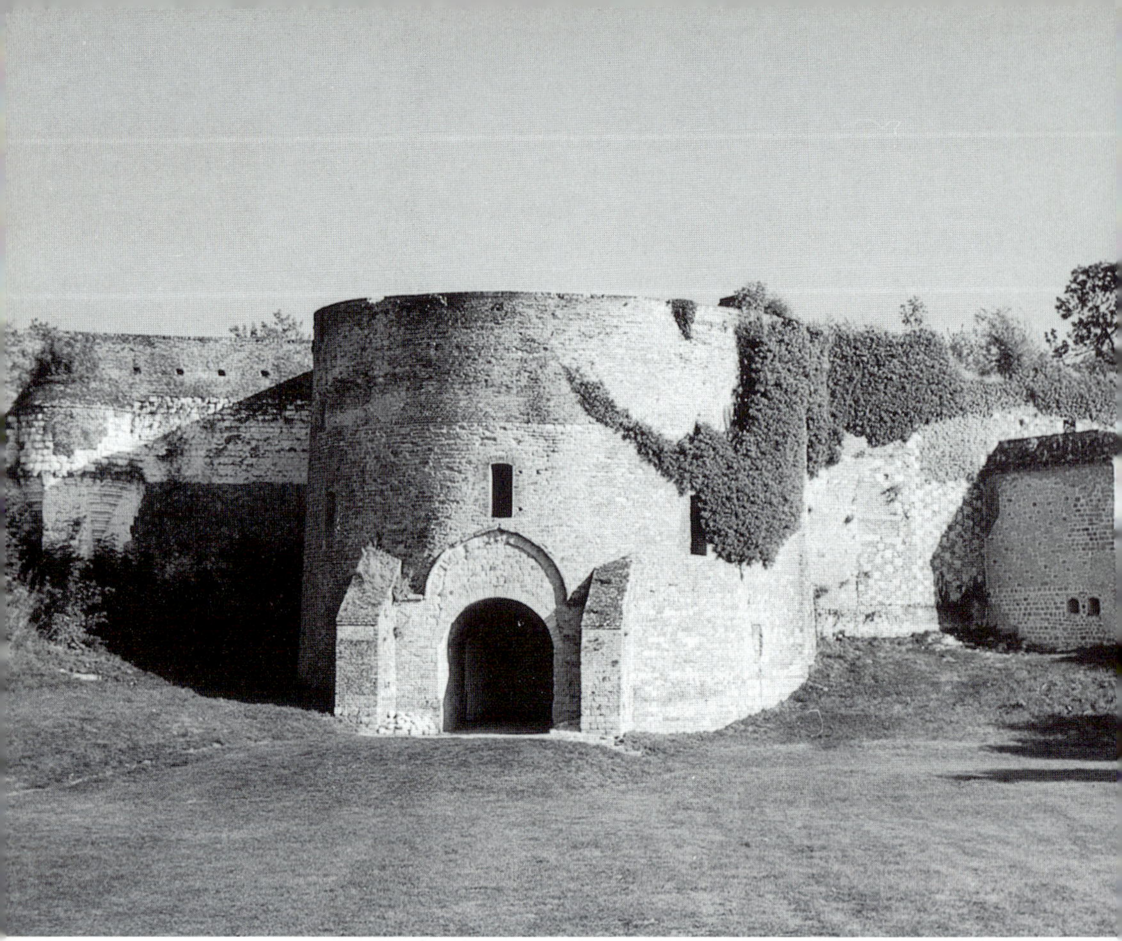

is that you can sometimes gain access to places which would be difficult or impossible for an avowed photographer travelling on his or her own. There are a number of regimes which will deny or restrict access to anyone whom they may suspect of being a journalist (including photojournalists), but who will admit tour groups. Provided you write 'company director' or 'teacher' or 'housewife' on your visa application form, you can get in comparatively easily and your movements may well be less controlled. You may need to give some thought to the equipment you carry, and to any identification you carry in your wallet: we would dump our press cards, our Ilford Pro cards, and so forth. But equally, many modern amateurs are equipped with bigger and more up-to-date outfits than many professionals, so you are unlikely to experience problems in the area.

The possible third advantage is that you can see exactly the kind of people who will be looking at your pictures if they are published: your fellow travellers constitute a sort of free market research.

## Tours with tuition

Moving on to the variety which offers tuition, these can again be divided into two categories. Many – perhaps most – are centred on fixed venues. They are in effect hotels with darkrooms and processing facilities, and the majority of

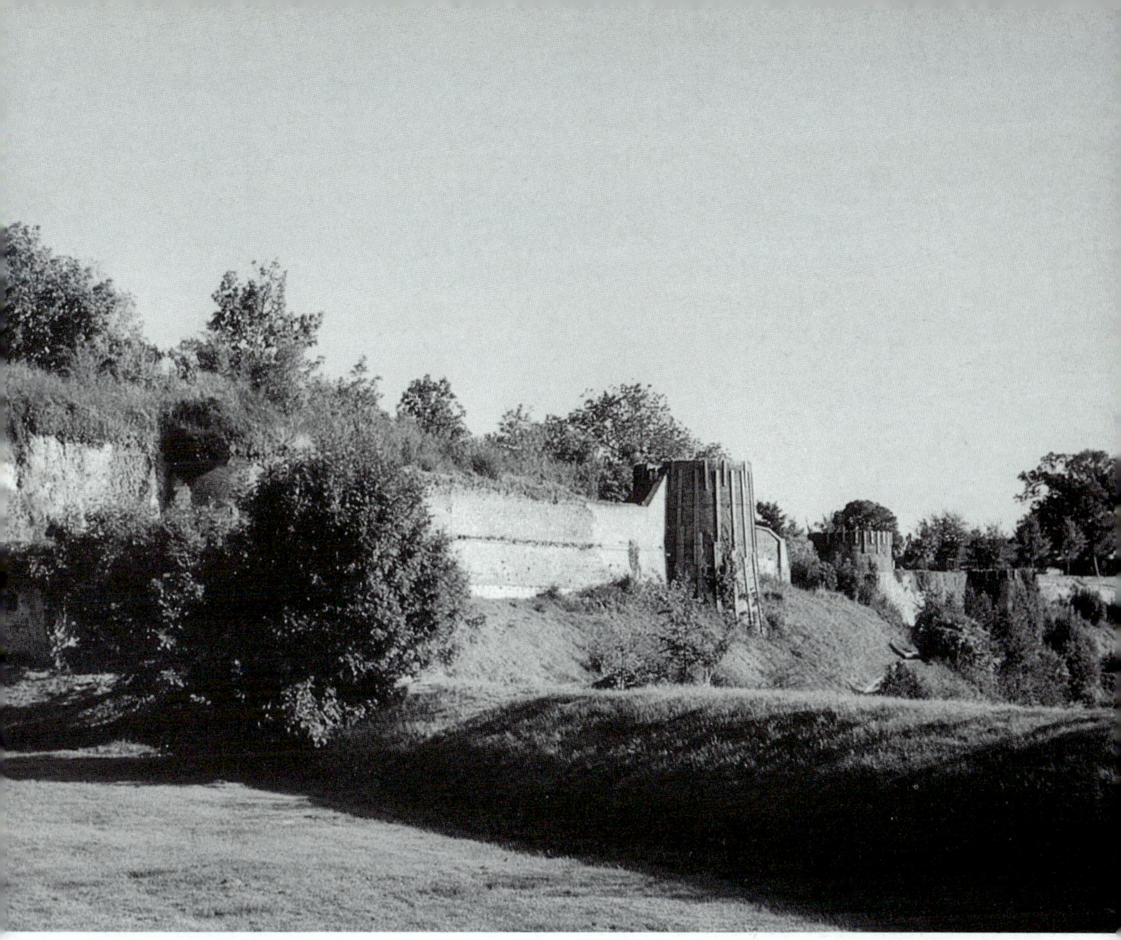

the courses are run by the proprietors. The main thing which makes them of interest is that many of them also have guest course leaders, whether to cover topics on which the proprietor is shaky, to provide additional courses on specific topics, or simply for variety.

From what we have been able to discover (the proprietors are understandably reluctant to divulge too much about their businesses), the guest course leaders are quite modestly paid, though of course their bed and board is provided.

## Running your own courses

If you can get on the wavelength of the people who attend courses, there is a very good chance that they will want to come on your courses, which you organize yourself and where you will see a significantly better chunk of the overall income.

What you need in order to organize a course is a venue, and processing facilities. The need for the latter can restrict the former, though the problems are not necessarily as great as they might seem. The type of venue will depend on the type of course that you want to run. Week-end courses, even long week-ends, can afford to be mostly in the form of lectures, or of lectures in the morning followed by shooting in the afternoon. A popular format is a lecture

**Figure 15.2** Panorama of citadel, Montreuil. *With a high quality roll-film camera, panoramic enlargements from sections of the negative are entirely feasible: enlargements to 50 cm or 20 inches wide are around 7 × from the Linhof 56 × 72 mm format. This allows several points to be made: how to compose for panoramas, the availability of a 'free' rising front (via cropping), actual versus nominal formats, and more. All you need to do is scout out the locations… (RWH)*

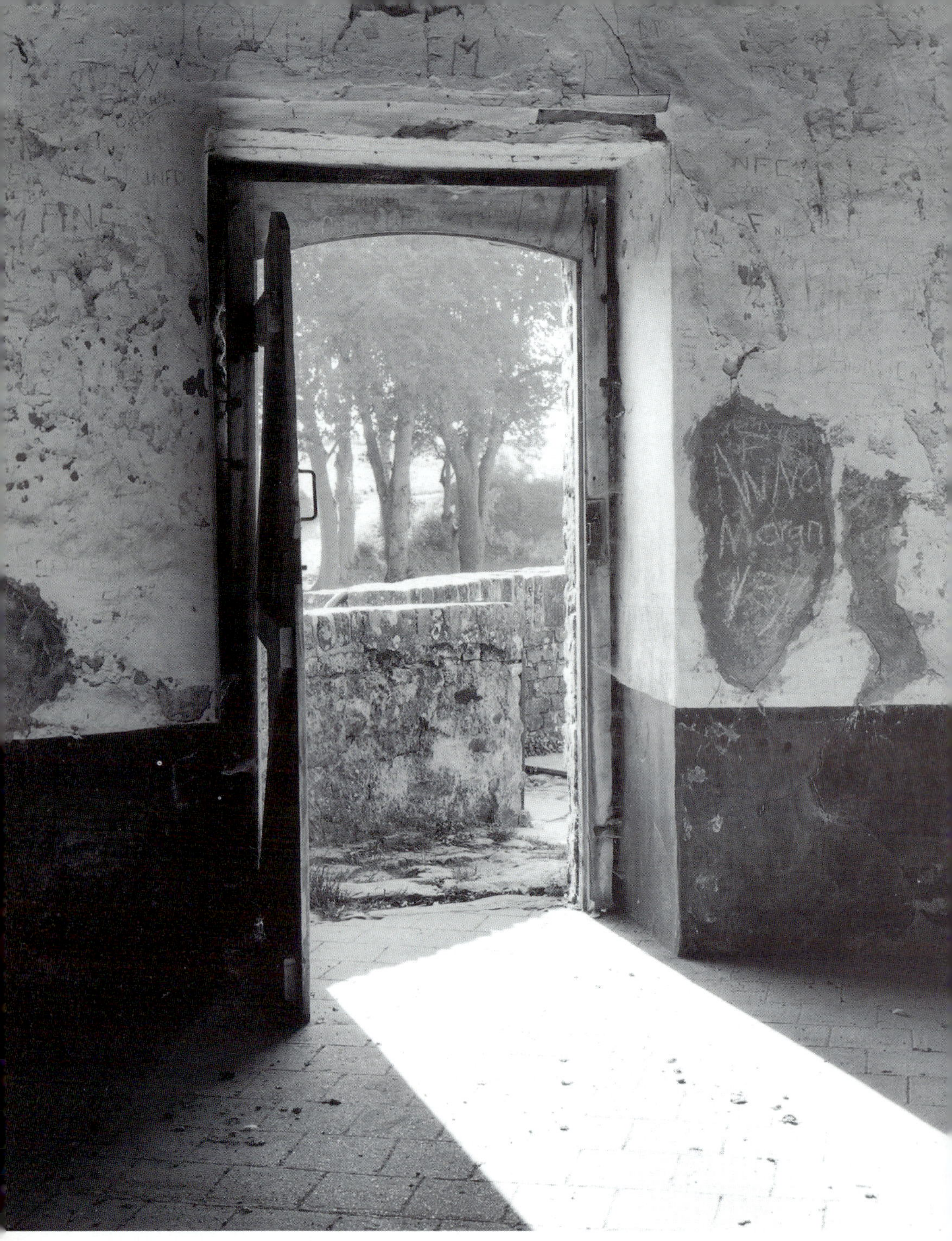


***Figure 15.3*** Door in tower, Montreuil. *Scout out as many places as possible – and work out how best to illustrate them. In this one shot alone you can see the raw material for discussions on texture; dodging and burning; using different contrast grades in one print; reducing development time to accommodate a wide range of subject brightness; and (of course) exposure determination. What is more, several of these points can be made even if the weather is not as sunny as it was on this day. (RWH)*

in the morning, individual shooting in the afternoon, and critique in the evening. Longer courses will typically involve less in the way of formal lectures, but more in the way of accompanied tours.

This means that you need sleeping accommodation; somewhere to eat; and somewhere to lecture and criticize. The first two are fairly easy, though you may have to give serious thought to what sort of lunch (if any) is to be provided, but the last can be trickier. If you choose the right place at the right time of year, you can give the lectures out of doors, but by the time the evening rolls around and you want to sit around criticizing their work and discussing photography in general, you will probably need to be indoors.

If you are going to project slides, you really need a room to yourselves – some sort of conference room – but arguably you will do better to take over the corner of a reasonably capacious bar and hold court there. The two main problems with this are unwanted guests (especially if you are running a glamour or nude workshop!) and the fact that some clients may have a problem with bars; a residual puritanism means that as well as refusing alcohol for themselves, they want to refuse it to other people as well. If you adopt this route, you must make it abundantly clear in the initial promotional material.

Also, of course, you need to clear your use of any bar or lounge area with the hotel proprietors. Be fairly probing: it is not unknown for people to say, 'Sure, no problem' – and then to throw you out of the area you thought you were going to use because there is a wedding reception there, or the local rugby club dinner, or something.

Another possibility, especially in more remote areas, is to look for places which you can borrow for a modest fee. The range is enormous. Many English pubs will have private meeting rooms; in the Third World, schoolrooms may be available; there are church halls... The list goes on. Talk to the local tourist information office, chamber of commerce or *syndicat d'initiative*, and to any contacts you may have, in order to find out what is available.

## Processing

When it comes to processing, there are three separate types to worry about: colour print, monochrome and colour slide. There is also the question of different formats.

The popularity of modern mini-labs means that they are far more widespread than one might expect, even in the most unlikely places, and provided the machines are reasonably well maintained and the chemistry is inside specification, you can rely on them to process 35mm film and to provide reasonable reference prints, including Ilford XP-2 black and white film. If you have any doubts about their process control, talk to them. Point out that your clients will be pushing a lot of film through their mini-lab, and that the chemistry had better be fresh. Volunteer to subsidize fresh chemistry if there is no alternative – but also consider talking to the mini-lab's supplier, to point out the advantages of tourism both to them and to their country. Anything larger than 35mm may however be a problem.

Monochrome processing may be easier in many countries than colour print. Countless towns and villages the world over have a local photographer, and if local wage rates are low enough to permit it, you may well be able to come to an arrangement about processing black and white. Depending on your assessment, you may wish to process the films yourself, or you may trust the local photographer to do it. All formats should be feasible.

For your own protection, and that of your clients, inspect the darkroom facilities to make sure that they are reasonably clean and dust-free and truly dark. If need be, bring extra chemistry and even processing tanks and reels, and warn your clients of the type of developer you will be using, making film recommendations accordingly. Bring several sizes of negative sleeves, too: these can be very hard to obtain off the beaten track. Photographic paper is probably best bought locally, as you are looking at reference prints rather than fine prints. If you are using the local photographer's services, make sure that there is plenty of paper in stock!

Processing E6 is likely to prove the biggest stumbling block, except in large cities, and there are two principal options. One is a courier service. Even under adverse conditions in a Third World country, it may be possible to dispatch the fruits of a day's shoot with a trusted courier who travels by train or bus, and have the results back next evening. The other is to set up your own E6 line, using a Nova hand-line. If you have a reasonably reliable power supply, E6 processing is not particularly demanding, and you can put about 12 to 16 films through a litre of chemistry. All roll-film formats are feasible, and you can even process 4 × 5 inch (in an FP54) if you want. We have done it, and the results are excellent. A similar approach could be used for C41, if the local photographer has colour printing facilities.

There are other possibilities, and perhaps one of the most interesting would be a large-format course based entirely around the use of Polaroid Type 55 P/N film. Processing and washing are not demanding, and can be done in daylight: the biggest single risk is dust. And although the optimum negative gives a somewhat over-exposed positive, the positive is still quite adequate for a critique. Another idea would be to process large-format film using a daylight tank (or a Paterson Orbital processor) and to make all prints on printing out paper.

Instead of organizing the whole thing yourself, you may care to hook up with an existing agency which will take care of bookings and the travel side of things generally. You will obviously get less of the profit, but equally, you can see how things are organized and how they work, and you can decide whether you really want to get involved in this sort of thing for yourself.

## Scouting and planning

Whatever approach you take, you will of course need to scout the area carefully on your own before you consider running any tours. As well as accommodation and processing facilities, you need to be able to recommend

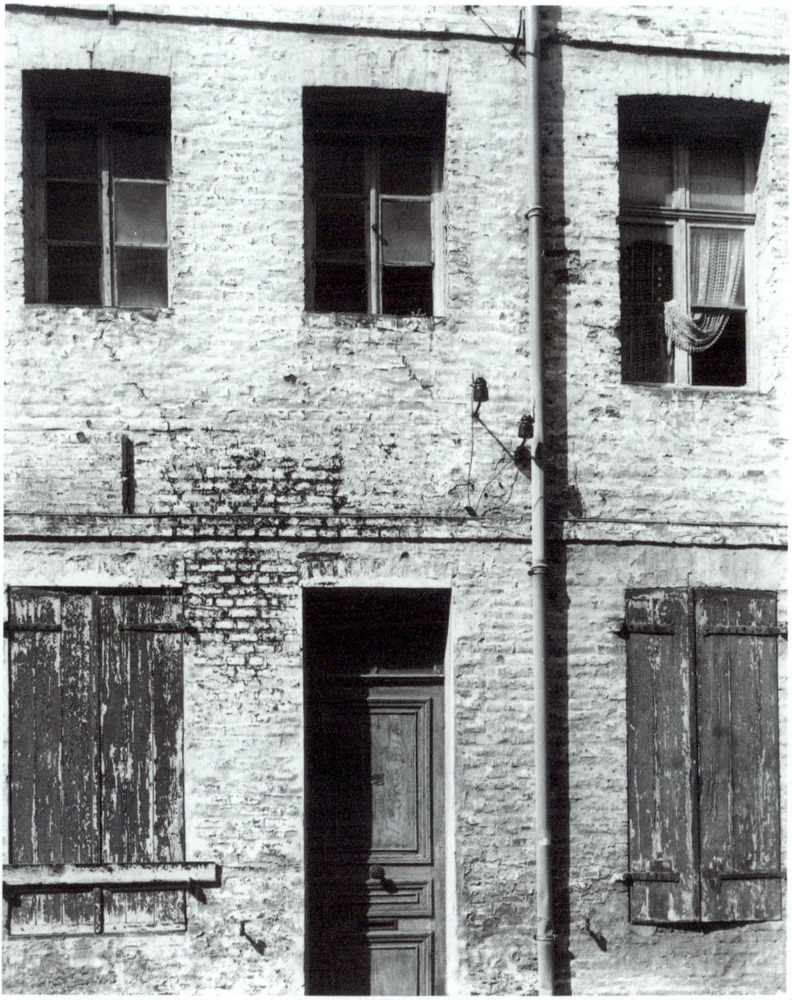

***Figure 15.4*** Semi-ruin, Montreuil. *Textures, tonal ranges, shift lenses/ camera movements, choice of focal lengths (this was 120 mm on 4 × 5 inch, and it wasn't wide enough) – all of these points can be illustrated with this photograph, and you can then lead the people on the course to the building in question and see what they make of it. (RWH)*

the best places to shoot, and to have made as many contacts as possible in order to smooth the way for your clients. You also need to have alternatives planned in the event of bad weather, non-appearance of models, or other mishaps.

The pictures which illustrate this chapter come from our own scouting trips to Montreuil, some 87 miles north-west of Paris, which we chose as a potential first centre for a number of reasons.

First, it is reasonably near us: about two hours away, via the Channel Tunnel. We were therefore able to check it several times, without undue effort or expense, at different times of year, and to shoot a lot of pictures with different equipment under varying conditions.

Second, it offers numerous photographic subjects, especially the citadel, which could form the basis of a whole tour in its own right. In good weather, the city walls are excellent, and so are the steep streets just inside the main city gate.

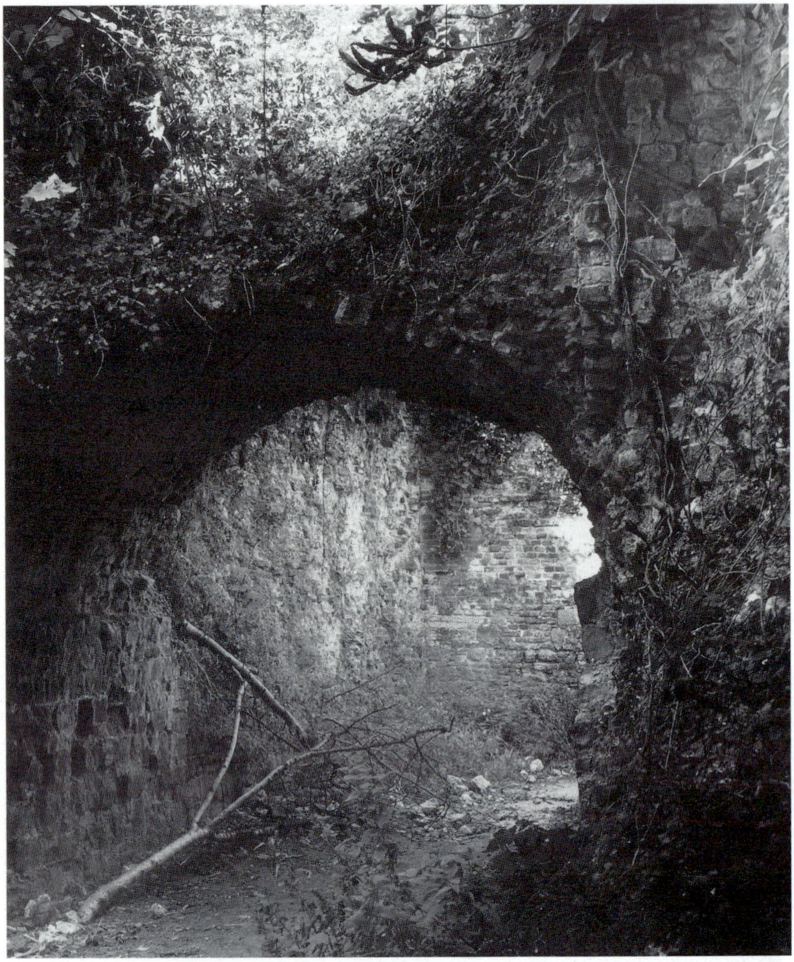

***Figure 15.5*** Ruined arch, Montreuil. *This is a textbook exercise in metering, and in how to interpret a negative when you make a print. In the negative (on Ilford SFX) there is texture in the underside of the arch, and in the sunlit wall glimpsed at the side of the arch. The well-prepared lecturer/group leader will make these points and more – and will come armed with pictures to show how interpretations can vary. (RWH)*

Third, there are no particular difficulties or expenses with admissions; some places are expensive to get into, and place unreasonable restrictions on photographers even when they have paid, but Montreuil is not like this.

Fourth, there is plenty of accommodation in a wide variety of hotels, and an adequate supply of good restaurants, and our French is reasonable; we would have more difficulty in, say, Portugal or Italy.

## Pricing and other considerations

In the United States, it is normal to quote prices exclusive of air travel to the destination (because fares can vary so widely from place to place) while in Europe it is normal to quote a fare-inclusive rate from a specified airport or airports.

Wherever you go, and whatever you organize, it is a sound idea to carry plenty of extra film: without doubt, some of your clients will run out, and the quality and indeed the availability of films cannot be guaranteed in many places. Insure yourself to the hilt, and make sure that your clients do the same: it can be very vexing when an uninsured customer threatens to die on you.

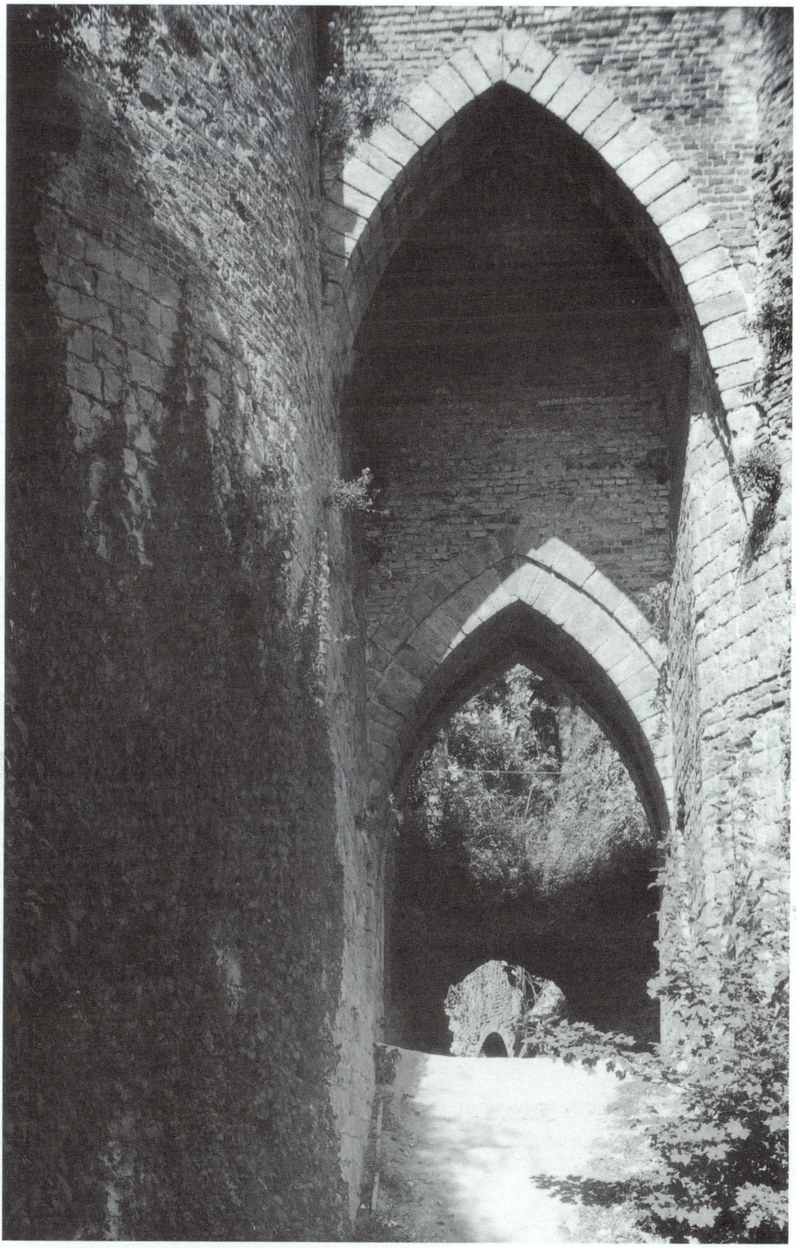

***Figure 15.6*** Citadel, Montreuil. *If you can, beg photographs from satisfied customers who have attended previous courses of yours at the same place, to show how interpretations can vary. Note the crop here, and also the poor resolution in the upper right-hand corner where the lens was still illuminating, though not sharp; the difference between circle of illumination and circle of sharp coverage could provide the material for a useful brief discourse. (FES)*

There is no doubt that running photo tours can be very demanding, nor that there is a learning curve involved which can be long and arduous; but equally, the profits can be well worth while, and the intangible rewards both in the form of gratitude from your pupils and in personal fulfilment can be equally great.

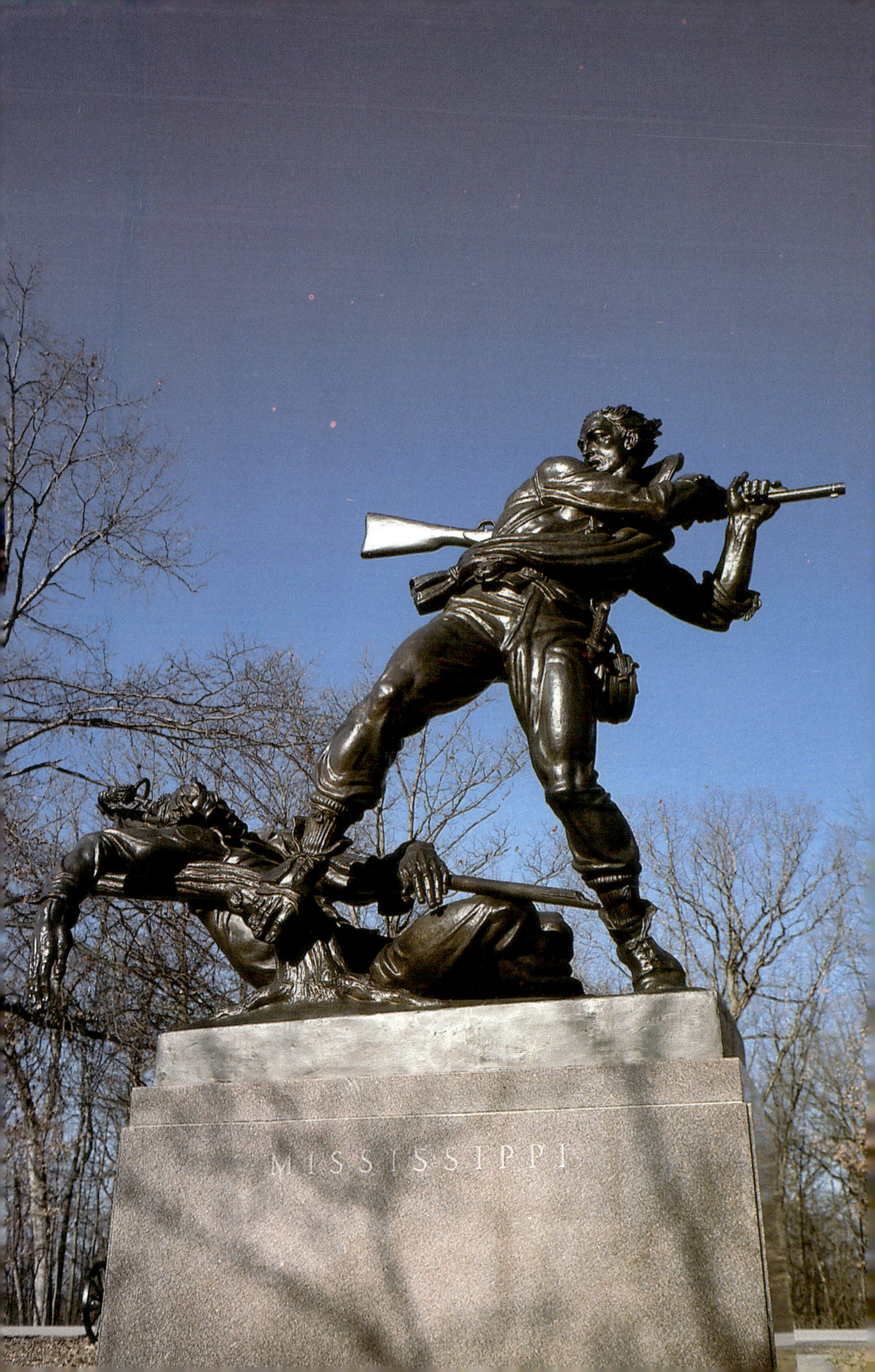
MISSISSIPPI

# 16 Books

The lavishly illustrated coffee-table book is the dream of countless photographers, but the reality is that books of pictures alone – even by great photographers – rarely sell well. If you want to see your pictures in a book, you are going to have to tailor the book to the market. For the most part, this means lowering your sights considerably, and reconciling yourself to the truth that (as ever) the travel market is essentially word-driven, not picture-driven.

To cheer yourself up, though, it may be as well to look first at that rare breed, the picture-driven travel book, and to see how and where it can succeed. A brief history lesson is particularly instructive, as it shows how pictures of exotic lands have gone from something enjoyed by the wealthy few to an everyday occurrence which passes all but unnoticed – which helps to explain why the demand for coffee-table books has declined so.

The lineage is old enough, in all conscience. As soon as the basics of photomechanical reproduction had been worked out, travel books were among the first to come off the presses. In those days, it was not merely the case that the sun never set on the British Empire. Rather, it was always noon, somewhere in the British Empire. Spanning three-fifths of the world's surface and two-fifths of the world's population, it constituted an enormous captive market which was headed by an affluent, book-buying élite. The Holy Land was always popular, as were historical sites in general (especially Greek and Roman sites, given the predominance of the classics in the rapidly expanding public schools) and, for sheer novelty and exoticism, the Indian Empire and its appurtenances, from the Khyber Pass to Burma.

Nor were books the only medium for publication. Boxed sets of lantern slides were sold for private and (still more) for public edification: church halls and similar venues were the scene of endless illustrated talks on different aspects of both the Empire and the 'benighted heathen' (the two were often synonymous). And perhaps the biggest market was for stereo views, typically with minimal captions, which allowed middle-class Victorians to marvel at the grandeur of ancient ruins, the majesty of restored monuments, and the sheer exoticism of sights from all over the world. The paterfamilias would presumably have provided some sort of instructive and improving commentary to accompany these, from general or specific reading; the idea of 'bundling' stereo sets and books, after the fashion of a modern book-of-the-TV-series, seems to have been exploited remarkably little.

The rise of the picture press, in the early twentieth century, changed the market considerably. The old 'penny dreadfuls', and even the middlebrow news magazines such as *Harper's* in the United States or the

***Figure 16.1*** Mississippi memorial, Gettysburg. *Civil War battlefields are fairly awash with memorials, and they can be very hard to photograph. You need the right time of day, and the right angle, and (above all) the right monument: some are very saccharine, while others are all but featureless blobs of white stone in anything but the most glancing light. Many Confederate memorials are much later than the Yankee ones, partly because it took longer for the impoverished South to raise the money, and partly because it took a while before memorials to the losing side were politically acceptable. (RWH)*

*Illustrated London News* in Britain, relied principally on woodcuts or engravings, often from photographs; but the picture press, led by publications such as the *Daily Mirror*, challenged the greyness of the traditional broadsheet newspaper. As was to become increasingly clear in the next half century or so, their challenge was very successful. The years between the wars were the days of scoops, of intense inter-newspaper rivalries, and of spending money like water: aircraft were hired, private trains were chartered, and no expense was spared to bring to the breakfast tables of millions the latest pictures of all that had happened in the world in the previous few hours or days.

Although at first the intrepid photographers had to rely on couriers, express trains and mail flights to get their pictures home, the wire machine soon made it possible to send pictures by telegraph. Extraordinary as it may seem, the first demonstration of sending pictures by wire was made by Alexander Bain in 1842, so 'phototelegraphy' actually antedates Morse code. What limited the process for many years was not the basic technology: it was the lack of an international wire network. In 1908, Belin demonstrated phototelegraphy using telephone lines, and thirteen years later (in 1921) he achieved the same thing by wireless. Until the ready availability of satellite broadcasting, the newspaper could still 'scoop' the television, so newspapers and magazines retained their supremacy well into the last third of the twentieth century.

Today, of course, it is almost a joke to watch the television news and to see the network's correspondent or stringer standing in front of some identifiable landmark – the Taj Mahal, say, or the Ginza – and delivering a piece to camera which could equally well have been recorded in the studio. Travel programmes proliferate, and talking heads take us on their own personal tours of Byzantium, the path of St Augustine from Rome to Canterbury, or around all the countries of the Pacific Rim. But it all helps to explain how today we regard the world as our backyard; and who pays serious money for photographs of his own backyard?

## Modern picture books

Now look at the picture books which are available in bookshops. First, discount all the historical material, from *Pioneers of Soviet Photography* to *1000 Nudes: The Uwe Scheid Collection*. No living photographer is likely to be making much money out of this. Next, discount the books which are clearly assembled from picture libraries. Usually, these pictures are bought in bulk deals which would barely pay for the film on which they are recorded.

Third, discount the books which are clearly exercises in public relations: somewhat self-conscious declarations by the publisher that they support photography, by supporting major photographers. You can spot these by touring the discount bookshops as well as the mainstream booksellers: books are regularly sold for a quarter or even a tenth of their nominal cover prices. This is not to say that such books have anything whatsoever wrong with them, but it is to say that in order to make any money the publishers have almost certainly printed copies which are actually intended to be sold as 'remainders', i.e. at a fraction of the nominal published price.

The mathematics of this are not immediately apparent to those outside the book trade, but they turn on the concept of Run-On At Same Time (ROAST). The origination costs of a lavishly illustrated book may be astronomical, but the additional cost of printing another 10 000 copies after the first 10 000 can be quite modest. If you do not know how many you are going to sell, but suspect that it may be (say) 8000 to 12 000, it can make sense to print 15 000; to sell as many as you can at full price; and then to sell the remainder at a cost which barely covers production. Because the marginal cost of printing 15 000 copies is not that much greater than printing 10 000, you will make your production cost back even on the remaindered copies, and the unit cost falls significantly, thereby allowing you to make a greater profit on the ones you sell at full cost. Crazy? Yes, but it works.

Touring the remainder shops will also reveal those books which are out-and-out mistakes, where the publisher thought there was a market, but got it wrong. We buy quite a lot of photographic picture books in remainder bookshops, which is one of the reasons why we have so few aspirations to produce them ourselves.

Finally, there are the books which clearly do make money, or which at least are not to be found at the remainder shops. There are very few names on the roster of photographers who can produce such tomes, however, and even they are not immune from the occasional remaindered title. Yoshikazu Shirakawa is one. Raghu Rai is another. Ansel Adams, of course. Sebastiao Selgado. But the very fact that one can name them – indeed, that one has to cast around for names – is revealing. Even though Shinzo Maeda has made a fortune out of his landscape books, we have bought his books as remainders. Likewise David Douglas Duncan. If masters such as this are not infallibly successful, small wonder that publishers are far from eager to commission

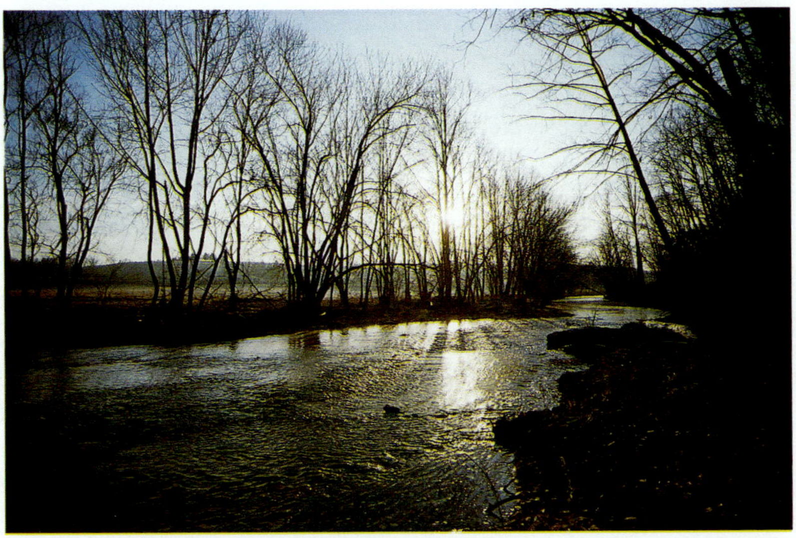

***Figure 16.2*** *We photographed this crossing at Bowman's Mill Ford very early in the morning, 125 years to the day after Confederate troops crossed it to attack the Yankees in what would become known as the Battle of Cedar Creek. It was cold, and the mist was just burning off. Although a picture can never fully convey a scene – the shivering cold, the icy water, the smell of damp earth – it can make it easier for the reader to exercise their imagination. (RWH)*

unknown names. The biggest market for very high-priced picture books seems to be in Japan, where prices of a quarter of a million yen do not seem to be particularly unusual (at the time of writing, $200–250 or £125–150).

Even at that, when we met Hiroki Fujita in the Himalayas in the early 1980s, he was not living a life of luxury. In fact, he was staying in a $5 a night hotel, despite the fact that his backpack contained Hasselblad and Linhof cameras. Despite his being a leader in his field, it was abundantly clear that he was (like most of us) supporting his habit, rather than making a fortune.

In other words, if you can make yourself a major name as a fine art photographer, usually in landscape but sometimes in reportage (think of Henri Cartier-Bresson), then you may in due course have a good chance of being commissioned to do a picture book. Before that, though, you will have to have proved yourself with countless magazine articles, exhibitions, sales to major collections, and (in most cases) major-league cosying up to the art establishment; you may find Tom Wolfe's *The Painted Word* of interest in the last context. It can be done; but it is far from easy.

## Illustrated books

A far larger market, and by and large more profitable to both photographers and publishers, is the illustration of word-driven books. After all, you are at this very moment reading a word-driven but illustrated book on travel photography. As ever, if you can provide the whole package, both words and pictures, you will be better placed than if you can provide only pictures, and in our case, where we travel together as a couple, the only way in which producing books is feasible at all is if we can provide both. If you want to work as an illustrator of travel books only, you had better learn to live in $5 a night hotels, even if you are among the best in the world.

A classic example of a word-driven picture book is our own *Battlefields of the Civil War*, now out of print. Following the success of *Battlefields of Northern France*, Martin Marix-Evans of Thames Head/BLA (now of Book Packaging and Marketing) approached us with an idea for a touring guide to what Southerners still call the War of Northern Aggression. There would be three categories of pictures: maps, contemporary pictures, and modern pictures of the battlefields as they are today.

The maps were either specially commissioned (mostly based on United States Geological Survey topographical maps) or 'lifted' from vintage sources, most particularly the massive four-volume *Battles and Leaders of the Civil War*, published in the 1880s.

In the event, the vast majority of the contemporary pictures were taken from the United States Army War College in Carlisle, Pennsylvania, an extremely generous and well-run institution which, in common with most American organizations, takes the charming and rational view that in a publicly owned institution, so long as material is out of copyright, there should be no reproduction fees. Better still, they allowed us to set up our own copying stand to photograph original material from their extensive collection, so there were no copying fees either. Copying is not a skill which one expects to have to exercise on location, but we had to.

The modern pictures – the ones we shot – were designed primarily to show the terrain over which the battles were fought, with (as far as possible) some idea of the mood of the place: the eerie, early morning mist at Cedar Creek, the buzzards sunning their wings at Gettysburg where once their ancestors must have fed so well, the rank swamp of the Seven Days, the lonely houses which served as field hospitals, the precipitous slopes of Chattanooga, and so forth.

As so often, this meant that before we could shoot the pictures we had to understand the subject. Fortunately, even Roger's rudimentary military training – in what used to be called an Officer Training Corps, dressed in World War II uniforms – was sufficient for a grasp of such basic concepts as dead ground, ranging, sniping, flank attacks and the like, the more so when combined both with modern reading (almost all of the battles of the War Between the States have been exhaustively analysed) and with the books which the commanders of the time would have read, such as Hardee. After all, many of those who rose even to general rank had no more military education than Roger, and some had less; some were natural soldiers, while others were the opposite.

Understanding the subject meant that we had to remember countless names, and who had come from where, when. Once we had that on board, we had to try to position ourselves where we thought a particular commander or corps might have stood, and to try to discover (from historical evidence, contemporary markers, and general observation) what the terrain might have been like a century and a quarter before. As far as possible, we tried to exclude battle monuments unless they were the subject of a picture, and we did our utmost to exclude road signs, telephone wires, parked cars and all the other appurtenances of modern life.

## Equipment and practicalities

One thing which surprised us was the sheer range of focal lengths which we found useful, from a 14mm wide-angle for interiors through to 400mm and even 800mm to show natural features as they would have appeared through the field-glasses of the combatants. Everything was shot on 35mm, because the biggest pictures in the book would be less than a 5 × blow-up and there was little point in using anything bigger.

Another strange lesson was nothing to do with photography, but related to local customs. In Pennsylvania, we found places where restaurants (so-called) admitted their last customers for dinner at six in the evening, and closed their doors at seven; while in parts of the mid-West, even reasonable-looking restaurants looked at us as if we were some sort of degenerates when we asked whether we could have a bottle of wine with our dinner. After a few experiences like this, we took to carrying both food and drink so that we could picnic if all else failed, as it surprisingly often did.

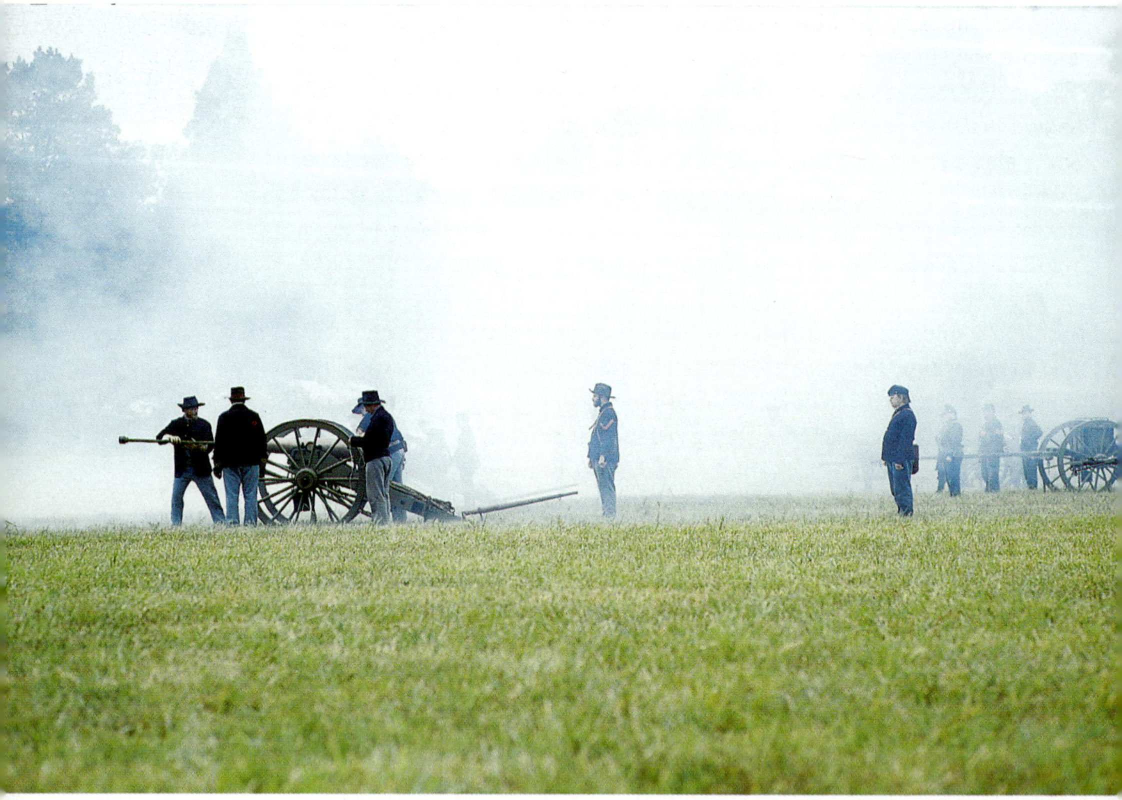

***Figure 16.3***
Re-enactors, Chickamauga. *'Living history' or re-enactment is very popular among* aficionados *of the War Between the States, and numerous excellent pictures are available. The main problem is that there is little or no provision for professional photographers, so you have to take your chances along with the hordes of amateurs and just plain spectators who also turn up for these events, which are publicized in several journals devoted to Civil War matters. (RWH)*

We also learned the unwisdom of having XP-2 processed in unknown labs – several rolls were scratched mercilessly by an allegedly 'professional' lab in Virginia – and we first acquired our trick of finding E6 labs by contacting local professionals, explaining our situation, and asking if they could recommend somewhere. Whenever possible, we liked to have our films processed en route, so that if necessary we could back-track and re-shoot. This is (or should be) more feasible in a reasonably developed country such as the United States than it is in somewhere like India; and it is also worth remarking that processed film is more stable than unprocessed.

Our book *Hidden Tibet*, about Tibetans in exile, required quite a different set of skills – after all, we were dealing more with people, and less with places – and we found that for the most part we needed a far more restricted range of lenses, mostly just 21mm to 135mm, with 35mm accounting for the vast majority of the pictures. We also had to travel lighter: in the United States we had our big old Peugeot 504 station wagon, while in India we had to fly, take taxis and jeeps, walk, and even on one memorable occasion ride while standing on the rear axle of a tractor. But the underlying lesson in both cases was the same, that unless you understand the subject and can structure your pictures to convey that understanding, you are pretty much wasting your time.

Rewards are not normally great: most journalists who also do books will tell you that they do books for credibility and for relaxation, because per-week income is likely to be laughably low, though royalty payments which come in after a year or two are very welcome and require no further work. You will generally do best to propose a book about a subject which is already dear to your heart, though if you have a good portfolio and a decent track record you may be able to get commissions for illustrating someone else's ideas: a friend of ours, for example, illustrated a book about Daphne du Maurier's Cornwall. As ever, proposals for books are normally word-driven, though you may be able to get commissions on the strength of your portfolio.

RUE
PAVEE

# 17 Fine art

'Fine art' is an elusive concept, the more so when allied to travel photography, and indeed we were of two minds about including it; but a brief chapter made sense, on at least four grounds.

The first is that if you can establish a reputation for fine art photography, your chances of having a book published are greatly increased, and your reputation feeds off both.

The second is that even if you cannot earn a full-time living from fine art travel photography, it can be a useful supplement to more conventionally commercial undertakings, including stock photography (Chapter 9).

The third is that the vast majority of skilled, creative photographers do personal work as well as paid work. This personal work is often experimental or exploratory. Some of it may be no more than technical exercises to establish the feasibility of a particular technique, while other aspects may result in saleable images, and it makes sense to sell them if you can.

The fourth is that some people actually do make a living from fine art photography, though to be fair this living is often supplemented by teaching courses and workshops (Chapter 15), by magazine articles, especially in the photographic press (Chapter 12), and even from a little commissioned corporate photography (Chapter 13).

Our definition of success in fine art photography is the simple working one of original print sales, regardless of artistic merit. If you can sell saccharine sunsets or Montmartre scenes, or vivid portraits of colourful ethnic groups, then you are by any working definition as much in the fine art market as the most refined photographer of monochrome landscapes or as the most relentlessly modernist archivist (in colour) of anomie and decay. Arguably, poster sales are a variety of fine art photography too, though the heyday of the poster is seemingly gone.

Very few photographers make much from print sales in the fine art market, though, and a quick examination of the economics makes it clear why.

Photography is still not widely accepted as a fine art on a par with (say) painting or lithography, so there is considerable price resistance, at least for works by living photographers. Those who are safely dead will often command much higher prices, but this is a rather drastic way to put your prices up.

Of the comparatively modest prices which most galleries can reasonably often command, the photographer sees something between 40 and 60 per cent; a lot depends on the precise agreement, and particularly on who pays for framing. Even then, sales are not rapid, and the gap between shooting and receiving the money may well be several months or even years.

*Figure 17.1 What makes this photograph of the Rue des Francs Bourgeois 'fine art'? Nothing, unless someone calls it so. The modern tautology, 'Art is what is produced by artists' could for our purposes be better (if more cynically) recast as 'Art is whatever you can persuade someone is art – especially if you can persuade them to part with money for it'. To us, this is both a pleasing image in its own right and (perhaps more importantly, as this will help it sell better) a good representation of a particular Parisian place and mood. (FES)*

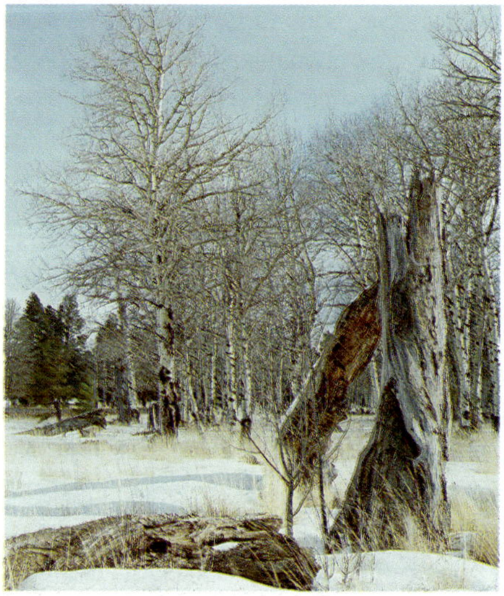

*Figure 17.2 Chocolate boxy? Yes. But also very attractive. You can almost hear the silence, smell the cool air; you do not need to have been there to 'remember' all this stuff. It is a long way from the kind of rarefied monochrome which is normally associated with fine art; but if someone is willing to buy it, don't argue. (RWH)*

We do however know one successful fine art photographer (who will remain nameless, for reasons which are obvious) who has worked out a method of producing reasonably permanent, highly attractive pictures in unlimited editions, with random variations which make each image effectively unique, at a very modest price. These sell into what is sometimes known as the 'wallpaper' market: pictures which are bought to match a particular colour scheme, but which are detectably 'fine art' instead of mass produced prints. Even though the final selling prices are modest, and even though the photographer sees only half of these selling prices, the mark-up is still very comfortable: several hundred per cent.

Some locales are definitely fashionable: Bob Shell, editor of *Shutterbug* magazine, refers to all the 'sub-Ansel Adamses and very Minor Whites' whose work he sees, and there is no doubt that in America in particular, photographs of wilderness and pseudo-wilderness are always popular, usually in monochrome though sometimes in vivid colour. Closely related to this is a nostalgic tendency, rooted to a very large extent in New England, which shows painted barns, covered bridges and other picturesque gewgaws, all photographed on large format and normally either in monochrome or (once again) vivid colour. The English equivalent of this is probably the Lake District. There is also an Anglo-Saxon tradition of photographing urban decay, as cheerlessly as possible but (as ever) in either monochrome or in vivid colour. For no very good reason, however, countless other places are simply ignored: for instance, rural France seems not to be a cult subject, despite its photogenic potential.

## EXHIBITIONS

Suppose, then, that you are interested in the fine art route to fame, if not necessarily fortune. What should you do?

The first thing is to get as many exhibitions as you can, wherever you can, preferably solo (or in our case, joint) but failing that, with anyone who will take your work. Do not be unduly proud: one of Roger's earliest one-man exhibitions was at a sort of up-market hamburger joint in one of the more self-consciously fashionable areas of Bristol. No-one, incidentally, bought a single picture, but someone did do him the honour of burgling the place one night and stealing, along with the few pounds that had been left in the till as a float, three of his pictures.

Another of his exhibitions was at a regional arts centre. The actual venues are less important than the fact that you have the exhibitions, as the technique is to build your curriculum vitae so that each subsequent place you approach is that much more likely to accept your work. At a certain point, which depends on the location of the venues, the number of venues, the type of work you shoot, the reviews you get (if any) and your own personal character, you achieve a sort of critical mass and become a 'known photographer'. Even if you don't make a penny out of it, this is rather gratifying.

Once you are a 'known photographer', you can afford to be slightly more selective about your venues, and you can start trying to persuade sponsors to part with money, or at least with equipment, materials and other support in kind. It is unfortunately entirely possible to reach this stage without any significant financial return from picture sales, though you may be invited to ornament your

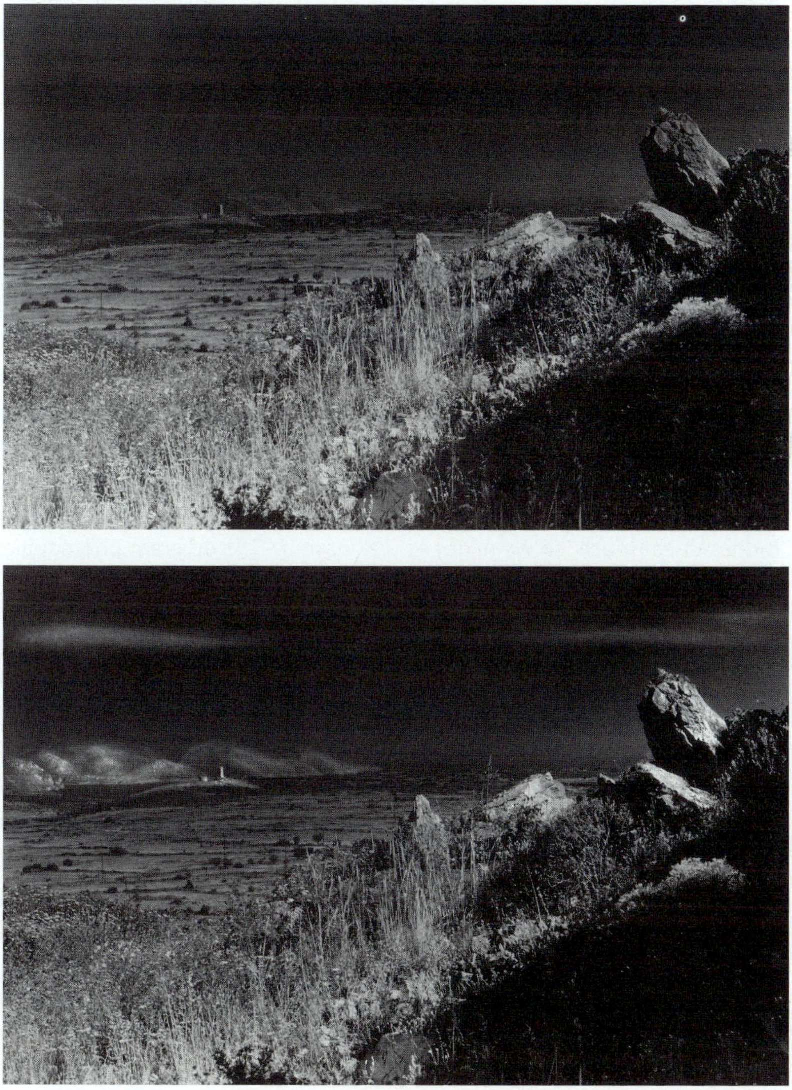

**Figure 17.3** Mani, the Pelopponese. *The term 'image manipulation' may conjure up electronics today, but traditional methods of manipulation – dodging, burning, bleaching and toning – are very much the stuff of fine art. A staple trick is the use of Farmer's Reducer on a slightly over-exposed image, as 'sunshine in a bottle'. In the straight print (top), the distinctive Mani tower and the hills in the background are all but lost; the rocks in the foreground are much less dramatic; and the clouds are barely noticeable. It is however a matter of taste how much you depart from what was actually there, in your putative quest for what your vision of it was. (FES)*

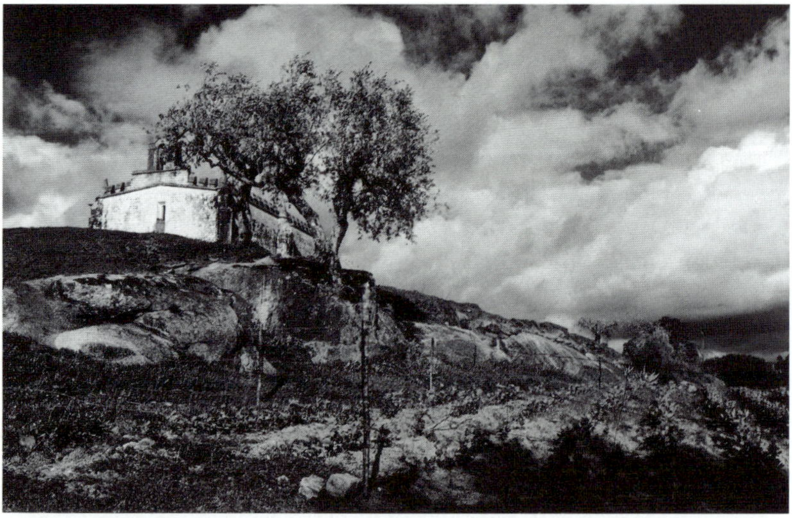

*Figure 17.4 Dramatic, stormy light and the counterpoint of the ruined chapel and the working farm in Portugal are the ingredients which make this picture strangely compelling. For our taste, some of the most highly regarded of current fine art printers are inclined to over-manipulation of their pictures: they stamp their personality on them so relentlessly that the subject matter is overwhelmed. Whenever possible, we prefer to let the subject have its head rather more. (FES)*

sponsors' stands at trade shows, which still further boosts your reputation; and so it goes, each stage building on the one previous to it, until (with any luck) you are selling prints, giving workshops, illustrating books and so forth.

This is also the stage at which you talk to commercial galleries, usually beginning with the newer ones – some galleries have the life of mayflies – before settling down with 'your' gallery which is the main source for those who wish to purchase your work. Perhaps needless to say, you will have to visit as many galleries as you can, and to make sure that your face is known. Also, whenever you have a chance to visit a new gallery, do not stop at looking merely at the current exhibition(s). In addition, find out what portfolios they have on display, and what their policy is. Different galleries have philosophies which range from the achingly high-minded through the blatantly commercial to the rather casual 'Well, another portfolio doesn't take up much space, and it doesn't eat much, so we might as well have it.' The different philosophies make less difference to commercial success than you might think.

You will also do well to cultivate the acquaintance of the art establishment – of critics and curators – and to learn to make the right noises about your work. Several options are open to you here, but at the time of writing, the two most popular and successful were the deconstructionist/ intellectual/psychological/ sociological (much favoured by those whose pictures are not, in fact, widely liked outside a narrow and often rather precious constituency) and the 'up yours', favoured by working-class lads made good and by those who found it easier to masquerade as working-class lads made good than to master the other sort of jargon.

## Self-promotion

If all of this seems unnecessarily cynical, consider for a moment that today the artist sells himself as much as his work; all art can be viewed as performance art. If in doubt, model yourself on Wilde: apply your talent to your art, and reserve your genius for the art of living. Your persona should be as carefully constructed as your pictures, and you either should not care a fig for convention, or should appear not to. It has done Roger's career, in particular, very little harm to affect a monocle, hand-made red Tibetan silk shirts (actually made by a Spaniard in Margate, from a Tibetan pattern), and cowboy boots; and convenience is not the sole reason why Frances prefers lorgnettes to spectacles.

From a purely technical point of view, you can, under the conventions of modern art, do pretty much anything you like. We know photographers who work (and sell) in all formats from 35mm to 11 × 14 inch and indeed beyond, and in media from platinum printing to colour photocopies. Some tone their images, some hand colour them, some use them as collages, some maltreat them in the most extraordinarily imaginative ways. To quote one, of an unusually experimental turn of mind, 'Don't microwave them, though, or they explode.'

The nearest thing to a universal commandment is, 'Thy pictures shall be archivally permanent', though this is perhaps based on a misunderstanding and on the historical debate about whether or not photography is art. In a world where the first thing they do in some galleries of a morning is to sweep up the bits that have fallen off the Pollock overnight, there might even be some capital to be made out of the impermanence of a badly-made photograph.

Whatever you sell, make a 4 × 5 inch copy transparency of it against the time that a catalogue raisonnée is produced; as a defence against copyright infringement; and as a tool for selling other pictures in due course. If you do not believe in yourself, then you may depend upon it that very few others are likely to do so either.

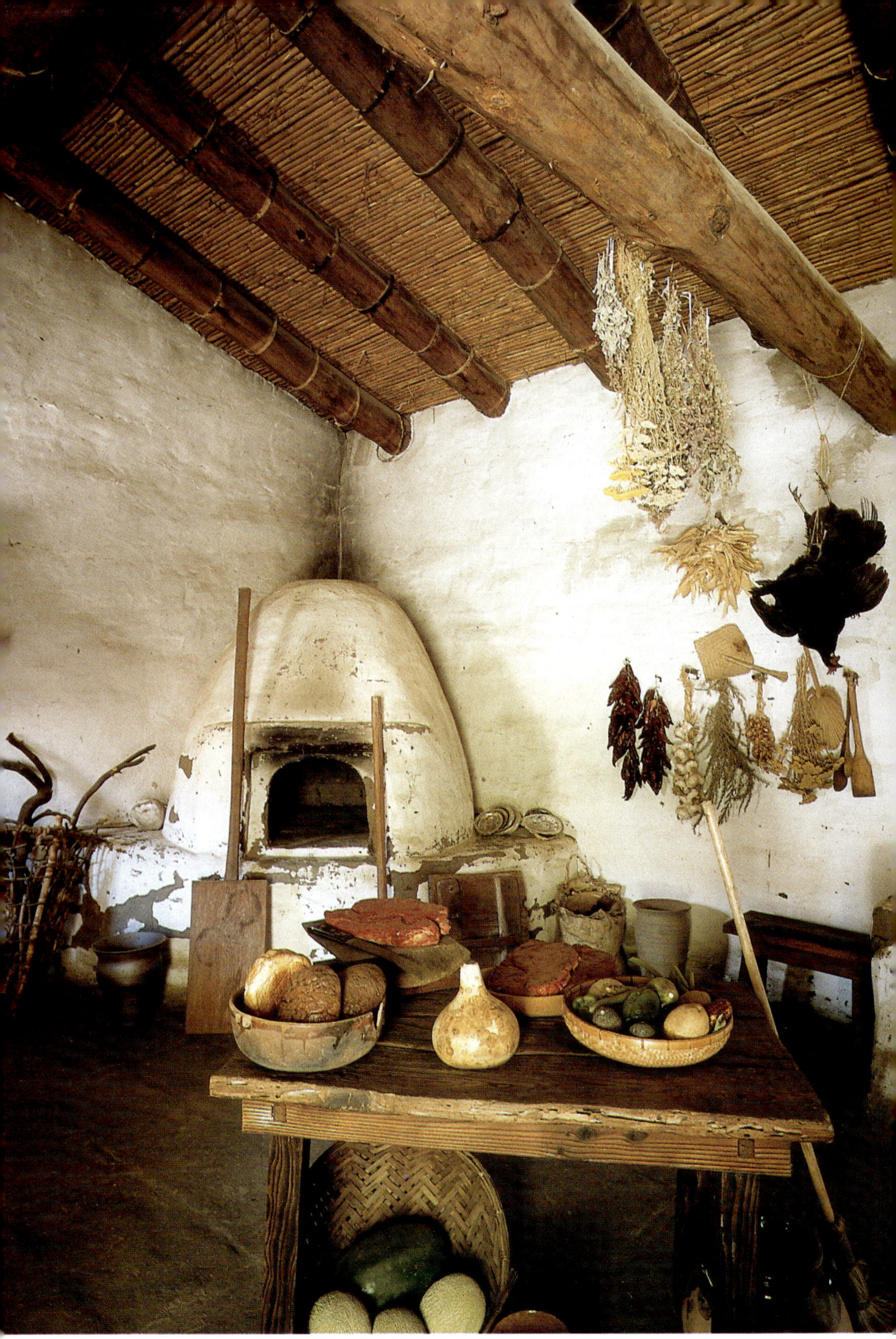

# 18 Travel at home



*Figure 18.1 When we lived in California, we frequently used to visit the Misión de la Purisima Concepción in Lompoc some twenty-five miles away. There were certain shots which became standard tests for new equipment and new films. This kitchen provided a good test for ever-increasing wide-angles, from 21mm to 17mm to 14mm, showing us how they worked with a known subject; it was also a good test of colour films of widely varying speeds. (RWH)*

A perennial piece of advice in books on travel photography is that you should endeavour to exercise your skills – and indeed, to shoot saleable pictures – at home as well as abroad. The less sophisticated version of the argument runs that there are as many things to photograph in your area as there are in (say) Paris or Yosemite. One cannot help wondering whether the people who advance this viewpoint have ever been to Paris or Yosemite, and also, what they think the market might be for pictures of the Isle of Thanet, California's central coast, and Bristol, to name only the last three places we have lived. At that, there is probably more interest in those places than in generic towns in the American mid-West, or in many of London's suburbs and dormitory towns.

A more sophisticated version of the same argument is that even if 'your area' is something of an exaggeration, there must surely be places which are reasonably accessible to you and which would be highly attractive travel destinations for people who lived elsewhere.

Well, yes. From where we live on the Kent coast, for example, it is but a short drive to Canterbury, or to the mediaeval town of Sandwich, one of the Cinque Ports. We could be in either of those places, traffic permitting, in half an hour. For that matter, we are less than two hours from London, even on the woefully slow East Kent railway line, which is roughly comparable with driving in.

The trouble is that places which someone else might give their right arm to photograph may completely fail to turn you on. This is nothing to do with distance. We find relatively little to photograph in Florida, either, and although we have never been there, we have no burning desire to go anywhere much in Australia (though New Zealand sounds more interesting).

Also, even if you do find a place photogenic, you can get stale. Sometimes this is a temporary condition, cured by a few months' or years' absence, while on other occasions it is either permanent, or lasts long enough that it might as well be. We have no particular inclination to revisit Los Angeles, except to see family and friends. By contrast, we can return again and again to Greece, whether to places we already know and love like Rhodes Old Town or Chania in Crete, or to islands we have never visited before. The same is true of most of India. Some places capture your imagination and your heart, and some don't, and that is all there is to it.

The first thing to do, therefore, is to get rid of any sort of guilt trip which anyone else may try to lay on you, whether deliberately or inadvertently, when they tell you how wonderful your part of the world is. If it doesn't interest you, it doesn't interest

*Figure 18.2 Testing new film is always problematic. You want something which is not too dull, but equally, you do not want to risk losing an irreplaceable image in an exotic location. Reculver Towers, about four or five miles from where we live, is a reliable place to experiment: this was one of our first tests of Ilford's then-new SFX 200 extended-red film. A fascinating aside is that where they are visible, the kite-strings are about 0.01mm wide in the print, so they must be under 0.002mm wide in the negative; about 80 millionths of an inch. (FES)*

you, and trying to drum up an interest which is not there is substantially a waste of time. In fact, it is worse than a waste of time. Because you cannot find pictures that you want to take, you begin to believe that you cannot take pictures, so the whole thing is a vicious circle: the kind of thing which Robert Pirsig so memorably described as a 'gumption trap'.

On the other hand, it is worth making an effort to find out those things which do interest you, and which you would, if you were travelling, love to photograph. It is all too easy to write off the whole of the area in which you live as dull or exhausted, and to neglect its potential. At the time of writing, we had a particularly good example of this. We went to see the Theatre Royal in Margate, the second oldest working theatre in the United Kingdom, and we were captivated by several aspects of it – not least by the fly-loft, where you can clearly see the nautical influence of the seaman who first built and managed the theatre, and the recycled ships' timbers which were used to build the place. When you are travelling, you often do not have time to explore such places, and if by chance you come across them, you file them away mentally as somewhere to which you will, when you have the opportunity, return.

Nor is this the only example of a place near at hand which has proved very rewarding. Around twenty-five miles from where we used to live in California was the Misión de la Purisima Concepción, in Lompoc. It was unashamedly a reconstruction, a legacy of the make-work projects of the Depression, but it is also a beautifully done reconstruction, and wonderfully photogenic.

## The value of practice

Instead of treating things like the Theatre Royal and Misión la Purisima as true travel destinations, you can instead use them to hone photographic skills which will be of use to you when you are travelling. That way, instead of making a note to come back to places which you 'don't have time to photograph', you may be able to take at least some pictures, based on skills acquired nearer home. Also, if you carry a 'postcard portfolio' you may find it easier to gain access to such places when you do come across them.

Admittedly, such an approach is not always applicable. In particular, it is generally easier to photograph total foreigners than it is to photograph one's own countrymen. Partly, this is down to the natural loss of inhibition (at least in some fields) which travel often seems to bring on. Partly, it is because we know we can take refuge in 'Sorry, I'm a foreigner, I don't know any better, and besides I don't speak your language.' And partly – probably the largest part – it is because the unfamiliar is inherently interesting. If something is familiar; if we do not want to get into explanations of what we are doing; and if (to be honest) we know that we may have to live with our photographic 'victims', we may find the whole thing a disincentive to taking pictures.

Thus, although we live a few hundred yards from a beach, and less than five miles from the famed Margate Sands (Margate is the oldest seaside

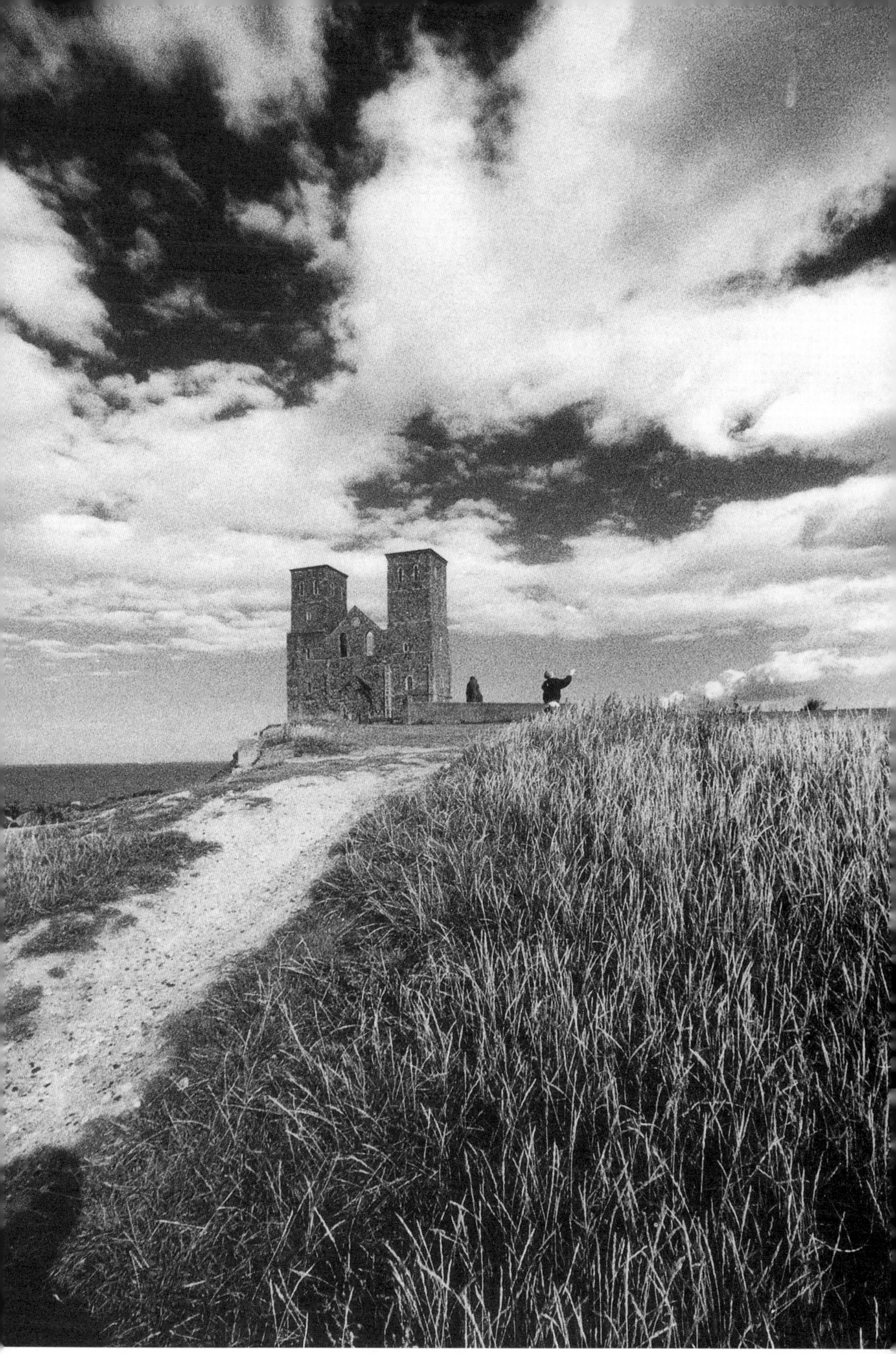

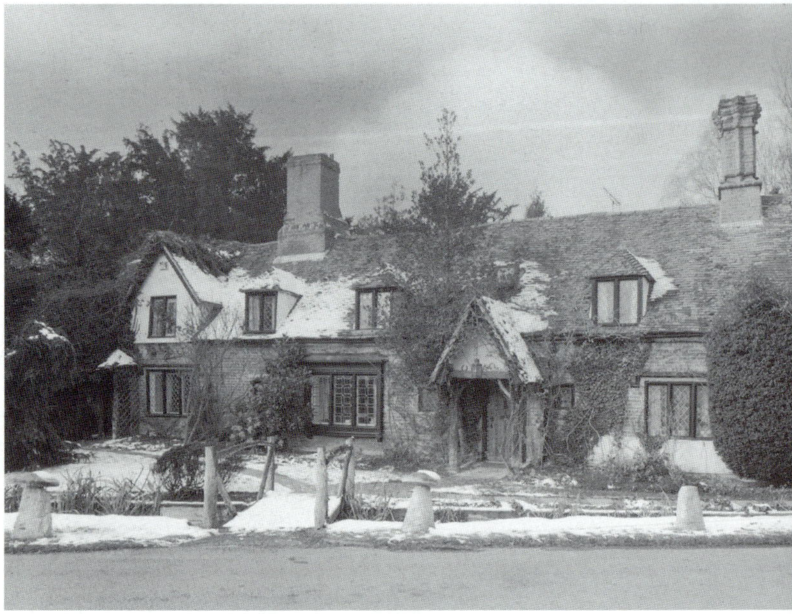

***Figure 18.3*** *One of the reasons for working with subjects near home is to practise techniques which will come in useful when you are somewhere more exotic. In the part of England where we live, snow is comparatively unusual and provides an opportunity to practise cold-weather photography; it was as a result of this shot that we had the shutters of our Linhof lenses cleaned, because they were sticking on the slow speeds. Better to discover this a few miles from home than at 2000 metres in the Himalayas! Also, the sky is printed in from another negative – a useful technique to master. (FES)*

resort in the United Kingdom, slightly antedating Brighton), we take comparatively few pictures at either location, though both might seem ideal for practising people photography.

## What is 'travel'?

There is also the question of precisely what constitutes 'travel' and what constitutes 'at home'. In a small country such as Britain, most people would regard a journey of 300–400 km (200 to 250 miles) as constituting reasonably serious 'travel', and indeed such a journey would see us in Paris, or Normandy, or Bristol, or most of the way to the Lake District. In Belgium, you would have considerable difficulty in staying in the country with such a journey, unless your path was fairly curved or crooked. In parts of the United States, however, you could drive for much the same distance and see hardly any variations in landscape, let alone ancient cities or different cultures.

Our view is that 'travel' starts when you spend at least one night away, and indeed, relatively short journeys where you spend just one, two or three nights away from home can be excellent practice for more extended trips. This is especially true if you are trying out new equipment or new techniques. We do it all the time, and it does indeed reveal periodical deficiencies in our planning. We once found ourselves in Belgium with everything we needed to shoot 4 × 5 inch pictures – except a tripod... Luckily, it was only a brief recce trip; but what we did was to buy the cheapest lightweight second-hand tripod we could find, rather than miss the picture-taking opportunities. As described on page 31, we now rely heavily on checklists, and indeed we have copies of several of our more important checklists pinned to the studio wall (our studio is the last room before the front door) so that we can check that we have everything.

From a purely technical viewpoint, it is worth pointing out that if you do decide to refine your photographic skills at locations near home, you may do well to restrict yourself to the kind of equipment which you would normally carry with you when you are travelling. Thus, if you normally carry only 35mm when you are abroad, there may be little to be gained from the point of view of practising your travel photography if you shoot at home on 4 × 5 inch.

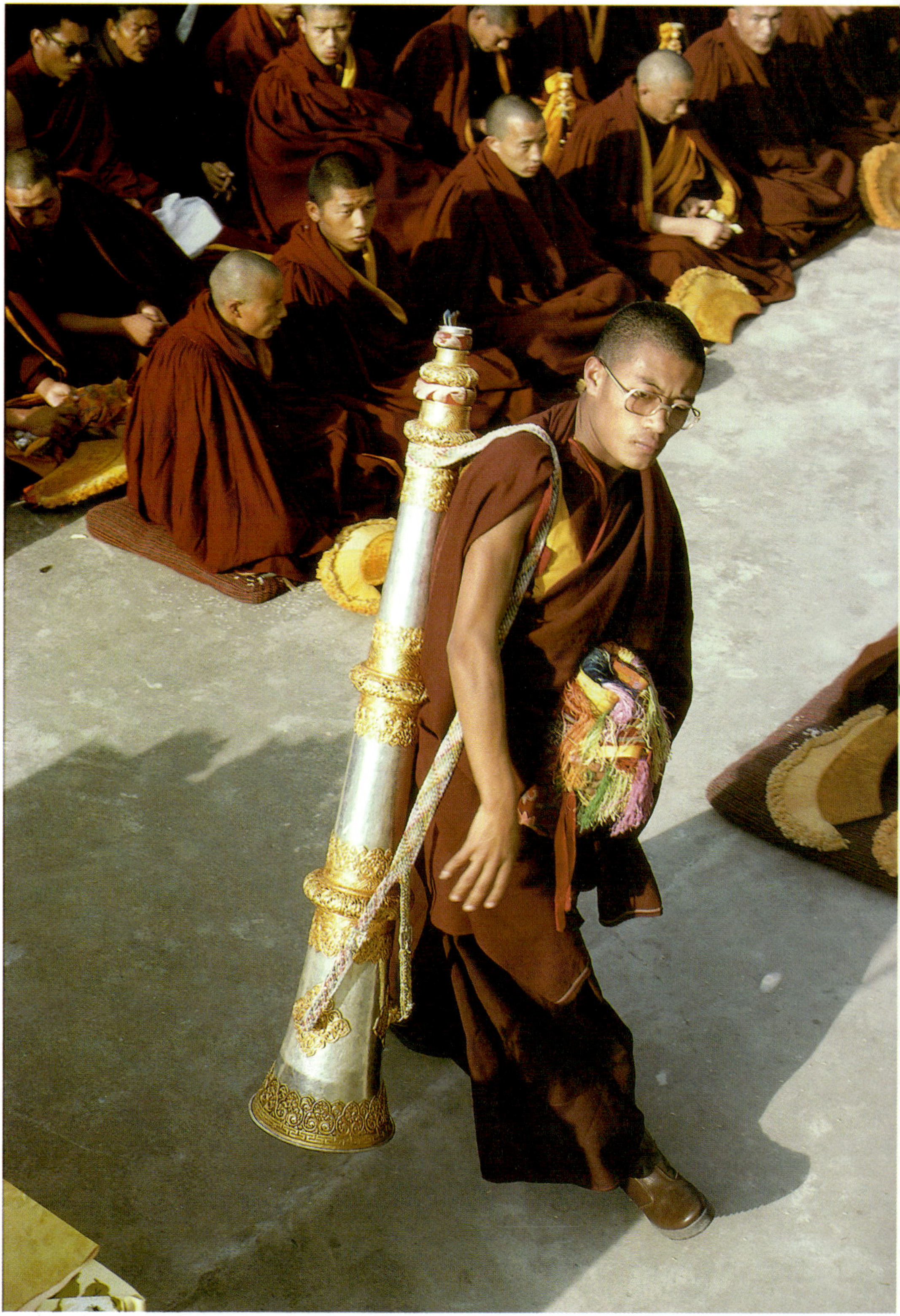

# 19 Working for nothing

After looking at commercial possibilities, but before looking at how to put together and present a travel portfolio, it is not a bad idea to look at the possibilities of working for nothing. One of the very best ways to hone your travel photography skills, in a very wide range of areas, is to work for a cause or organization that is important to you. You will in general be assured of cooperation from your subjects (though you may face opposition from others) and on those occasions where you do have to exercise your powers of persuasion, you should in most cases have some moral support.

The choice of cause is obviously intensely personal, and it needs to be sincere, because this is going to cost you money, time, effort and no small measure of frustration. For us, the cause is political, but for others it could be ecological, historical, charitable or artistic.

The primary value of working for a cause is that you have to convey a message – and to be thoroughly cynical, if you can persuade people to care about the plight of Tibet, or to come to an arts festival in Greece, or to give money for medical care in the Third World, you are acquiring and refining the skills you need to persuade people to take their holidays in Spain, or to persuade shareholders that the directors of a multinational mining corporation are doing a good job.

Also, because you are trying to convey a message, you learn the value of your pictures as a part of a campaign. A little humility in this area can be extremely useful: it is an important antidote to the purist approach which is sometimes adopted by those who smite their brows and cry that they are Artists, with a capital 'A'. If you want total control of your work, without ever having it cropped, then stay out of commerce.

This is an important part of the secondary value of working for a cause, which is that you have to work with other people. You have to learn when to charm, when to cajole, when to accede, and when to refuse. The importance of the last of those, of knowing when to refuse, should not be underestimated. On a commercial shoot, there is always the fear that unless you are compliant, you will not be paid. Admittedly there is the risk on a 'pro bono' shoot that you may be more of a prima donna than you should, because you have nothing (save esteem) to lose, but seeing how people react to refusals and suggestions is easier when there is no money at stake.

Also, you learn that even when you are nominally on the same side as someone else, there are all kinds of political considerations and hidden agendas. This is where frustration comes into it. When someone blocks one of your best ideas, you have to decide whether to hold on to it, or let go. If you decide to hold on, you need to find

**Figure 19.1** *Monk carrying* dungchen. *A* dungchen *is a 'great horn', a sort of telescoping Alpenhorn which extends to three metres or more but collapses to a metre or so for transport: many Tibetan religious artifacts have their origins in a nomadic society and are designed for portability. This is the sort of detail which many people find fascinating: the unfamiliarity of the subject matter will attract them to the photograph, and the caption will still further capture their interest. This was shot on the roof of the temple in Dharamsala at the end of the Losar ceremonies which greet the sunrise on the first day of the year. (RWH)*

out why they are blocking it. Can they be persuaded? Can you go over their head? If you do go over their head, will it have more adverse effects than positive ones in the long run? These are all real-world lessons which you will never learn at college, or as an amateur who just takes pretty pictures; and even if you are an established professional in another field, the skills you need in order to deal with (say) advertising clients are not necessarily the same as the skills you need to gain access to a monastery or a school.

## Start small

Wherever you start, start small. Don't come into an organization with promises that you will take over all their publicity – or indeed any of it. Leave room for both sides to change, to save face, and to back out if necessary. In the very nature of things, there will always be some people who are happy with the status quo, and who will see you as an unwelcome interloper. There will be others who will expect you to deliver the moon, gift-wrapped, on Tuesday, and who will castigate you if you do not.

Begin with something like, 'Do you need pictures of so-and-so?' Sometimes, the answer is even 'No', though very often this simply means that you are talking to the wrong person or that the person you are talking to has failed to understand your question. Make it as clear as possible, as soon as possible, that you are offering your services (including materials, in most cases) for free. If they start asking for things which you cannot provide for free, or which you do not wish to provide for free, then say so. For example, tell them that if they want frames, that is their responsibility.

If the answer is 'Yes', then shoot the pictures in question and deliver them as soon as possible. If they are not very good, and if you have the slightest chance, then re-shoot. Of course, an alternative to asking if they want you to shoot pictures for them is simply to present them with pictures which you have already taken, and to ask if they want more. Even if you have no pictures of them or their work, have something available to show them: something related, or at least in the same style as you wish to do for them.

## Suss the politics

Early in the relationship, find out who else is doing what, and how, and when. There may well be professionals who are charging to do what you are willing to do for free. Consider that they have a living to earn, and also that unless you stick around, the organization may have to go back to those professionals. Do not put people's backs up unnecessarily. If there are other volunteers, try to work with them as far as possible. Some of them may be better than you, and you can make a fool of yourself by showing off pictures which you think are pretty good, but they think are rather ordinary. Others may not be as good as you, and you may be able to do as much by teaching them as you can by taking pictures.

The whole thing is a self-perpetuating cycle. Tendzin Choegyal, youngest brother of His Holiness the Dalai Lama, summed it up beautifully. 'The first time you come, we ignore you, because we see so many people who promise things and don't deliver. The second time, we start to take you seriously. The third time...' Well, the metaphor was extremely vulgar, because Tibetans tend to be a bit earthy, but suffice it to say that one could hardly get closer.

And indeed, this was pretty much what happened with us. Our initial reception was in fact somewhat better than average, because we already had a book contract in our pockets and we had written to as many people as possible before we arrived, but even so, it was not until we returned on the second trip that we began to be taken really seriously. Eventually, at the request of the Tibetan Administration in Exile, we shot pictures at a number of refugee camps, and they even provided accommodation and transport; but that took a while.

The important thing to remember is why you are there: you are trying to help them. This generally means bringing in support in some way, be it in the form of paying customers, public opinion, or simply money. It also means doing something for them better, cheaper or easier than they could do it themselves (preferably all three). If you are more trouble than you are worth, or if you fail to deliver, you are not only going to make yourself fairly unpopular,

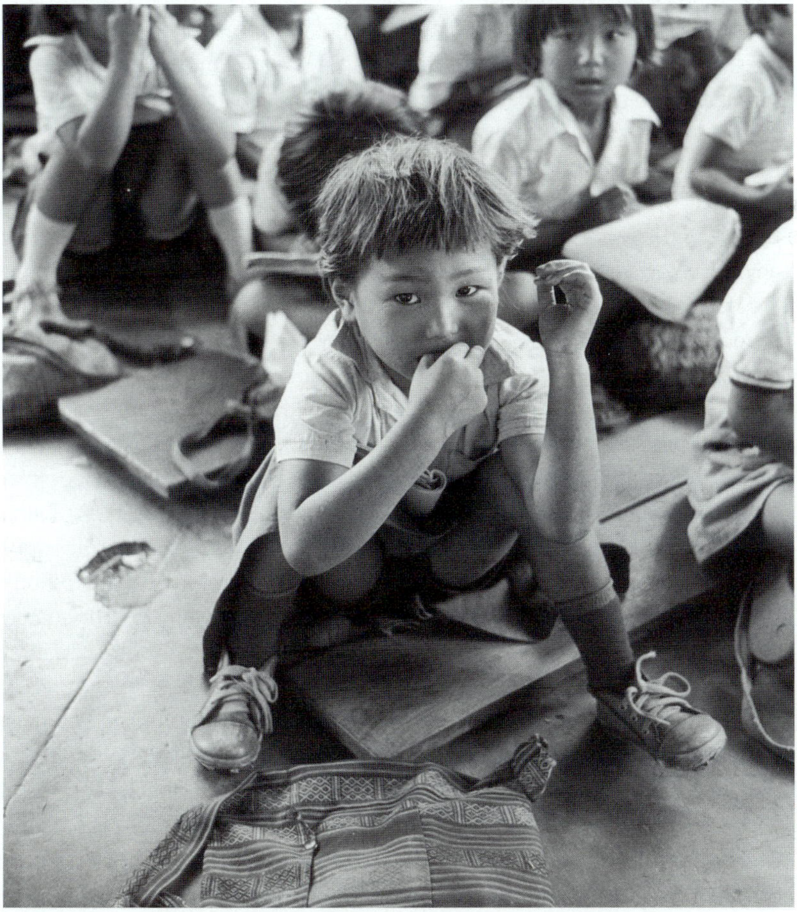

***Figure 19.2*** *Tibetan children are unusually appealing, and (let's be cynical) you want to press every sympathy button you can when you are working for a cause. Most people will do more to help an attractive child than they will for almost anyone else: this is, after all, one of the mainsprings of being human. We were working with a letter from the Office of His Holiness, which made access particularly easy, but a word with the headmaster, village head man, or whoever, will often get you access almost everywhere. (RWH)*

fairly smartly, but you are also going to make life more difficult for the next person who comes along, and you are going to have wasted everyone's time, including your own.

## GETTING A RESPONSE

Exactly how you play it will depend on your chosen cause, your personal skills and what the organization needs, but essentially you need to treat the whole thing in much the same way as an advertising campaign, or even as a training course. You need to decide whom you want to influence: the 'target audience'. Then you need to decide what you want them to do: the 'target behaviour' or 'target response'. Then you need to work out how to deliver a message which will make them do it.

In the case of the Tibetan Administration in Exile, this is comparatively simple. Most people are dimly aware of a number of things about Tibet. They have heard of His Holiness the Dalai Lama, and of Tibetan Buddhism. They are acquainted with the bright colours and striking iconography of the religion. They have some idea that the Chinese are involved, and at fault. The would-be publicist therefore has a very easy ride indeed – much easier, for example, than someone who is trying to publicize the Kurdish cause, or the plight of the marsh Arabs.

Our target population was for the most part reasonably well educated, liberal in political views (though the far right is sometimes pro-Tibetan, too, because they stand against the communists), and self-selecting: they would read anything which looked interesting.

Our intention, therefore, was to elicit a sequence of reactions. The first can best be summed up as 'Wow, this is interesting'. The second, which can be very important if there are existing prejudices to overcome and which is in any case the heart of the matter, is 'These people are not only interesting; they are not doing any harm to anyone, so why are they being persecuted?' The third, the logical consequence of the first two, is 'What can I do to find out more and to help?' This was our target behaviour.

Fairly obviously, this cannot be done with pictures alone; and equally obviously, there is no sense in re-inventing the wheel, or in keeping a dog and barking yourself. As mentioned above, you have to work with other people, so try to make sure that each of you does what he or she does best, but with a leavening of what he or she loves best. There are always unrewarding jobs, and many of them are done by volunteers. There is no reason why you should take over part of another volunteer's work, unless you want to, but equally, you must make sure that you are not adding unacceptably to someone else's work-load, be they volunteer or paid employee.

Nor is there any inherent reason why you should not mix commercial work with volunteer work. As already mentioned, what first took us to the Himalayas was a biography of His Holiness the Dalai Lama, already contracted with Element Books (it appeared as *Great Ocean*, an abbreviated translation of His Holiness's title, which means 'One whose wisdom is as great as the ocean' or 'Great ocean of wisdom').

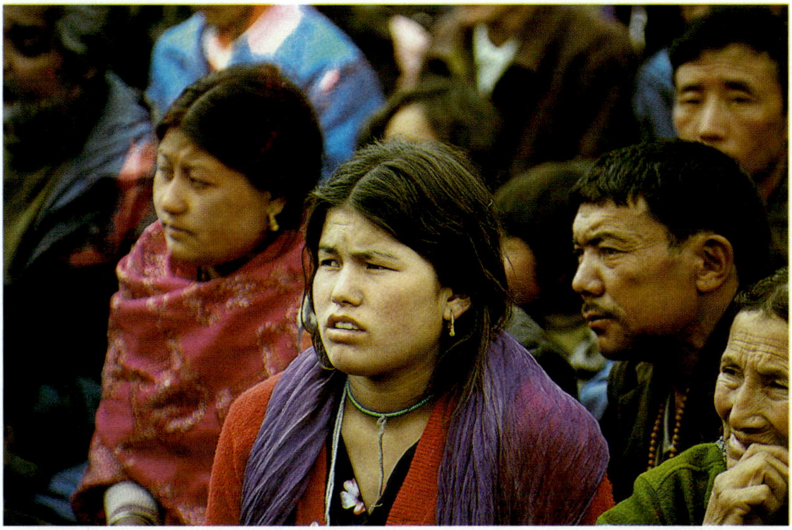

***Figure 19.3*** *Monlam is the great prayer festival after the Tibetan New Year, and all ages and conditions come to the main temple to hear His Holiness the Dalai Lama leading the prayers. In the West, this girl might be into clubs, pop music and boyfriends, with no spiritual dimension whatsoever; in Dharamsala, an interest in boys, dances and pop music by no means implies an absence of interest in spiritual matters. (RWH)*

The original advance was nothing like sufficient to cover the costs involved, so the book was to some extent subsidized by other work. But as the pictures we took were used in various books and magazine articles, and a few sold for stock, so it became a viable proposition. When Penguin took up the book, there was no question that overall our numerous trips to India paid for themselves. Also, without the volunteer work, we would not have had access to many of the places we went, so in the long run volunteer work and commercial work became almost indistinguishable. In due course, we also produced a propaganda book for the Administration, *Hidden Tibet*, and contributed to a major exhibition about Tibetans in exile.

An interesting aside here is that we have never actually been to Tibet. As running-dog lackeys of the reactionary Dalai bandit clique, we strongly doubt that we would get visas. It might seem that this was a major obstacle, but as soon as you realize that the people we photographed were likewise excluded from Tibet (or at least, could not return there safely), it makes sense.

## Choosing subjects

To return to our three-point plan, the most obvious question is what sort of pictures we took. Because Tibetan culture is so impossibly colourful, we were spoilt for choice, but even so, we went in for some unashamed pushing of emotional buttons.

Religious ceremonies were obviously central to the original biography, as indeed they are central to the whole of Tibetan culture; and as so often, there was plenty to show here. Imagine, if you will, the Losar ceremonies which greet the rising sun on the first day of the new year.

Long before dawn, in full darkness, people make their way to the temple, dressed in their best clothes: the men in *chubas* and polished boots, the women in their *chubas* with bright blouses and (for the married women) multicoloured aprons. There are flash shots to take on the road to the temple.

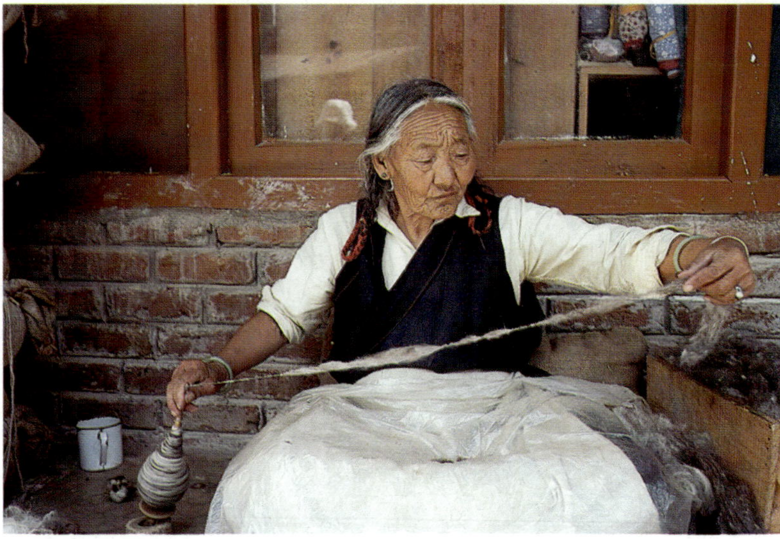

***Figure 19.4*** *There are certain archetypal images which seem to go beyond the intellect and to reach deep into the psyche. An elderly woman spinning wool is one of them: it is the stuff of fairy-tales, of folk memory. It is, therefore, a surprisingly easy subject to photograph. Each person who sees the picture is likely to supply at least as much meaning from their own emotions and experience as was contributed by the photographer when he took the shot in the first place. (RWH)*

Message: simple dignity, regard for tradition, exoticism.

At the temple, they make their *mendel tensum*, circumambulate the temple, and spin the prayer wheels. The monks gather on the roof, in their maroon and yellow robes. There may be just enough light for fast film and fast lenses; otherwise it's flash again. Message: religion is central to the lives of these people.

His Holiness arrives; the ceremonies start. The sun rises, illuminating the roof of the temple. Message: the analogy between sunrise and religious enlightenment.

The ceremony moves down into the temple. Musicians, dancers, ceremonial debate. Message: peaceful activities (there are very few glorifications of war in Tibetan culture).

At the temple, and elsewhere, we photographed children as often as possible. Children of most races have an inherent appeal, and Tibetan children (even those with runny noses, which many of the smallest ones seem to have) are particularly appealing. We also photographed child-monks, some of whom are orphans because their parents were killed by the Chinese or perished in the escape. Words are needed here: these children may or may not remain as monks, and no-one thinks any the less of them if they quit. Many of our friends and acquaintances are ex-monks, often happily married. Message: children are the hope of the future – but their future has been blighted.

The celebrations continue, all over Dharamsala and the other settlements. At the Tibetan Institute of Performing Arts, the courtyard is covered with the great Inner Sky canopy, and Lhamo (Tibetan opera) goes on all day. People drift in and out to watch. Message: Tibetan culture is not one-dimensional and religious, but embraces music, dance, acting.

But the poverty cannot be denied. Pema Dorje-la lives in one room, the walls papered with magazine pages against the cruel Himalayan winter: this is at almost 2000 metres, around 6000 feet. She is lucky: there is a tap outside her hut, though she shares it with many others. Her toilet facilities are however a choice of a communal latrine almost a hundred yards away, or (slightly closer) an area which is widely used for this purpose but which is also used by the monkeys. We set up a shot: Pema-la is fond of *chang*, barley beer, so we buy some to show her offering it in the traditional two-handed Tibetan manner. Poor as she is, she puts a dab of butter on the side of the glass to show that her guests are offered the best of what she has. Message: hospitality is central.

We also photographed Pema-la and her daughter Yuden on the precipitous steps which lead up to her hut. Pema-la wore traditional Tibetan dress, as many of the older women do at all times and as most of the women do on special occasions, but Yuden wore corduroy trousers and a T-shirt. Message: this is not a theme park, but a living community. Message: this is desperate, if picturesque, poverty. Message: Tibetans in exile build villages which are very much like Tibetan villages at home.

Examples could be multiplied without end, but we have given enough to make our point. Also (we hope) we have shown that unless you understand what is going on, unless you have a message that you are trying to convey, your pictures can all too easily be empty and meaningless. You learn the importance (and the difficulty) of captioning. In Tibetan, captioning is particular fun because of the spellings, which are phonetic but extremely complex, such as rDorje Sems.dpa (pronounced 'Dorje Sempa'). Get it wrong, and someone will notice and write to the editor!

It is not hard to take pretty pictures of Tibetans; but pictures which say something are more use to everyone, and (to return to crass reality) they are more saleable. From an exercise like this, you learn what people actually want to know, which stands you in good stead for every other branch of travel photography.

Perhaps the most important thing you learn, too, is that pictorialism is only one component of travel photography, and often the least important component at that. A picture which is sadly deficient from an aesthetic viewpoint may convey more than the loveliest composition you have ever shot. You learn to mix pretty pictures and informative pictures, so that the pretty picture can be the 'hook' which grabs someone's attention and the informative picture is what keeps them reading the article or book.

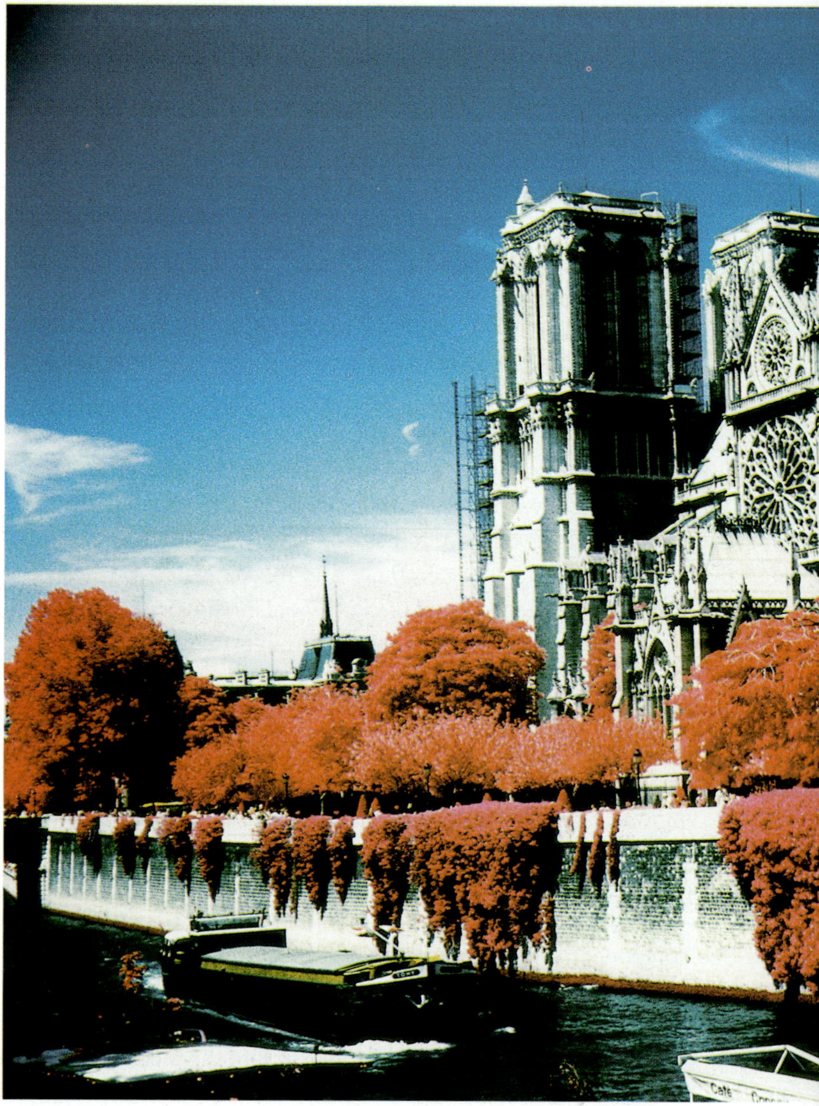

# 20 Selling yourself and your travel portfolio

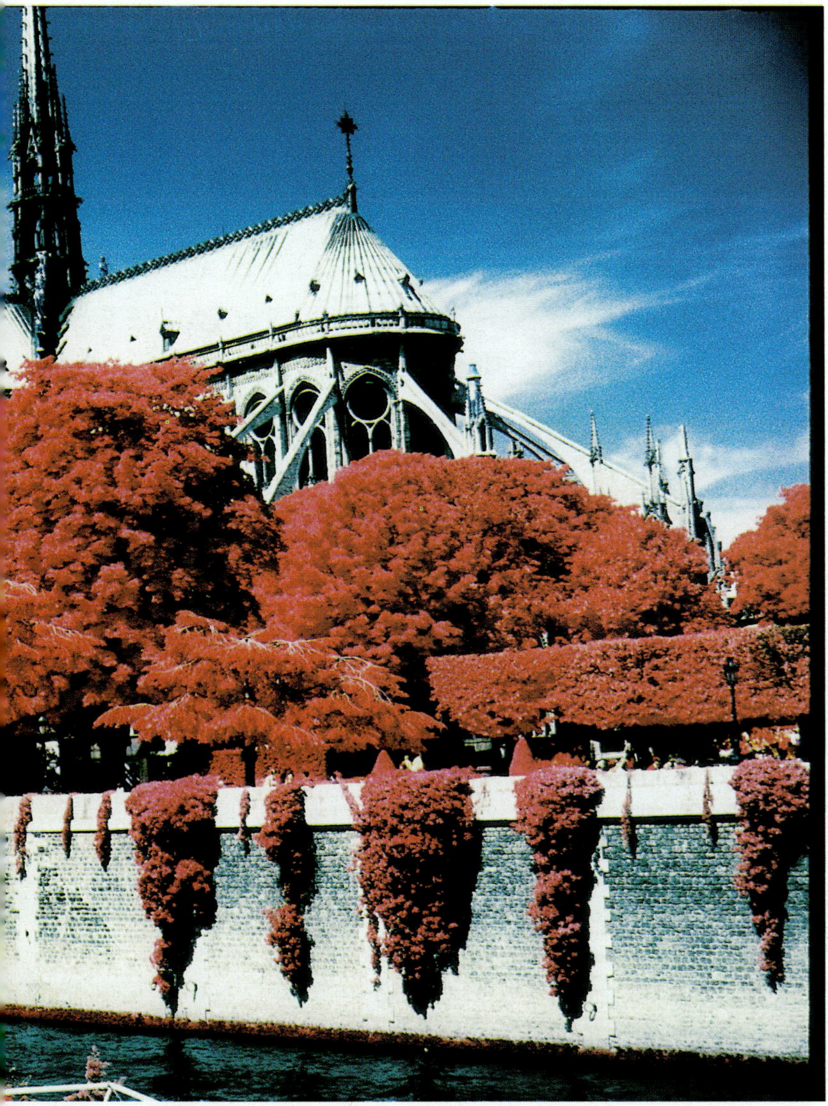

# Selling yourself and your travel portfolio

*Figure 20.1 Photographs taken with unusual lenses (such as fish-eyes) or on unusual film stocks (this photograph of Notre Dame is on Kodak E6 infra-red) should be used sparingly, as technique can all too easily overwhelm subject matter and the pictures end up looking 'samey'. Even so, there is a good case for one or two exotic pictures in the portfolio: you never know what may catch someone's attention. (RWH)*

A photographer's portfolio or 'book' can be his or her most potent selling tool – but it is not the only selling tool, nor is it invariably the most useful for a particular market. This is particularly true in travel photography, where we must repeat (at the risk of sounding like a broken gramophone record) that most projects tend to be word-driven.

All too often, in fact, the only thing which the travel photographer can sell is the finished product, produced at his or her own expense. There are essentially four levels of commissioning, though the first (and most advantageous to the photographer) is very rare, and growing rarer all the time.

This first level is the commissioned and funded trip, where the commissioning editor actually puts money up front. Only a very few

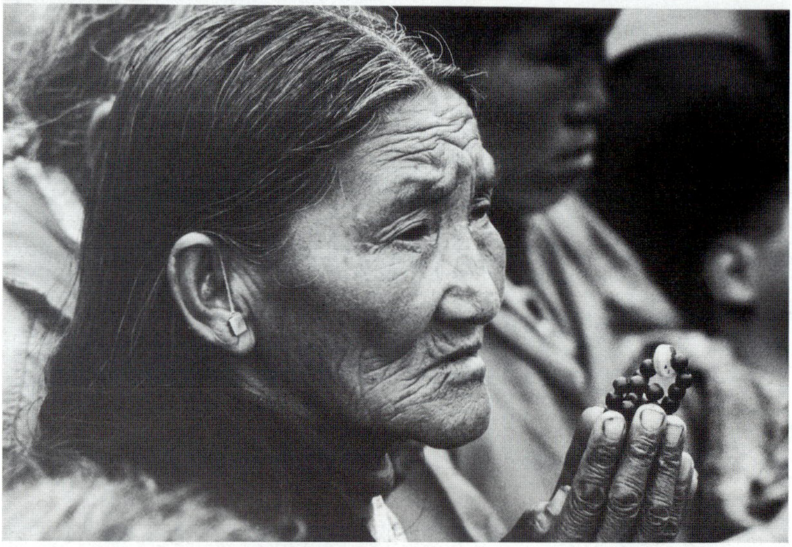

***Figure 20.2*** *Only you can decide on the balance between 'people' and 'places' in your portfolio. The words are put in quotation marks because, of course, the distinction is not always clear-cut. Be wary of putting one-off shots into the portfolio, too. If you habitually photograph people in close-up, then by all means use the best examples; but if you only have one or two such pictures, ask yourself if you could replicate them if you were commissioned to do so. (FES)*

photographers are likely to be able to pull a deal like this, though it has occasionally happened to us in the form of a book contract where the first tranche of the advance actually did pay for the photography that was needed; the American Civil War book, described in Chapter 16, was funded on that basis. Although advances are nominally refundable, the convention in publishing is that unless the photographer wilfully refuses to deliver, or unless the pictures are patently unusable and far below the normal standard of the photographer's work, the advance is not returned.

The second level is the commissioned trip with kill fee. With these, the commissioning editor undertakes either to publish at an agreed fee, or to pay a smaller 'kill fee' if the material is not used, though the photographer is responsible for funding the trip. Again, you generally need to be reasonably well established to get this kind of deal.

The third level is 'if we like it, we'll buy it'. For the beginner, and all too often for the established photographer as well, this is the normal deal. The only difference is that the established photographer is more likely to make a sale, partly because he or she is established, and partly because he or she knows the market better and is therefore more able to place it. This may sound like a classic case of 'it's not what you know, but who you know', but it really is not quite like that. Being established means that your reliability and the quality of your work are already known quantities, and knowing the market is an inevitable consequence of being involved in it.

The fourth level is the speculative job, fully funded and produced by the photographer before the prospective buyer is even approached. Even if you have one of the other deals, you may also decide to do this sort of thing in order to generate additional income. We do.

Regardless of which level you are operating on, we have always found that major considerations are pure luck, and personal rapport. Sometimes you hit an editor right; sometimes you don't. If the rapport is there, they will take you on, regardless of the fact that you hardly know each other and that your portfolio is far from ideal. If the rapport isn't there, you can submit the most brilliant proposals, the most stunning images, and completely fail to get anywhere. The old saying that 'Winners never quit, and quitters never win' is at best a half-truth, and at worst a flat lie; and it is more often quoted by losers than by winners. Knowing when to quit, and when to apply your energies to something else, is as important a component of winning as knowing when to persist.

An aside which is worth making here is that regardless of what ideas you have, what pitch you make, you very rarely have to worry about people 'stealing your ideas'. Indeed, this whole mind-set is very much an indicator of amateurism. On those rare occasions when you propose a particular idea, or show a particular style of photography, and despite your being turned down you see something very similar in the same publication a few days, weeks or months later, you will usually find upon closer investigation that the other photographer's ideas antedated yours – there is a good deal to be said for the theory that ideas are 'in the air' or 'waiting to happen' and can occur to several people at once – or, hard though it may be to admit to yourself, that he or she simply came along with a better proposal than yours, or is a better photographer.

Even when an idea is unquestionably stolen (and it can happen, though very rarely), ask yourself first, whether it matters all that much, and second, what you can do about it. Ideas are, after all, ten a penny to the creative mind: if you do not, on a regular basis, have more ideas than you can possibly realize or follow up, you will be a most unusual photographer. As for what you can do about it, is it worth trying to find out whether the idea was genuinely stolen; then trying to establish your priority; then trying to bring an action for damages; then trying to recover the damages? If you fail to sell one idea, well, sell the next one. It is not worth grieving over 'stolen' ideas, the more so because (as already emphasized) they probably weren't stolen anyway.

## Presentation

With the question of 'stolen ideas' aside, we return to the question of the portfolio; and there are several options.

Probably the most impressive portfolios, as portfolios, are the ones which are laminated onto large, uniform-sized boards (typically 20 × 16 inches, 40 × 50 cm) and carried in an appropriately sized portfolio box or case. We know a number of excellent photographers who adopt this approach, and who regularly get magazine work from it, by the traditional expedient of making an appointment with an editor and running through the 'book' with him or her.

If you are selling pictures and only pictures – in other words, if you are not selling word/picture packages – this is probably the best route to take. You may however prefer to go to a smaller size such as 12 × 16 inches (30 × 40 cm) in the interests of expense and ease in carrying; our own experience is that once pictures are beyond a certain size, editors are not necessarily impressed by area alone. This size can be surprisingly small: the actual image can be as small as 4 × 6 inches (10 × 15 cm), though a reasonably substantial mount (at least 10 × 12 inches, 25 × 30 cm) does add gravitas.

It is important not to have too many pictures, lest you bore your prospective employer, but equally, you do not want too few, or the portfolio looks too skimpy and lacking in variety. Ten or a dozen pictures is probably the absolute minimum that you dare show, and twenty-five or thirty is the absolute maximum. Even worse than boring an editor – the first risk of an overlarge portfolio – is the second risk, which is being asked to leave your book behind, so that he or she can give it the attention it deserves. At worst, you may never see it again; at best, it is likely to be days before you do, and it may well be weeks or months.

Some photographers mount tear-sheets in the same way as other pictures, while others carry magazines, and yet others mount the tear-sheets in sleeves; glass-clear acetate sleeves are a much better bet than polythene or similar sleeves, which dull down the images and take away much of their impact. Having tear-sheets mounted is probably the most impressive approach, and carrying magazines is probably the worst, as the magazines rapidly get dog-eared. An option we have found useful is colour photocopies in acetate sleeves. Colour copying brings all tear-sheets to the same size, and saves you having to carry often irreplaceable originals around with you.

## Words and pictures

If you are selling words and pictures, or if you want multiple copies of a portfolio so that you can leave them with editors, then colour photocopies can be very effective indeed. We habitually have colour photocopies made of tear-sheets and black and white prints, and we have had excellent colour photocopies made from scanned-in 35mm slides. It is however essential to find someone with a proper scanner, as the usual method of copying 35mm slides (via a projector attachment to the photocopier) is a complete disaster and will give you 'blown' highlights, funny colours, and blocked-up shadows. If you are calling around from the *Yellow Pages*, be warned that many copy shops will flatly lie about how they copy 35mm transparencies, and will tell you that they use a scanner when they actually use a projector.

If your proposals are primarily word-driven, then pictures can become almost incidental: original (or duplicate) transparencies, either in black mounts or even in multi-pocket sleeves, can be perfectly adequate. If you are selling a finished idea, this is of course all you need: the editor wants to see the finished pictures, in the form in which he or she will be using them. Even if you are

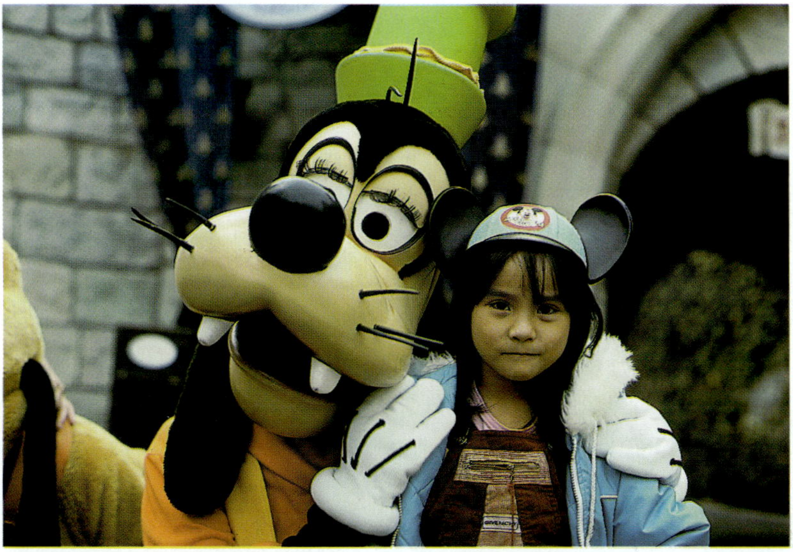

*Figure 20.3 Disneyland may be one of the most hackneyed subjects on earth – but when a publisher wanted to launch a new magazine about the United States for British readers and holidaymakers, he fell on this image like a hen on a blackberry. A few reliable clichés are unlikely to do your portfolio any harm whatsoever. (RWH)*

selling an idea on the basis of 'if we like it, we'll buy it', you may need no pictures at all for your initial pitch. You write proposing the idea; you mention publications in which your work has appeared (if appropriate); and you just do not need pictures.

An option which we had not at the time of writing taken up, but which was becoming so attractive as to be almost inevitable, is to scan in your images yourself, and output them using an ink-jet or other colour printer. This has further advantages if you are preparing proposals, in that you can 'dummy up' covers and sample spreads with comparatively little effort.

## The 'postcard portfolio'

Building your portfolio requires little comment, except to suggest a way in which you may find it easier to persuade people to grant you access to things. A small, travelling portfolio or some samples of your work will often make it much easier. In the past we have used examples of our books, and copies of various magazines for which we write, but at the time of writing we had just embarked on a 'postcard portfolio', which is exactly what its name implies: a set of postcard-sized images, in both colour and black and white, carried in a postcard-size paper box.

The 'postcard portfolio' has the advantage that you can show a wider range of your best work, in a more compact space, than any other way; it can even go into all but the smallest camera bags, or into the pocket of a photographer's vest, without taking up significant space. Combined with a book or magazine, it is even more effective. The only real drawback is that you may have difficulty in avoiding requests for pictures. Giving people pictures in return for access or for their cooperation is a fine and commendable thing, but a professional photographer literally cannot afford to make a habit of it, as it

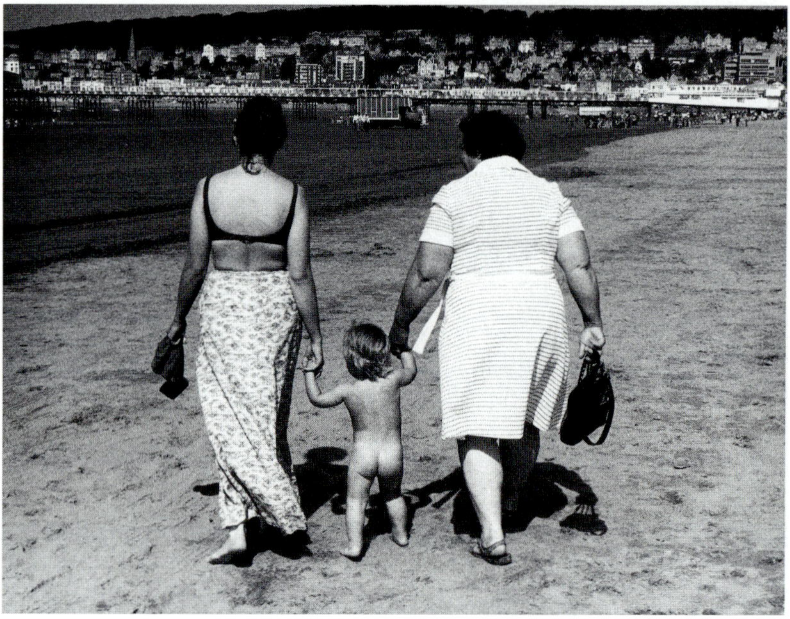

***Figure 20.4*** *There is a certain school of photography which deals with everyday life – but with everyday life taken almost to the point of parody. It can perhaps be described best as grittiness with an edge of nastiness. This sort of shot (usually in colour) is often used to illustrate the sort of slightly supercilious and pseudo-psychological article which is so popular in the Sunday newspaper supplements. (RWH)*

takes up too much time and costs too much money in both printing (especially from transparencies) and postage.

## The business of travel photography

The question of what you can and cannot afford to do is an excellent illustration of the most important thing to remember about travel photography as a business: that it is, indeed, a business. In one sense, the professional travel photographer is doing what countless amateur photographers do, going to attractive places and taking attractive pictures of them, so it is all too easy to lose sight of the fact that it is not feasible for the professional to work in the same way as an amateur. Lazy days, prolonged lunches and dinners, sunbathing, late mornings: work like this and you will take very few pictures, and you will not earn a living.

This does not mean that travel photography should be an unrelenting grind. If it is, or if you find it so, you would be well advised to go and do something else, because as we said early in the book, you can earn more money doing many other things, and the rewards of travel photography must to a considerable extent be other than financial. Put it this way: a substantial proportion of our income has, for many years, come from travel photography, and although there have been times when we would willingly have changed our lifestyle for one which is either easier or more profitable (or preferably both), we cannot readily imagine one which we would, taking everything into consideration, actually prefer.

# Index

Note: Entries in italics refer to photographs in the text